Illustrated Encyclopedia of Freshwater Fishes

Opposite *Hyphessobrycon pulchripinnis*
Above *Carassius auratus* var. Veiltail Goldfish

Illustrated
Encyclopedia of
Freshwater Fishes

George F Hervey   Jack Hems

Doubleday & Company, Inc.
Garden City, New York

Library of Congress Catalog Number 73–80340

Published by
The Hamlyn Publishing Group Limited
London · New York · Sydney · Toronto
Astronaut House, Feltham, Middlesex, England
Copyright © The Hamlyn Publishing Group Limited 1973

ISBN 0 600 33916 5
ISBN 0 385 02327 8 Doubleday

Printed in Great Britain
by Jarrold and Sons Limited, Norwich

Contents

Preface

Although keeping an aquarium of fishes in the home was known in Victorian and Edwardian days, it did not become a popular hobby until after the First World War. What brought it to the front, at all events in England, was the publication of the *Amateur Aquarist* (now the *Aquarist and Pond-keeper*) in 1924. Thereafter a large number of books on how to set up and maintain an aquarium in the home were published.

Most of these books were (and those published today still are) written by practical men, well experienced in the handling of fishes. For easy reference much that has been written about aquarium management is admirable, and for he who aims at nothing more than to set up and maintain an aquarium with his right hand, while holding a book of instructions in his left, they can hardly be bettered.

In this book we aim at something higher. We believe that an aquarium consists of no more than a glass-sided tank of adequate size, water to fill it, fishes to swim in the water, aquatic plants to keep the water healthy and a planting medium for the plants to take root in. These five fundamentals constitute an aquarium. If we are reminded that for an aquarium to be successful more must go into it, we agree, but with the qualification that it is largely dictated by common sense, and that a great deal of it is so much a matter of the choice of the individual that it is for him alone to decide what is to be done.

The reader who comes to this book, therefore, will find in it all about how to set up and stock an aquarium. He will find a large range of aquatic plants from which to choose, and a still larger range of fishes. He will find an account of how these fishes breed, and some advice on how to feed and keep them in health and how to diagnose and treat them in sickness.

What he will not find is a wealth of trivialities. So much has already been written (elsewhere we have written it ourselves) that rather than repeat it *ad nauseam* we leave it unwritten, with the firm conviction that the reader will already have some knowledge of the subject, gained either by practical experience or from reading other books, and that his own gumption will be enough to fill any gaps that he may find in our story.

In accordance with current practice we have given temperatures in degrees centigrade. The formula for converting centigrade into Fahrenheit is $F = \frac{9}{5}C + 32$ and, by contrary, the formula for converting degrees Fahrenheit into centigrade is $C = \frac{5}{9}(F - 32)$.

American readers are reminded that the gallon mentioned is the Imperial gallon and that the US gallon is equivalent to approximately $\frac{4}{5}$ths the Imperial gallon.

Where sea water has been mentioned, that which is derived from salt mixtures is quite satisfactory.

George F. Hervey   Jack Hems

Part 1
The Aquarium

It began on 4 March 1850, for it was on this day that Robert Warrington read a paper to the Chemical Society in which he described how he had found it possible to keep fishes (goldfish) in tanks for months, with no need to change the water so long as growing plants (*Vallisneria spiralis*) were present.

This, the basis of the balanced aquarium, had been known for at least a generation. As early as 1819, W. T. Brande wrote in his *Manual of Chemistry*: 'Fishes breathe the air which is dissolved in water; they therefore soon deprive it of its oxygen, the place of which is supplied by carbonic acid; this is in many instances decomposed by aquatic vegetables, which restore oxygen, and absorb the carbon …; hence the advantage of cultivating growing vegetables in artificial fish-ponds.' Robert Warrington, however, was the first to experiment on the practicability of aquaria. Before his time fishes had been kept in bowls. Writing in his *Diary* in 1665, Samuel Pepys mentions '… fishes kept in a glass of water …', and still earlier, in 1596 to be precise, a young Chinaman of the name of Chang Chi'en-tê, wrote the *Chu sha yü p'u* (*Book of Vermilion Fish*) in which he explains how he cared for and bred his prize red-and-white goldfish, or what he called vermilion fish. In all these cases, however, and others, the water had to be changed frequently, and the aquarium proper cannot be said to have begun until 120 years ago, as we write, with the experiment of Robert Warrington. Simultaneously, a Mr Price conducted some very successful experiments on the principle of balance, and, during the decade that followed, the work of Gosse, Hibberd and Sowerby carried it further forward and did much to popularize the keeping of fishes, and other aquatic animals, in aquaria.

The principle of balance

Shorn of fustian phraseology, the principle of balance is not difficult to explain, nor to understand. The representatives of the animal kingdom inhale oxygen and exhale carbon dioxide, and under the influence of light, the representatives of the vegetable kingdom take in carbon dioxide through their leaves (using the carbon to manufacture carbohydrates as food) and liberate oxygen. It follows from this, therefore, that if the aquarium is not overcrowded with animal life, if it is amply but not overstocked with plant life, and if it receives sufficient light, a balance between animal and plant life will be struck and the aquarium will remain in a healthy condition more or less indefinitely.

Although this is a close approximation to the truth it is not the whole truth, because the value of aquatic plants as oxygenators is much overrated: their more important function is to absorb the carbon dioxide that the fishes produce. This is not to say that there is no need to select plants for their oxygenating properties. Far from it. The more carbon dioxide present in the water the greater must be the concentration of oxygen if the fishes are not to die of suffocation. The important factor in the balanced aquarium is a large surface area of water, not so much for oxygenating the water (though oxygen is drawn from the air that comes into contact with the surface of the water) but to facilitate the escape of carbon dioxide as quickly as possible.

The tank

The first fundamental is a tank. Some might call it an aquarium but by definition it remains a tank until it is stocked and fishes are swimming in it.

The most satisfactory tanks are those made of angle iron, painted or protected against rust with a coating of nylon or polythene, chromium plated or of stainless steel; the sides, back and front and base glazed. A tank should be at least 24 inches long and 12 inches wide; its depth is of no great importance, so long as it is not out of proportion to the length and breadth. It is the surface area that matters, particularly if the tank is to be stocked with the so-called coldwater fishes, because they need considerably more oxygen than tropical species.

A newly acquired tank should be tested for leaks and then washed, disinfected (kitchen salt is recommended), and finally rinsed clean of the disinfecting agent before it is set up in the position that it is to occupy.

Planting medium

The second fundamental is a planting medium in which the aquatic plants are to be rooted. In a sense no one planting medium is ideal; for some plants (for example *Vallisneria*) flourish best in a mixture of one-third sand, one-third clay and one-third leaf-mould or peat, others (for example *Cabomba*) prefer a mixture of one-third sand, one-third garden soil and one-third leaf-mould, and still others (for example *Cryptocoryne*) prefer a mixture of equal parts of peat and clay.

It is, of course, possible to give each plant the soil that it prefers by planting it in a small pot. The result, however, is not altogether a happy one because the art of aquarium design is to create a natural scene and flower-pots are impossible to hide. Fortunately there is no great need to use pots. Practically all aquatic plants will flourish well in a fine, non-calcareous grit or coarse sand with a little leaf-mould or peat added.

The tank, therefore, should be layered with fallen beech leaves (other leaves may be poisonous) or soaked peat, over which the sand or grit should be placed to a depth of about 2 to 3 inches at the back, sloping to a depth of about 1 to 1½ inches at the front.

Sand with grains about the size of a pin's head is satisfactory. Fine sand, such as silver sand and bird sand, is to be avoided, as is builder's red sand which, for one reason or another, never proves satisfactory.

The sand should first be well washed by standing it in a bucket under a running tap and stirring it until the water runs from it clearly.

Water

The chemist knows water as H_2O; the rest of us know very little about it. To the fishes it is the elixir of life, although against all the evidence of our eyes, they do not drink it.

Of all liquids water is the most general solvent, and in nature it is never found pure. It is pure as formed in the upper atmosphere, but as it comes down to us as rain it brings with it atmospheric gases, mainly oxygen, nitrogen and carbonic acid, and near towns and cities compounds of sulphur and other industrial pollutions. Then, after it has filtered through rocks and soil and returned as spring or river water, it is always charged to a greater or lesser degree with dissolved salts. When the quantity of these impurities in water is small the water is said to be soft; when larger the water is said to be hard. The degree of hardness and softness may be determined by the effect that the water has on soap; soft water lathers more easily than hard water. It is for this reason that soft water is preferred for washing and hard water for drinking.

If the dissolved salts in water are chlorides or sulphates the hardness is described as permanent: if they are bicarbonates the hardness is described as temporary. Most aquarium fishes favour soft water and only a few, notably the White Cloud Mountain Minnow (*Tanichthys albonubes*), the glass-fishes (*Chanda* species), the Australian Rainbowfish (*Melanotaenia nigrans*), and fishes that normally inhabit brackish water (for example *Scatophagus* and *Monodactylus* species) flourish better in hard water. Dissolved calcium bicarbonate is precipitated from water as calcium carbonate (the well-known fur in kitchen kettles) by boiling, and temporary hard water may be rendered soft in this way and made suitable for fishes by allowing it to cool and then aerating it. Too soft a water, however, is unsatisfactory not only for fishes but also for plants, because all life needs dissolved salts to maintain growth. They may be replaced in water that has been boiled by adding to every 10 gallons of water three teaspoonfuls of sodium chloride (kitchen salt) and one each of potassium sulphate and magnesium sulphate. To provide a water suitable for those fishes that flourish best in soft water, a half-and-half mixture of distilled water and medium-hard tap water may be used.

The hardness and softness of water are not to be confused with its alkalinity and acidity. In broad outline water may be acid, neutral or alkaline, and a simple chemical test enables the degree of acidity or alkalinity to be determined. It is expressed by a number (*p*H value) that ranges on a scale either side of 7·07. Water with a *p*H of 7·07 (usually taken as 7) is neutral; if the *p*H is lower the water is acid, if higher it is alkaline. Natural waters range from about *p*H 4 to *p*H 9, and most aquarium fishes favour a water that is acid. Few fishes will tolerate a *p*H of less than 6 or more than 7·6, and a *p*H of 6·7 or 6·8 is recommended for most. Some prefer a slightly alkaline water, with a *p*H of 7·1 or 7·2.

The problem is not altogether an academic one, for the *p*H value of water can be altered artificially. Acid water may be made alkaline by the addition of sodium bicarbonate, and alkaline water may be acidified by the addition of potassium hydrogen tartrate (cream of tartar). We are, however, not in favour of it, except in certain circumstances, because any alteration in the *p*H value of water must be done by degrees. It involves the risk that if the adjustment is overdone it is extremely difficult to rectify. We have seen many disasters when amateur chemists add alkalis and acids to aquarium water, and it should be enough to improve water that is too acid by adding a teaspoonful of powdered egg-shell to every gallon of water, and by straining through peat, water that is too alkaline.

The most satisfactory water for an aquarium is that taken from a pond or stream in which healthy fishes are known to be living, with the precaution of boiling it to rid it of any unwanted small life. On the whole, however, water drawn from the mains supply is satisfactory. At worst it may contain chlorine, but rarely enough to harm fishes, and in any case most of it escapes as the tank is filled. It is considered desirable to mature tap water by standing it outdoors for two or three days before filling the tank.

The tank should be filled very slowly. A satisfactory way to do this is to stand a cup and saucer on the bottom and pour the water very gently into the cup.

Aquarium plants

Plants are an essential feature of an aquarium. It is not only that they are decorative, and without them an aquarium would look bare, but that an aquarium largely depends on them for success. As we noted at the beginning, under the influence of light plants take in the carbon dioxide exhaled by the fishes and liberate oxygen that fishes breathe; it is this exchange of gases that helps to keep the water healthy and suitable for fishes to live in. A

Acorus gramineus var. *pusillus*

further factor in the exchange between animal and plant life is that the plants feed on the excreta of the fishes. The submerged plants furnish the fishes with a natural surrounding and provide shelter for the more timid; the floating plants furnish the fishes with shade; both serve as a spawning ground because most freshwater aquarium fishes scatter adhesive eggs that attach themselves to the leaves and stems of aquatic plants as they gravitate to the bottom.

Plants for the aquarium may for convenience be divided into two groups: submerged plants, which take root in the planting medium and throw their stems and leaves to the surface, and floating plants, which float free on, or just under, the surface of the water. Botanists have classified a very large number of species in each group, but only a comparative few are suitable for the aquarium.

Submerged plants that have roots are planted by

spreading these out and pushing them gently into the planting medium. If the plant has a crown (for example *Vallisneria*) it should rest on the surface of the planting medium and not be buried in it. Those plants that are propagated as cuttings should be planted by pushing about an inch of the stem into the planting medium. It is a mistake to plant too deeply and every plant should be planted separately, never a number tied together in a bunch. Plants that tend to ride to the surface may be held down with a small strip of soft lead. No other metal should be used as some are toxic to fishes, and even lead should be used in limited quantity. Planting is simplified if a couple of notched sticks (one in each hand) are used. The plant can be held in position with one and the planting medium raked back with the other.

For the standard 24-inch tank about thirty-six plants are required for a start. Very pleasing effects may be obtained with a selection of suitable species from the list that follows. It must be pointed out, however, that selection has to be made with discretion because aquatic plants are indigenous to different parts of the world, so that their requirements, in the matter of water, light and heat, vary very greatly.

Acorus gramineus var. *pusillus* (Japanese Dwarf Rush) and the variegated form *A. gramineus* var. *variegatus* have narrow, sword-shaped leaves, arranged like a fan. The latter is a particularly attractive plant because the grass-green leaves of the type are striped pale sulphur-yellow. Both plants call for a good light and an optimum temperature of 18°C, with a range of 10 to 12°C. Above this they tend to die in a short time.

Aglaonema simplex (Malayan Sword Plant) though essentially a bog plant, like many other bog plants, will grow submerged. It is indigenous to south-east Asia, from Malaysia to the Philippines, and therefore needs a heated aquarium. The firm, shiny and ovate leaves – about 4 inches long – are mid-green on the upperside, paler on the underside. They are held either stiffly erect or at right angles to the stem, which normally reaches a length of about 5 or 6 inches, but exceptionally 15 inches. It is at its best in a mixture of peat and clay in part shade.

Alternanthera sessilis like the foregoing species is a bog plant that may be grown submerged. It is indigenous to the tropics (chiefly India) and flourishes best in a bright light and a mixture of peat and clay. The narrow leaves (about ½ inch across) are lanceolate, about 1 to 3 inches long, rather fleshy, green in colour shading to wine-red

Aponogeton ulvaceus

Bacopa amplexicaulis

on the upperside and bright red on the underside. They are borne in opposite pairs on a branching, red stem that may grow to a length of 15 inches or more.

Amblystegium riparium is an amphibious moss, mainly to be found in peaty bogs. As a submerged plant for the aquarium, it is seen at its best when anchored to a piece of sunken tree bark or a small log. It is indigenous to Europe (including Great Britain*) and although it is normally to be grown in an unheated aquarium it is an accommodating species that can be acclimatized to a heated one. It has thin, thread-like stems and very small, scale-like, pale green leaves. It needs soft water and a fairly good light.

Anubias lanceolata (Water Aspidistra) from tropical Africa has remarkably thick, shiny, green leaves, very similar in appearance to those of the well-known aspidistra of the suburban parlour. They are about 5 or 6 inches long and borne on short, stout stems which rise from a rhizomatous tuber. Propagation is by division of the tuber. Its

congener *A. congensis* is very similar in appearance but is taller growing. In the wild it grows up to 20 inches, but reaches only about half this height in the aquarium. Propagation is the same as for *A. lanceolata*. Both species grow rather slowly, favour slightly acid water, a soft light and a temperature range of 20 to 30°C, optimum 25°C.

The genus *Aponogeton* embraces a large number of species indigenous to the Old World, from Africa (including Malagasy) through India (including Ceylon) and Malaysia to Australia, with one solitary species in Mexico. *A. fenestralis* from Malagasy is the well-known Lace Plant, so called because the leaves consist of a mere lattice of longitudinal and tranverse veins sometimes far enough apart to allow the passage of a small fish. It is not an easy plant to grow: the water should be soft and slightly acid, the light subdued and the temperature not less than 18°C or more than 22°C. *A. ulvaceus*, also from Malagasy, is commonly known as King of the Aponogetons. It is indeed a very handsome plant with pale green, translucent leaves, wavy at the edges, and up to 18 inches long and 4 inches wide, held on a 10-inch stem.

---

* J. H. has collected it in the Peak District of Derbyshire.

Sometimes it is mistaken for *A. natans*, a species from Ceylon, because when young both plants look much alike. *A. natans*, however, is a much coarser plant and grows into an untidy tangle of submerged and small floating leaves oval in shape. *A. crispus* and *A. rigidifolium* are two attractive species from Ceylon and easier to cultivate than the species from Malagasy. *Aponogeton* species should be planted in a mixture of peat and clay. They will not tolerate continuous culture and for several months of the year they must be rested in a reduced temperature. Propagation may be effected by seed but more usually by division of the rhizome. As *A. fenestralis* is rather expensive we have not tasted it ourselves, but we understand that the rhizome when grilled makes very good eating.

Bacopa (*Herpestis*) species are bog plants that are not difficult to grow submerged. They have bright green, thick, fleshy leaves, circular to oval in shape, arranged in opposite pairs on stout stems. Branching is sparse so that to obtain the best effect planting should be in clumps. They flourish best in a good light and at a temperature range of 18 to 22°C, optimum 20°C. They are not particular about a planting medium. Of the two species known to aquarists, *B. amplexicaulis* is indigenous to the southern and Atlantic states of the United States; *B. monnieri*, which is a slightly smaller plant, has a cosmopolitan range.

Cabomba species (Fanwort) are indigenous to the tropical and subtropical areas of the New World. All have finely divided, submerged leaves. *C. aquatica* has kidney-shaped floating leaves and sulphur-yellow flowers held above the surface of the water. *C. caroliniana* is the species most usually in cultivation: its floating leaves are narrow and linear; its flowers white with two yellow spots at the base of each petal. *C. caroliniana* var. *pulcherrima* has a reddish-purple stem and bright purple flowers. For *C. aquatica* a temperature range of 18 to 25°C (optimum 20°C) is recommended: *C. caroliniana* prefers slightly cooler water, 12 to 22°C, optimum 18°C. All species demand a good top light, particularly during the winter months and soft, acid water.

Cardamine lyrata from eastern Siberia, through China and Korea to Japan, has delicate, pale green, circular leaves, and heads of small white flowers. It flourishes best in a temperature range of 15 to 22°C, and in fact is more for the unheated than the heated aquarium. Its congener *C. rotundifolia* (American Watercress) has darker coloured leaves. It is indigenous to North America and is essen-

tially for the unheated aquarium. *Cardamine* species are propagated as cuttings but new plants may be struck by placing a leaf in damp soil.

Ceratophyllum (Hornwort) is represented to aquarists by two species: *C. demersum*, indigenous to Europe (including Great Britain) and North America, and *C. submersum*, indigenous to Europe (including Great Britain), tropical Asia and Florida. A temperature range of 10 to 18°C is advised because those in cultivation are essentially for an unheated aquarium; in a heated aquarium they do not last long. As the stems are very brittle they have to be handled with care. Propagation is very easy. Small pieces broken off from the stem will grow if pushed into the planting medium or allowed to float on the surface of the water.

Ceratopteris thalictroides has a number of popular names, but Sumatra Fern is probably the most appropriate because the plant is indigenous to south-east Asia, and resembles nothing so much as brack fern. It is at its best in a soft to medium-hard water, slightly acid, and with a temperature range of 20 to 30°C. *Ceratopteris* species are viviparous and propagation is by daughter plants that form on the margins of the leaves.

Crassula intricata (*Tillaea recurva*) is indigenous to Australia and flourishes well at a temperature of 20°C with a range of 5°C each way. It has light green, needle-like leaves, about 1 inch long, and therefore should be planted in clumps if it is to be seen at its best. It needs a good light, and although it is not particular about a planting medium, clay is recommended.

Cryptocoryne species (Water Trumpet) in general call for soft water, a temperature range of 18 to 30°C (optimum 25°C) and a subdued light. The genus is a large one and at least forty species and subspecies, mainly from the islands of south-east Asia, are known to botanists. *C. affinis* (sometimes given the erroneous name of *C. haerteliana*) is the plant most usually offered for sale. The leaf is lanceolate, up to 6 inches long and rather more than an inch wide, the upperside dark bluish green, the underside wine-red to pale green. *Cryptocoryne* species are ornamental rather than useful, although a few species of fishes favour the leaves on which to deposit their eggs. Among the more ornamental species, and which are not difficult to grow, mention may be made of *C. becketti* var. *latifolia* with narrow leaves about $2\frac{1}{2}$ inches long and $1\frac{1}{4}$ inches broad, on stems about twice the length of the leaf blade; *C. becketti* var. *angustifolia* with ovate leaves about 3 inches long and 1 inch broad; *C. blassi* with ovate leaves about 3 inches long, the upperside reddish to dark green, the underside deep purple to bright red; *C. lucens* with lanceolate leaves about 3 inches long and a mere ½ inch across, mid to dark green in colour; and *C. wendti* with leaves about 4 inches long, dark olive-green on the upperside and pale green to reddish on the underside.

Echinodorus species are generally known as Amazon sword plants because the majority of them are indigenous to the Amazon basin and their leaves are sword-shaped. *E. tenellus*, however, extends as far north as the Great Lakes of the United States. It is popularly known as the Pygmy Chain Sword Plant, and erroneously as *Sagittaria microfolia*. The pale green leaves are about 3 inches long and so narrow that a clump of plants has the appearance of grass growing under water. It favours soft water. *E. grisebachi*, popularly known as the Chain Sword Plant, has lanceolate leaves about 8 inches long. *E. paniculatus*, the Amazon Sword Plant of the aquarist, is suitable only for a very large aquarium; for the pale green leaves grow up to 15 inches long and 3 inches wide. *E. paniculatus* var. *gracilis* is known as the Narrow-leaved Sword Plant, and *E. paniculatus* var. *rangeri* as the Broad-leaved Sword Plant. Although *E. tenellus* will withstand a temperature as low as 15 °C other species need a temperature of 20 °C or higher.

Eleocharis acicularis (Hair- or Needle-grass) when grown submerged reaches a height of about 5 or 6 inches, and planted in a clump looks very pleasing against a large stone. The pale green needle-like stem terminates in a dark brown oblong spikelet. In the wild it is found throughout the temperate and warmer regions of the New World as well as the Old, and will withstand a temperature up to 24 °C.

Elodea (*Anacharis*, *Egeria*) species are the well-known waterweeds, sold in every pet shop because they are good oxygenators, easily propagated by cuttings and grow profusely if the light is good. *E. densa*, the Argentinian Waterweed, tolerates a temperature range of 10 to 25 °C, *E. canadensis*, the Canadian Waterweed, and *E. callitrichoides*, from the Argentine and Chile, favour slightly cooler water, 10 to 20 °C, and will not survive in a heated aquarium.

Fontinalis antipyretica, the well-known Incombustible Willow Moss, derives its name from the fact that at one time it was used in Sweden to pack the air space between chimney and walls, and so lessen the risk of fire. It is a pretty little plant – not unlike seaweed – that attaches itself to a sunken log or porous stone, and looks well in the front of an aquarium, with the added advantage that it collects sediment. It does best in a subdued light. It is widespread in Europe (including Great Britain) and is therefore suitable for the unheated aquarium. A large number of species have been described by botanists, but only a few are available to the aquarist. A form of *F. antipyretica* known as *F.a. gracilis* has bright green leaves much finer than those of the type species, and will withstand the temperature of a heated aquarium (24 °C). It amounts to the fact that *Fontinalis* species are not normally in cultivation and have to be collected from the wild. Even botanists find identification exceptionally difficult and whatever the species, that taken from cold running water is unlikely to survive when transferred to a heated aquarium, but that taken from the shallow water of a pond or lake warmed by the sun during the summer months will.

Heteranthera (Water Star-grass) is represented to aquarists by the two species *H. dubia* (*graminea*) and *H. zosteraefolia*. The former is indigenous to the central and southern states of the United States, and does best in medium-hard to hard water and a temperature range of 15 to 25 °C. The latter is indigenous to Brazil and Bolivia. It favours soft water and a temperature range of 22 to 28 °C. Both resemble the better known *Elodea densa* but the leaves branch alternatively from both sides of the stem, instead of growing in whorls. If the light is good both species will produce small flowers that lie flat on the surface of the water. Those of *H. dubia* are light yellow in colour; those of *H. zosteraefolia* are pale blue.

Hydrilla verticillata is another species that closely resembles *Elodea densa*. It has a very wide range that extends from south-east Europe through Asia and western Africa (including Malagasy) to Indonesia and Australia. It grows well in a good light and a heated aquarium. In an unheated aquarium it will not survive the winter months.

Hygrophila species, represented to aquarists by *H. polysperma* from India and *H. salicifolia* from south-east Asia, need a good light, soft to medium-hard water, and a temperature range of 18 to 30 °C. In appearance both species are similar to the better-known *Ludwigia* although the leaves of *Hygrophila* are larger, narrower and more pointed, and the undersides are not flushed red.

Lagarosiphon muscoides var. *major* (*Elodea crispa*) flourishes well at a temperature up to 20 °C, but will not withstand a prolonged heat. Its robust, green leaves are set in whorls along the stem and are strongly recurved. It is indigenous to South Africa.

Lagenandra species are bog plants very similar in appearance to *Cryptocoryne* species but the leaves are tough and thick to the touch, not soft as in *Cryptocoryne*. The leaves of *L. lancifolia* are dark green on the upperside and pale green with numerous white spots on the underside. Two forms are recognized: one grows to a height of about 15 inches, the other to about 8 inches. The latter is the one most usually offered for sale. Its congener *L. thwaitesi* is particularly decorative, with a long-pointed leaf, 4 to 6 inches long and up to 1½ inches broad, on a 6-inch petiole. The upperside of the leaf is dark green, the underside light green. The leaf edge is slightly wavy and sometimes, but not always, marked with a silvery-white pattern.

Limnophila (*Ambulia sessiliflora*) is indigenous to tropical Asia. It is a handsome plant that strongly resembles a compact growing *Cabomba* of a beautiful vivid green. Growth is slow, but once established, side branches develop and the plant soon obtains a bushy appearance. A good light is essential (particularly during the winter months) and a temperature range of 22 to 30°C. Given the right conditions, small bluish-white flowers develop in the axils of the leaves.

Littorella uniflora is indigenous to Europe (including Great Britain) and is essentially for the unheated aquarium with an optimum temperature of 18°C and a maximum of 20°C. In a good light it forms tufts of bright green circular leaves up to 4 inches in height.

Ludwigia species were at one time very popular among aquarists. Today they are rarely seen in aquaria; their place has been taken by plants of similar leafage but of better and more profuse growth. From time to time a form known as 'mulertii' is offered for sale; it is the horticultural form of the natural species *L. natans* from the United States and Central America. It is an attractive plant with oblong-lanceolate leaves, bronzy green on the upperside, flushed crimson-purple on the underside. A good light and a temperature range of 18 to 25°C are desirable.

Marsilea species (the Nardoo Plants of Australia) are aquatic flowerless plants related to the ferns, with four-lobed leaves that resemble those of clover. A large number of species are known to botanists, but only a few are represented to aquarists. The easiest to grow is *M. hirsuta* from northern Australia, with grey-green to silvery-green leaves that are covered with a nap of fine

hairs. It grows to a height of about 9 inches. *M. drummondi* from central and southern Australia is much the same in appearance but demands a bigger aquarium as it will grow to a height of 18 inches. Both plants need a good light and a heated aquarium.

Micranthemum micranthemoides is an attractive little marsh plant, not unlike the well-known Creeping Jenny, from North America. Bright green in colour it looks well in the foreground of an aquarium although, like most marsh plants when planted in an aquarium, it tends to grow erect instead of carpeting the bottom. It needs a good light and a temperature range of 16 to 22°C with an optimum of 18 to 20°C.

Microsorium pteropus (Java Fern) is a true aquatic fern widespread in tropical south-east Asia. The frond (leaf) is a deep green, elongated-lanceolate in shape, up to 8 or 9 inches long and 2 inches broad. The stem is woody, short and sometimes absent. Reproduction is by daughter plants that form on the fronds. It requires a subdued light and a temperature range of 20 to 28°C. Although it may be grown anchored to the bottom of the aquarium with a few twists of lead wire, it is seen at its best when attached to a sunken log.

Myriophyllum species (Water Milfoil) are probably the best known of all submerged plants for they have much to attract the aquarist. They are decorative, offer a first-class spawning ground for egg-laying fishes, the hair-fine divided leaves furnish the fry with cover, propagation is easily effected by cuttings from the main stem, and there are many species from which to choose. *M. hippuroides* (*scabratum*), from North and South America, flourishes at a temperature range of 15 to 26°C and is not difficult to grow. *M. heterophyllum*, from North America, will stand a lower temperature and is a very satisfactory plant for the unheated aquarium. The lower leaves are divided into hair-like segments, the emergent ones are arranged in whorls of three or four: they are linear and sharply serrated. In bright sunlight the normally green leaves acquire a bronzy-red tint. *M. elatinoides* has very fine leaves that vary in colour from grass- to blue-green. It does best in soft water. In the wild it is found in the Old World from Australia, through Tasmania, to New Zealand: in the New World it extends from Mexico in the north, through northern Brazil and Chile, to the Argentine and Falkland Islands in the south.

Najas species are rather slender and brittle plants that are seen at their best when planted in clumps. They are not very particular in their cultural

Potamogeton species

requirements, but they need a good light, soft to medium-hard water and a temperature range of 18 to 25°C. *N. kingi*, from Malaysia, has narrow, linear leaves of a translucent green, minutely serrated and slightly reflexed. They grow in whorls of three or four. *N. pectinata*, from tropical and subtropical Africa (including Malagasy), varies in colour from a translucent pale green to reddish brown. The leaves are coarsely serrated and grow in whorls of four or five.

Nitella species are decorative plants best suited to a small aquarium but quite attractive in a large one that is inhabited by small fishes. *N. gracilis*, the most common species, and *N. flexilis* are indigenous to Europe (including Great Britain), Asia and North America; *N. megacarpa* is indigenous to the eastern states of the United States. All three species are of a translucent colour that varies from pale olive to a dark brownish green. The last is striped white. *Nitella* species have no true roots, stem or leaves, but small cuttings, anchored to the bottom of an aquarium or pushed into the planting medium, will grow well in good light and a temperature range of 18 to 25°C, optimum 20°C. Some aquarists find them a little difficult to establish; once established, however, they release oxygen in quantity and are excellent spawning plants for those fishes that scatter their eggs at random.

Nomaphila (Hygrophila) stricta is indigenous to tropical south-east Asia, and makes an excellent centrepiece for a large aquarium with medium-hard water and a temperature range of 20 to 30°C. The leaves are broadly lanceolate to narrowly elliptical, from 2 to 4 inches long and up to 1¼ inches broad, pointed at the tip, the upperside light green, the underside whitish green.

Nuphar species (Spatterdock) are closely related to the water lilies and in the main are large plants more suited to the outdoor pond than the aquarium. *N. sagittifolium*, however, known as the Cape Fear Spatterdock, from the Atlantic coast of North America, makes an excellent centrepiece for a large aquarium because it always remains submerged. The elongated arrow-shaped leaf reaches a length of about 7 inches and a breadth of about 2½ inches. It is pale translucent green in colour, the tip slightly rounded, the edges deeply ruffled. It needs a heated aquarium and a subdued light.

The genus *Potamogeton* (Pondweed) is a very large one with a cosmopolitan range. Many species are indigenous to Great Britain and Europe, but they are altogether too weedy to merit a place in an aquarium. For the heated aquarium *P. gayi* from South America, mainly Uruguay, is to be recommended. The linear leaves are a translucent pale green to reddish brown. Frequent pruning and a strong light encourages bushy growth.

The genus *Sagittaria* (Arrowhead) is an important one for the aquarist; not only are *Sagittaria* species good oxygenators but their roots help to keep the planting medium healthy. The foliage is interesting because the submerged leaves are narrow and grass-like, the floating leaves ovate and the aerial leaves typically arrow-shaped. Some twenty species are suitable for the aquarium; the best are indigenous to the Atlantic coast of the United States with a temperature range of 15 to 25°C. *S. subulata (natans)* is represented to aquarists in two forms: *S.s. natans* with light green strap-like leaves up to 15 inches long, and *S.s. pusilla*, a pygmy form, with leaves only about 4 inches long. *S. teres* has stiff, submerged leaves, rarely more than 7 inches long, and no floating leaves. *S. platyphylla* has submerged leaves about 11 inches in length with rounded tips. All *Sagittaria* species have white flowers and increase by stolons.

Synnema triflorum (Water Wistaria) is indigenous to south-east Asia from India to Malaysia. The leaves are very variable, ranging from oval with serrated margins to finely divided and fern-like with deep serrations. It needs a good light, soft water and a constant temperature of 25°C, with a few degrees either way, to produce the admirable large rosettes of finely divided leaves, pale green on the upperside, whitish green on the underside.

The genus *Vallisneria* is particularly well known to aquarists, for since 1850, when Robert Warrington conducted experiments on keeping fishes in aquaria without changing the water (see page 8), *V. spiralis*, indigenous to North America and southern Europe, has been the stock oxygenating plant introduced into every aquarium. It will withstand a temperature range of from 15 to 26°C (optimum 18 to 20°C) and is undemanding in most other respects, although it will not flourish if the water is very soft. The strap-shaped leaves grow up to a length of about 22 inches but a cultivated variety, usually known as twisted, and to horticulturists as 'torta', has slightly broader leaves that grow only up to about 15 inches long in close spirals throughout their length. *Vallisneria* species increase by stolons.

Vesicularia dubyana is an aquatic moss indigenous to south-east Asia from India to Indonesia. It is commonly known as Java Moss. It flourishes in a temperature range of 10 to 30°C (optimum 25°C) and is not particular about water or light. Reproduction is by fragmentation of the cushions and these moss-cushions look very attractive when allowed to spread over the bottom of the aquarium and attach themselves, or are anchored, to stones. In appearance it is very similar to *Fontinalis* with translucent, pale green, very small leaves, ideal as a spawning ground for egg-laying fishes and for furnishing cover for fry.

Floating plants need no planting; they are placed on the surface of the water and allowed to float free. Not too many should be introduced into a decorative aquarium, however, because their roots hang down and look unsightly, and what is much more important, they multiply very rapidly and exclude a lot of the top light that is so essential for the growth of the submerged plants.

Azolla caroliniana (Fairy Moss) is indigenous to the New World from California and the southern states of the United States, southwards to Buenos Aires. It has been introduced into Europe. The lace-like fronds are about $\frac{1}{2}$ to 1 inch in length and of a pale green colour in the summer darkening to a bronzy red later in the year. A good light is necessary and the water should not be too hard with a temperature range of 10 to 25°C.

Ceratopteris cornuta (*pteridoides*) (Floating Fern) is a favourite with aquarists of experience, partly because it is very decorative and partly because

the anabantid fishes find its fronds and long feathery roots ideal among which to build their bubble nests. The sterile fronds, of a pale green colour, have wavy margins and lie flat on the surface of the water in the form of a large rosette: the fertile fronds are much divided and stand up from the centre of the plant. Reproduction is by daughter plants which develop on the margins of the fronds. A heated aquarium is essential as the plant is indigenous to the tropical swamps of Africa and South America.

Eichhornia crassipes (Water Hyacinth) is indigenous to tropical America but has been introduced into other warm parts of the world. Sometimes this has had disastrous results; for once established it increases so rapidly that it has been known to choke rivers and impede shipping. It is a particularly handsome plant for a large heated aquarium (20 to 30°C). It has shiny green leaves that grow in rosettes and ride on the surface of the water by virtue of the petioles inflated with a spongy tissue. The roots, purplish in colour, are long and feathery and make an excellent spawning ground for egg-laying fishes. The hyacinth-like flower is very beautiful but in the aquarium is rarely to be seen for flowering occurs only if the light is intense, the air damp and warm, and the stolons, by which the plant increases, have been removed.

The genus *Lemna* (Duckweed) is cosmopolitan but most species are altogether too weedy to be worth a place in an aquarium. *L. trisulca*, the Ivy-leaved Duckweed, is probably the only species worth more than a passing mention: it forms clusters of pale green, translucent foliage with young fronds growing at right angles to the old ones, and one root fibre to each plant. It remains partly submerged and is an ideal plant for keeping water crystal clear. It needs a good light (but will not die if the light is poor) and a temperature range of 5 to 20°C, optimum 18°C.

Limnobium stoloniferum (American Frog-bit) is very similar in appearance to our native Frog-bit (*Hydrocharis morsus-ranae*) but the leaves are rather larger in size and paler in colour. It is a charming little plant, very suitable for small aquaria, but the light must be good and the water very soft or it will not survive for long. It is indigenous to tropical America and therefore will not stand a low temperature – a range of 15 to 25°C (optimum 20°C) is recommended.

Pistia stratiotes, from tropical America, is a very handsome plant for the heated aquarium with a temperature range of 18 to 30°C. It is commonly known as Water Lettuce, a name that is parti-

Above *Limnobium stoloniferum*

Below *Riccia fluitans*

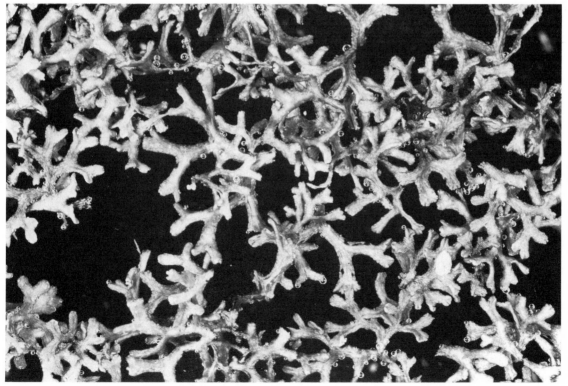

cularly well chosen, because not only are the leaves similar in shape to those of a small Cos lettuce, but they are also of the same pastel, grey-green shade. A good light is essential, and this plant flourishes best if the water is sufficiently shallow to allow the long, white, feathery roots to reach the planting medium.

Riccia fluitans (Crystalwort) is a plant much favoured by those aquarists who breed live-bearers; for the plant packs tightly, remains always partly to wholly submerged and is an excellent oxygenator. As a result, the fry have the advantage of finding shelter in particularly well-oxygenated water. Of cosmopolitan range, it is very plentiful in Australian waters and undemanding in its requirements: normal light, water that is not too hard and a temperature range of 8 to 30°C suits it well enough.

The genus *Salvinia* contains about a dozen species indigenous to the temperate and tropical regions of the world. The species most usually introduced into the aquarium is *S. natans* from the temperate regions of the northern hemisphere, including Europe but excluding America. It is a pretty plant with small, almost kidney-shaped leaves, the upperside bright green and covered with a nap of fine hairs, the underside matted with shiny brown hairs. It increases rapidly under a good light and in a temperature of 16 to 25°C, optimum 20°C.

The genus *Stratiotes* contains only one species *S. aloides* (Water Soldier) that is indigenous to Europe (including Great Britain). It is a rather large plant, resembling an aloe, and suitable only for a large aquarium. The leaves, borne in rosettes, are long, sword-shaped and serrated. The flowers are white and about 1½ inches in diameter. If the light is intense, the water slightly acid (*p*H 6·8) and the temperature range 10 to 20°C, optimum 18°C, the plant will flourish and increase by stolons from which daughter plants break away.

The genus *Utricularia* (Bladderwort) is a large one that contains more than 200 species of cosmopolitan range. The chief feature of the plants is that their stems are furnished with small bladders by means of which they capture minute animal life and convert it into food. *U. gibba*, commonly known as Pygmy Bladderwort, from South Africa and Australia, is the species most usually introduced into the heated aquarium. It grows just under the surface of the water in a tangled mass, but for decorative effect a few stems may be anchored to the bottom of the aquarium and allowed to grow to the surface.

Stonework

Stones in an aquarium are not necessary for success but there is no doubt that, suitably chosen, they add to the decorative effect and always interest to the general picture. If they are to be included the arrangement should be done at the same time as the planting because plants and stones are complementary to each other.

Decorating an aquarium can be, and by some has been, brought to an art. Plants, stones and fishes are chosen to echo a mountain stream in south-east Asia, the waters of an African rainforest or perhaps an Alpine lake. Such work, however, calls for a skilled hand, the unerring eye for beauty of the artist and the technical knowledge of the limnologist. It is beyond the capacity of most of us, who must rest content with the ambition to go no further than to create a pleasing underwater scene, free from such artificialities as gaudily coloured lumps of glass and such childish trivialities as sunken galleys, treasure-chests and divers, incongruous and absurdly out of proportion.

With this in mind, when it comes to choosing stones for an aquarium, it is not so much a matter of what to choose but of what to avoid. In the first place, stones should not be too big nor too many as they restrict swimming space for the fishes. In the second place, they should be devoid of sharp or jagged edges against which a fish might injure itself. In the third place, calcareous stones, such as marble, alabaster, spar and gypsum, should be rejected because water dissolves the lime in them and increases its hardness. Sandstones, such as Westmorland, Somerset and York, are most satisfactory; granite, quartz, flint and slate may all be used with confidence. They are particularly attractive when accompanied by chippings of the same stone or of a contrasting one. For bizarre and novel effects, well-washed coke and coal may be used, also cork-bark and the scrubbed roots of long-dead trees soaked in several changes of water. The most suitable species for use in the aquarium, because they are not toxic, are oak, willow, hazel, alder and pine.

An aquascene is largely a matter of the individual taste, and although it is usual to place large stones at the back of the tank and small ones at the front, very attractive effects may be obtained by reversing this rather obvious arrangement. In particular, every stone, large or small, is best seen from one angle and this should first be determined by holding it at arm's length and turning it this way and that, tilting it forwards and backwards, until the desired angle is found.

Choosing the fishes

The fifth and final fundamental of an aquarium is the fishes. There is a very large number from which to choose, and in the second part of this book we mention those that are usually available and from which selection may be made. Here, in this section, it is not so much a matter of giving advice on which fishes to choose but on how to choose them.

As a start, the decision has to be made whether tropical, sometimes called exotic, fishes are to be chosen or those that are commonly known as coldwater fishes. The difference is important because tropical fishes need a heated aquarium and coldwater fishes do not. From this it might be assumed that coldwater fishes are easier to keep than tropical ones. The very reverse is the case because coldwater fishes make a greater demand on the oxygen in the water, and those that do not die young for lack of oxygen, grow to a size uncomfortably big for an aquarium. When choosing fishes for an aquarium, whether tropical or coldwater species, attention must be paid to size because fishes are notorious bullies. Large fishes should not be allowed to share the same aquarium as smaller ones. Even if all the fishes are about the same size it is not always wise to keep them in the same aquarium. Some small fishes are pugnacious by nature with the bad habit of attacking more peaceful ones.

Although what makes a first-class fish is one of those things that is to be learnt only by experience, it is by no means difficult to choose fishes suitable for an aquarium if a little common sense is applied to the job and a few simple rules are borne in mind. The buyer will not go far wrong if he insists on fishes that swim on an even keel, are active, clear-eyed, and hold their fins away from the body and not drooping and lifeless; the body should be in good colour and free from blemishes. Although in some species (for example *Betta splendens*) the fins are normally drooping, it may be said that for all practical purposes any fish that fails to measure up to these requirements is to be rejected without a second thought; such fishes are certainly ailing even if they are not moribund.

One important point remains to be considered. The number of fishes to be bought must be restricted by the size of the aquarium because there is a limit to the number of fishes that a given body of water will support, and if that limit is exceeded the weaker fishes will die one by one until the working balance is reached.

For coldwater fishes the general rule is to allow 1 inch of fish (excluding the caudal fin) to every 24 square inches of surface area. Tropical fishes can manage with considerably less room because they require less oxygen and are accustomed in nature to more crowded conditions. As a rough and ready guide it may be said that for tropical fishes the minimum surface area should be 10 square inches for every inch of fish. Some fishes, however, will thrive in less space. The labyrinth fishes, for example, by reason of an accessory breathing organ, can manage with about 5 or 6 square inches of surface area to every inch of fish; and the Guppy (*Poecilia reticulata*) will tolerate a lot of crowding: 3 square inches of surface area is probably enough for it. Even though more fishes can be kept in the same amount of water by the use of a pump designed to drive air into the water through a porous stone, the limit imposed by nature should never be greatly exceeded, for overcrowding is the most fruitful source of disease.

Fishes should never be introduced into an aquarium until the plants have had time to take firm root, a matter of a fortnight to three weeks.

Ideally, a newly acquired fish should be carried home in some of the water in which it has been living and kept isolated for a period during which it should be inspected daily for any signs of disease or parasites. At the same time, to avoid too abrupt a change of water, it may be acclimatized to the water in which it is to be kept by partial changes of water every other, or every third, day. When the time comes to introduce the fish into the aquarium it should be taken in a jam-jar, small bowl or other container, and floated on the surface of the aquarium for about a quarter of an hour, in order that the temperatures may equalize. The jar may then be sunk and the fish allowed to swim out of its own accord.

Lighting

Every aquarium, whether heated or not, needs light and the natural assumption is that daylight is best. As a result, inexperienced aquarists place an aquarium close to a window in order that it may receive the maximum amount of daylight. No worse place could be chosen. In theory daylight is best for lighting an aquarium; in practice it is not because biologically the light is filtered through glass, important ultraviolet rays are lacking, and artistically it is too diffused to give the pleasing effect of strong shadows.

Some daylight is beneficial, however, and ideally an aquarium should be situated where it will receive an hour or two of direct sunlight either in the early morning or late afternoon. This means that it should never be placed close to a window, particularly one that faces south, but always about 2 or 3 feet away from one that faces either east or west. If necessary, the back and sides should be shaded so that the light enters the aquarium only from above, as it strikes water in nature.

For the rest, artificial lighting by electricity is necessary. Ordinary room lighting is not enough. The electric lamp must not be more than 5 or 6 inches above the surface of the water and should be fitted in a reflector shade. Ten hours a day is about the right length of time to keep an aquarium lighted. Water has a limited capacity for storing oxygen and it is better to provide slow oxygenation by the plants over a long period than rapid oxygenation over a short one. On the other hand, if the aquarium is lighted for more than ten hours a day, the plants grow lanky and look unsightly.

If tungsten lamps are used, a lamp should be placed towards each end of the aquarium, or a striplight should be used to give a more even illumination. The wattage may be determined by multiplying the length of the tank in inches by 3·25, but for the best result some experimentation must be made. Some plants need more light than others and the depth of the water will affect the amount of light needed to support the fishes and plants, as also will the amount of daylight that varies greatly with the seasons.

Fluorescent tubes are now available for lighting aquaria. A warm-tint tube is best for the plants and gives the aquarium a most attractive appearance. Initially these tubes are more expensive than tungsten lamps but they are cheaper in the end because very much less wattage is necessary. A 20-watt fluorescent tube is ample to light a 2-foot or 3-foot aquarium. There is the further advantage that fluorescent tubes generate insufficient heat to discomfort coldwater fishes, or to crack the cover glass if rested on it.

Heating

If an aquarium is to be stocked with tropical fishes the water must be heated. The handyman will be able to think of many ways of doing this but he will never be able to improve on an electrical immersion heater with thermostatic control. They are sold in a number of different types and wattages.

The heater should not be buried in the planting medium but placed on top of it at the back of the tank, where it, and the flex to the house supply, may be hidden by stones and plants.

Powerful heating equipment is not necessary; for when it comes to heating an aquarium it is not so much a matter of raising the temperature of the water, but of preventing it from becoming too cold. There is a difference. Once the aquarium has been filled with water at the required temperature, it takes very little heat to retain it at the same temperature within a few degrees either way. The wattage of the heater, therefore, will depend on the size of the aquarium and the temperature of the room in which it is situated. Postulating that when the weather is cold the room will be heated, a 60-watt heater is enough for the standard 2-foot aquarium. If the room is not heated during the winter months, or if the aquarium is a large one, two such heaters (one at each end of the tank to distribute the heat more evenly) are to be advised.

A temperature of 24°C, with a range of a few degrees either side, is enough for most tropical fishes. It is wrong, however, to keep the temperature at a steady 24°C, for in tropical countries there is quite a wide range of temperature between midday and midnight, and most tropical fishes, with a few exceptions, are at their healthiest when acclimatized to a temperature range of 21 to 25°C made gradually over the twenty-four hours of the day.

In a heated aquarium a thermometer is a necessity: in an unheated one it is a desirability. The most useful types are those that may be attached to the glass by a suction disc and read from the outside, without removing them from the water.

Filtration

Filtering the water in an aquarium is not necessary, except for a few species, but if a pump is available, filtration is a worthwhile refinement. It helps to keep the water clear by removing the suspended matter that occurs in every aquarium, and also the sediment that is churned up by the movements of the fishes.

Various types of filters are to be bought. The simplest is known as the internal filter because the chamber is installed inside the aquarium. For obvious reasons it can only be of very small size and therefore strictly limited in its efficiency.

A more advanced type is known as the external filter because the chamber is outside the aquarium. As the chamber can be as large as one likes, it is far more efficient. Both filters operate on the same principle: air from the pump lifts the water from the aquarium into the filter chamber and returns it to the aquarium after driving it through a layer of nylon wool and layers of medium and coarse

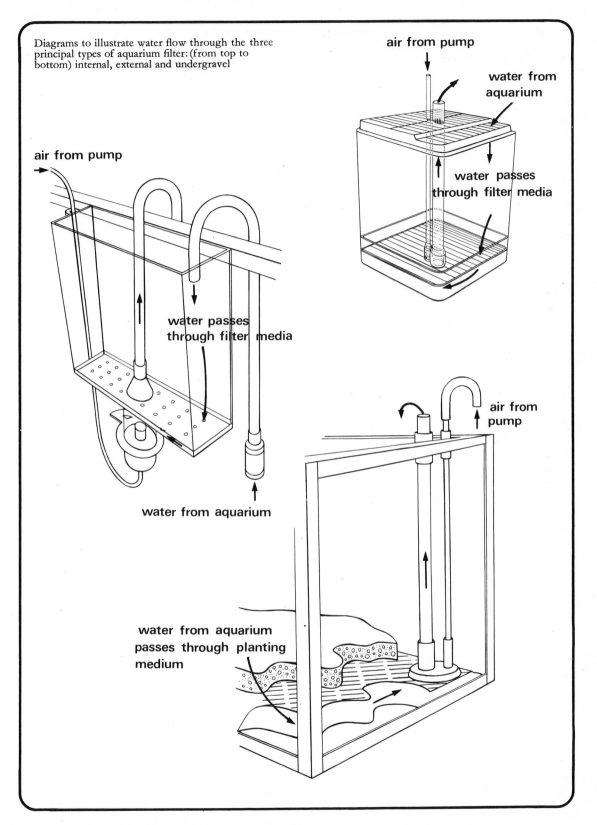

Diagrams to illustrate water flow through the three principal types of aquarium filter: (from top to bottom) internal, external and undergravel

air from pump

water from aquarium

water passes through filter media

air from pump

water passes through filter media

water from aquarium

air from pump

water from aquarium passes through planting medium

sands, fine shingle and carbon. The nylon wool requires frequent renewal as does the carbon which, because it is an absorbent, loses its efficiency in a few weeks.

A third type of filter is known as the substrate or undergravel filter because the water in the aquarium is filtered by being drawn through the planting medium, leaving the waste products to be broken up, and rendered harmless, by aerobic (oxygen-consuming) bacteria. It is an efficient form of filtration, and indeed some say that it is too efficient because it deprives the plants of food at their roots.

Feeding

That fishes kept in aquaria have to be fed is not altogether the glimpse of the obvious that it may seem. On several occasions we have met people whose fishes have died through failure to be given food. When we have explained to them the facts of life, that all animals need food if they are not to die, they have explained that they always thought that fishes found things in the water. This is one of those half-truths that is all the more dangerous because it is only half true. Very young fishes do live for the first few weeks of their lives on the minute organisms present in all waters. However, just as young mammals eventually need more solid food than their mother's milk, so in time fishes need more solid food than is to be found free in aquarium water.

It is as well for those who keep fishes that feeding them is no great problem. The majority of cyprinids, characins and catfishes are omnivorous and will eat more or less anything that comes their way. The cyprinodonts are also omnivorous, and most of the live-bearing poeciliids must be given some plant matter in their diet. The anabantids and cichlids are chiefly carnivorous and cannot be kept in good condition unless living food, or substitutes for it, are included in their diet. The nandids and polycentrids are strictly carnivorous and must have living food if they are to survive: in the wild they eat small fishes almost exclusively.

It will be seen that fishes, like man, abuse their stomachs, and if feeding them is no great problem one or two general principles must be observed. Fishes kept in aquaria remain active all the year. There is no hibernating period as there is in the wild. Feeding should therefore be regular, at least twice a day, and more often if the food is readily taken. Much depends on the species; carnivorous fishes seem to do better if given a big meal and then left with no food for some time: by contrary,

ideally herbivorous fishes should be given small meals every two or three hours during the daytime. Food should never be thrown haphazardly into an aquarium but always dropped into it at the same place, so that the fishes know where to find it. It is better to drop the food into the aquarium in two places at the same time; for in this way the slower fishes have a chance of getting a look in. Dried food that is left uneaten should be removed with a dip-tube or sediment-remover. Finally, as no one food will supply fishes with all the proteins, carbohydrates, vitamins and minerals that are necessary to keep them in health, the key to good feeding is to vary the diet as much as possible.

Foods for fishes fall into three main categories: living foods, dried foods and vegetable foods. We do not have space to give a complete list of all the foods that may be offered to fishes. A selection may be made from the following.

Living foods Water fleas (*Daphnia* and *Cyclops*) are among the best foods for small tropical fishes for their main source of food is algae from which they obtain oil. This gives them a laxative property which is beneficial for fishes kept in the confined space of an aquarium. Most dealers sell water fleas but during the summer months they are to be found in the shallows of stagnant ponds, particularly those near farms. They can be taken in quantity with a sweep of a fine-meshed net.

The Freshwater Shrimp (*Gammarus*) is an excellent food for the larger tropical fishes and coldwater species. It is to be found crawling among the roots and on the stalks or plants in almost every stream and ditch.

The Waterhog Louse (*Asellus*) is very similar in appearance and size to the Common Woodlouse (*Oniscus*). It is to be found in much the same places as the Freshwater Shrimp and, as a food for fishes, serves the same purpose.

The Earthworm (*Lumbricus*) is one of the best of all foods for aquarium fishes; it has slightly laxative properties, it is readily eaten by all fishes, it may be obtained at all times of the year, and if too big to be given whole it may be killed by dropping it into boiling water and chopped to a suitable size. Small pink worms and the red ones found on lawns are best. Those found on compost-heaps and heavily manured soils should not be given to fishes. Worms may be brought to the surface by watering the ground with a solution of permanganate of potash.

The Mudworm or Sludgeworm (*Tubifex*) thrives in running, preferably tidal, waters. Collecting it is a troublesome and very messy job. It is, therefore, better to buy a quantity from a dealer. The worms can be kept for some time in a shallow pan under a dripping, coldwater tap, but they soon die if kept in stagnant water or if the water is warm. After soaking in several changes of water they should be fed to fishes in a perforated basket (very cheaply obtained from dealers) that floats on the surface of the water.

The Whiteworm (*Enchytraeus*) is creamy yellow in colour, about ¼ inch long, and to be found under dustbins and similar unpleasant places. To maintain supplies, the worms may be bred in a shallow wooden box filled with sifted garden loam, kept moist, and in a place where the temperature does not fall much below 10°C or rise much above 18°C. The box should be kept covered with a sheet of glass to retain the moisture, and a piece of sacking or cloth to exclude light. Two or three times a week, the worms should be fed with a small quantity of mashed potato, bread soaked in sour milk, porridge, or similar mess.

The Grindal or Dwarf Whiteworm (*Enchytraeus*) is considered superior to its congener as it is more digestible. It may be bred in the same way.

The larva and pupa of the Gnat (*Culex*) are excellent foods for fishes. They are to be found throughout the summer months in most stagnant waters. The town-dweller need look no further than the nearest rainwater-butt. They are easily taken with a fine-meshed net.

The Bloodworm is the larva of the Midge (*Chironomus*) and the Glassworm or Ghostworm of the Plumed Gnat (*Chaoborus*). Both are very much alike in appearance, but the former is bright scarlet in colour – due to haemoglobin in its blood – and the latter is transparent. They are found in much the same places as gnat larvae and may be taken in the same way. They should not be given to very small fishes which have been known to choke to death on them.

The crustaceans, worms and insect larvae that we have mentioned are more or less the regular living foods for fishes. They are, however, not the only ones, and when unobtainable they may be replaced by gentles (maggots), mealworms, houseflies, small caterpillars, slugs and much else. In these days of toxic sprays, however, care should be taken to ensure that no insect that has been in contact with a spray should be offered as food to fishes. Scraped raw beef and horseflesh, chopped liver and white fish, as well as chopped shellfish are excellent substitutes for living foods, but no longer as essential as they once were; for today most dealers sell freeze-dried foods which are available all the year round. According to some authorities freeze-dried foods are better than living foods. They are just as nourishing and there is no risk of introducing parasites and diseases into an aquarium as there is with living foods, most of which come from polluted waters. The drawback to freeze-dried foods is that they encourage laziness among fishes. 'Fresh live foods', Hellmuth Wachtel writes in his *Aquarium Hygiene*, 'has the great advantage that it moves and attempts to escape, thus arousing the hunting instinct which is natural to most fish, and so does not allow the mechanism of prey-catching to lie dormant.' In the confined space of an aquarium physical exercise is very important to fishes.

Dried foods If given to fishes at all, dried foods must be given sparingly and only as substitutes when, for one reason or another, other foods cannot be obtained. For one thing, uneaten dried foods decompose very quickly and pollute the water; and for another, some of those that are factory packed in jars, cartons and packets are overloaded with starchy material, resulting in fishes, already restricted in exercise, developing fatty degeneration of the heart.

There is a large range of dried foods on the market, and if some are unsatisfactory, others offer an excellent balanced diet. Many aquarists like to prepare their own. There is no limit; for the best foods are a mixture of many ingredients. Fats should be excluded as fishes cannot digest fat, but mineral salts, carbohydrates and proteins (in that order) are essential for the health of fishes.

A very good food for all-round purposes may be made by mixing together one cup each of dried and pulverized codfish, shrimp, daphnids, spinach and wholemeal flour, two heaped teaspoonfuls of agar-agar and one of precipitated chalk. When thoroughly mixed the food should be kneaded into a stiff paste with a beaten egg and a little milk. The paste is then rolled out thin and dried in a slow oven. When dry it is crushed and the crumbs graded to suitable sizes; some fishes need bigger food than others. Although much depends on the size of the mouth, the general rule is that 1-inch fishes need food about the size of a grain of millet, 2-inch fishes food a little larger, and 3-inch fishes food about the size of a lentil. If the food is too big the fishes cannot eat it, and if too small they will ignore it. Either way it will be left to pollute the water.

Brown bread-crumbs, oatmeal dry or as porridge, the proprietary health food known as Bemax, dried shrimps and dried daphnids may also be given to fishes, although none is ideal nor as satisfactory as one made by mixing many ingredients.

Vegetable foods It is always as well to give omnivorous fishes a feed of green food about once a fortnight, and most live-bearers are very partial to green algae. Mollies and *Scatophagus* species can hardly live without some green food in their diet. Some fishes will eat Duckweed (*Lemna minor*) as a substitute for algae. It is unwise to take it from the wild as it grows in stagnant ponds and, unless very well cleansed, there is the risk that trematodes (parasitic flukes) and other pests will be carried into the aquarium with it. If Duckweed cannot be obtained from a safe source, good substitutes are the boiled and finely chopped leaves of spinach, nettles, cabbage, sprouts and lettuce. The last may also be given raw.

Maintenance

In every house the carpets have to be swept, the furniture polished and periodically the paint washed. In every garden the beds have to be hoed, the grass mown and periodically the paths swept. It is only common sense, therefore, that an aquarium must be kept clean by regular attention, just as a house and garden must, if it is not to deteriorate into a nuisance.

It seems hardly necessary to point out that a dead fish must be removed from an aquarium before it decomposes and pollutes the water. It is more necessary to point out that any fish that shows signs of ailing should be transferred at once to an aquarium by itself, not only to facilitate diagnosis, but because an ailing fish in an aquarium is a potential danger to the healthy fishes.

Much the same may be said of the plants. Decaying leaves should be cut off as close as possible to the main stem, and a dead plant should be uprooted and replaced with a fresh one. A dead plant in an aquarium is a danger to the fishes and not just the eyesore that it is in a garden. Even plants that are growing well should be pruned from time to time and not allowed to grow so luxuriantly that they hamper the movements of the fishes. Plants that increase by runners (for example *Vallisneria*) should have them cut as soon as the new plant has taken firm root. Plants that are not growing well may be manured with a dried pellet of excreta (rabbit's, guinea-pig's or hamster's) pushed into the planting medium near the roots.

At least once a week the front glass should be cleaned of algae, using a wad of cottonwool, or a razor-blade in stubborn cases. On stones the mossy types of algae look very attractive and are to be encouraged, but the hairy or filamentous types are not and should be scrubbed off.

Dust is harmful to fishes and that which settles on the surface of the water may be removed by laying a clean sheet of absorbent paper on the surface and removing it when the water has soaked through.

A considerable amount of sediment collects on the bottom of an aquarium in which fishes are kept. It is a good food for the plants but they can never cope with all of it, so that about once a week it is as well to remove the excess before it gets out of hand.

Sometimes a patch of the planting medium turns black and develops a cobweb-like appearance. As the main cause is uneaten food left to go bad, it is usually to be seen in a corner where feeding takes place. If vigorous plant life is present it is not particularly dangerous, but it is very unsightly and it is as well to siphon it off. The planting medium may be replaced, after it has been thoroughly washed and dried in the sun, by sliding it down a tube.

Although an aquarium should be kept covered at all times, much water is lost by evaporation. Periodically, therefore, the aquarium should be topped up. For this purpose distilled water raised to the same temperature as that in the aquarium, or water that has been boiled and allowed to cool to the same temperature, should be used. Salts in the water do not evaporate and unless the precaution of using distilled water is taken, the salinity of the water will be continually increased by topping up with tap water.

We have outlined the main jobs to be done in order to keep an aquarium clean. It is important to remember that if an aquarium has been properly set up in the first place, with adequate plant life and no overstocking with fishes, the less it is fussed with the better. Moving the plants from one position to another, wiping the glass, scrubbing the stones, removing some of the planting medium and making partial changes of water, for no better reason than that something seems to be wrong, does more harm than good. The more harm that it does the more the inexperienced fuss, making the situation worse. There is, for example, no need for alarm because the water in an aquarium turns green. It is due to the presence of algae (most freshwater algae are green) and, as they flourish best in strong light, the control is not to make a change of water but to reduce the light (either in wattage or hours) for about a week or ten days.

Algae in excess, however, can be dangerous. If the water, while clearing, takes on a turbid appearance – just as though a little milk has been added to it – and a faint but unpleasant smell is detected, it is a sure sign that if deaths have not occurred they may be expected at any moment. Provided that the water is not too badly polluted it can be cleared if an adequate filtration system, with activated carbon, is available. If not, or if the water is very badly polluted, it is time to throw it away, give everything in the aquarium a thorough clean, and start again.

Diseases

The diseases of fishes (embracing parasites) are many. The cures are few. This is inevitable because you cannot cure if you cannot treat, you cannot treat if you cannot diagnose, and the diagnosis of fish diseases is remarkably difficult. The fish cannot tell you where it hurts and, apart from a few obvious exceptions such as fungus and white spot, it is sometimes impossible to diagnose with certainty until it is too late. A post-mortem will reveal the cause of death but that helps no one, least of all the fish.

The biologist can always explain these things for the benefit of other biologists, but not always to the satisfaction of the layman. He sees things through a different pair of eyes, and even if he sees them through the same eyes he lacks the high-powered microscope, and other paraphernalia of a well-equipped biological laboratory, to confirm his diagnosis.

It is fortunate, therefore, that for the most part aquarium fishes are healthy, and that if the aquarium was properly set up in the first place and well looked after, diseases rarely strike them.

A good deal has been written about the diseases that affect fishes and the parasites that infest them. Perhaps too much has been written; for much of what has appeared in print about the treatment of diseases and control of parasites is nonsense. It could hardly be otherwise when the study of fish diseases, ichthyopathology for those who prefer the long word, is still in its infancy.

In this section, therefore, we are not aiming at being comprehensive. Rather we prefer to cut the subject down to size by mentioning only those diseases and parasites that are most likely to attack fishes kept in aquaria.

It may be said that the first sign that a fish is off-colour is the collapse of the dorsal fin. Such a fish should be transferred for further observation to what is called a hospital tank. A hospital tank is a small tank, devoid of plants and stones, that holds about a gallon of water of the same quality, and at the same temperature, as that in the aquarium from which the fish has been taken.

The faeces tell us much about the health of a fish. In a healthy fish they are short and drop from the vent soon after appearance. If they are long and filamentous, and contain air bubbles, it is a sign that the fish is constipated, usually as a result of too much starch in the diet. (Intestinal disorders are frequently caused by feeding dried foods that have been stored for more than a year in containers that are not airtight.) It is probable that a change of diet, to a variety of living and vegetable foods, will correct the condition, especially if the fish is a small one. If it does not the fish must be purged because constipation leads to indigestion and more serious complaints, such as derangement of the air bladder. To purge a fish normal food should be withheld and a small pill of bread soaked in a drop of halibut oil, or a few crystals of Epsom salt, should be dropped in front of it at feeding time. If necessary this should be repeated daily.

Parasites are sometimes introduced into an aquarium with plants obtained from a doubtful source and insufficiently cleansed or, more likely, with living foods such as *Daphnia* that have not been adequately inspected. The most common parasites that are to be seen with the naked eye are anchor worms (*Lernaea*), fish lice (*Argulus*) and leeches (Hirudinea). It is essential to control them as soon as noticed, and before they multiply to such an extent that it is impossible to eliminate them without wrecking the aquarium.

Anchor worms appear like very short lengths of dark thread protruding from the skin. The fish should be given a bath in a solution of 4 ounces of kitchen or sea salt in a gallon of water for about twenty minutes (less if it shows signs of distress).

Fish lice have flattened, disc-shaped bodies, greenish grey in colour and up to $\frac{1}{4}$ inch across. They attach themselves to a fish in order to feed on its blood, and are therefore most likely to be seen in the region of the gills. The fish should be held in the wet net, the lice touched with a drop of paraffin oil or turpentine and removed with forceps. The wounds should be dabbed with acriflavine. If the infestation is a bad one, it is better to immerse the fish for five or six seconds in 2 millilitres of Lysol in a litre of water.

Leeches are slug-like worms that vary in length from $\frac{1}{2}$ to $1\frac{1}{2}$ inches. They may be removed from an aquarium by hand, but when attached to a fish they must be picked off with forceps after first

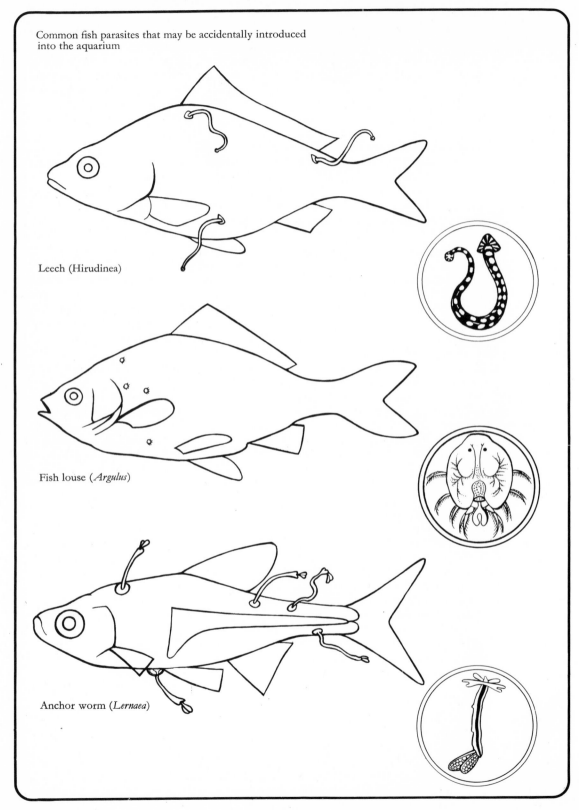

Common fish parasites that may be accidentally introduced into the aquarium

Leech (Hirudinea)

Fish louse (*Argulus*)

Anchor worm (*Lernaea*)

touching them with a drop of paraffin oil or turpentine. The wounds should be dabbed with acriflavine.

Frayed fins are often the result of attacks by other fishes. They may, however, be the result of bacterial infection and are therefore not to be neglected. Prolonged baths in various drugs have been recommended, but for large fishes surgical treatment is probably best. The affected part of the fin should be cut off with sharp scissors or a razorblade, and the stump painted with acriflavine or Friar's Balsam. Care must be taken to remove all the affected part of the fin; it will regenerate in time.

Frayed fins, indeed any wound on the body of the fish, should always be carefully watched for signs of fungus. The hyphae of *Saprolegnia* and *Achlya* readily settle on the damaged areas of skin in weakened fishes; they are easily identified by their cottonwool-like appearance. The standard treatment is to keep the fish in a salt bath (1 ounce of kitchen or sea salt in a gallon of water) for twenty-four hours. The strength of the bath is then increased to 2 ounces of salt in a gallon of water for a further twenty-four hours, and finally to 3 ounces of salt in a gallon of water and retained at this strength until the fish is clean. The salt content may then be gradually reduced daily before the fish is returned to fresh water. As some fishes (for example *Corydoras* species and those of the family Cobitidae) will not stand a lot of salt, an alternative treatment is to immerse the fish for up to eight hours in a bath of 50 to 80 milligrams of chloromycetin in a gallon of water.

The so-called fungus of the mouth is a slimebacterium infection that attacks the mouth of a fish after injury and destroys the jaws and gills. If neglected it quickly proves fatal. Aureomycin at the concentration of 50 milligrams to every gallon of water is recommended. The fish should remain in the bath until the treatment is effective.

A healthy fish swims on an even keel. One that swims with undulating motions, or otherwise shows an inability to balance itself, may have some disorder of the inner ear, but far more likely a derangement of the air bladder associated with chilling, constipation or an intestinal infection. Fancy goldfish with round fat bodies are particularly liable to the complaint because intensive breeding has distorted their internal organs. The recommended treatment is to transfer the fish to very shallow water (just enough to cover the dorsal fin), add sufficient kitchen or sea salt to make the water taste salty, raise the temperature to 30°C and give artificial aeration. Fast the fish

for a week and when feeding is resumed give relaxing foods such as daphnids and earthworms. Treatment should continue until the fish regains normal and for some time afterwards. No great things, however, are to be expected of it. There are records of complete cures having been made but they are few and far between, and were successful only when treatment started when the complaint was in its early stages. Normally the treatment will do no more than give the fish relief for a time, and once a fish has developed the complaint it remains susceptible to it at any time. A fish that swims with undulating motions and sinks to the bottom like a stone is a hopeless case and should be destroyed without hesitation.*

A fish that trembles, wobbles clumsily from side to side, seemingly swimming but making no forward progress and constantly resting on the bottom of the aquarium or on a plant, is popularly described as suffering from the shimmies or shakers. It should be purged (see page 25) and given a raised water temperature; nearly always the cause is due to its having been kept at too low a temperature. If this treatment fails, keeping the fish in very shallow water for about a week should be tried.

Fishes that persistently dash wildly about, scraping their bodies against stones, plants and even the planting medium, are almost certainly infested with gill flukes, trematodes of the genera *Gyrodactylus* and *Dactylogyrus*. These parasites can barely be seen without a magnifying glass for they are less than $\frac{1}{16}$ inch long. They attach themselves to soft spots on the body of the fish, most usually to the gills, causing hyper-secretion of mucus that is frequently fatal to it. The standard treatment is to immerse the fish in a quart of water, add five drops of forty per cent formalin and up to ten drops more (each drop at one minute intervals), the treatment not to exceed ten minutes in all. Four treatments, given at intervals of forty-eight hours, should effect a cure. An alternative treatment is to immerse the fish for several hours in a solution of 0·6 gram of trypaflavin in a litre of water. The

---

* The fish should be held by the tail, using a piece of dry cloth to prevent slipping, and the back of the head brought down as sharply as possible on to a hard surface, such as the corner of a kitchen sink. If this method of destroying a fish is impractical, owing to its small size, the head should be snipped off with very sharp scissors. For those who are squeamish, the fish may be dropped into a five per cent solution of formalin. Probably the simplest and quickest of all methods is to dash the fish with great force on to a stone floor. To flush a moribund fish down a drain is a very cruel practice.

aquarium in which the outbreak occurred should be disinfected with a strong solution of kitchen salt. The plants should be thrown away and the planting medium and stones boiled if they are to be used again.

Fishes are the hosts of a number of microscopic parasites. The flagellate *Costia* and the ciliates *Chilodonella* and *Trichodina* (*Cyclochaeta*) appear on their bodies as patches of grey slime. The salt treatment, as recommended for fungus (see page 27), causes them to leave the fish. It does not kill the parasites, however, and for this, protosil, or a similar silver-protein compound, is recommended. It is bought as a powder and a five per cent stock solution is made up in water. The fish is then immersed for two minutes (up to five if it will tolerate it) in a gallon of water to which 1 ounce of the stock solution has been added. The treatment should be given daily for three days. If no improvement is shown, it should be continued with a double dose of the stock solution, or an immersion in trypaflavin, as recommended for gill flukes (see page 27), may be tried.

The microscopic parasite *Oodinium* shows itself on the fish in yellowish or yellow-brown patches of a velvety texture. The most suitable control is with acriflavine. A tablet that contains 0·46 grain should be dissolved in 8 ounces of hot water and a teaspoonful of the solution added to every gallon of water in the aquarium. The dose should be repeated a week later.

White Spot is a parasitic infestation by the ciliate *Ichthyophthirius*, and it is very easy to diagnose because the infested fish shows gravelly white spots, each about the size of a pin's head, where the parasites have lodged in the skin. For tropical fishes the control is very simple. The temperature of the water is raised during the day to 32°C, and lowered at night to 24°C to give the fishes some relief, and two or three drops of five per cent medicinal methylene blue are added to every gallon of water in the aquarium. (As methylene blue at this concentration is likely to kill the plants, expensive ones should first be removed from the aquarium.) The fishes are kept in this solution until they are clean, more dye being added from time to time to retain the light blue colour of the water. The water is then changed. In the unheated aquarium it is not practical to raise the temperature of the water, and control consists of merely adding methylene blue to the water. Without increasing the heat, however, the cure will take longer, for drugs are not effective against the parasites in the skin, but only against the spores, so that treatment

must continue until the last parasite has been released.

Sometimes an opaque white spot appears on the eye of a fish and spreads slowly over the cornea. Popularly called a Cataract, it is not a true cataract but is not altogether a misnomer for, if neglected, it has the same effect of blinding the fish. Twice a day the eye should be wiped dry with a wad of cottonwool and either painted with a tincture of one part iodine to nine parts glycerine, or one of equal parts of argyrol and glycerine.

In some cases the eye protrudes, rather like a bubble. Known as Exophthalmia, or Pop-eye, it is sometimes associated with gases in the eyeball due to a sudden change in the temperature or *p*H of the water, and sometimes to an excess of artificial aeration. The fish should be immersed for three hours (or longer if it will tolerate it) in water to which five drops of ammonia have been added to every four gallons. The precautions must be taken to transfer the fish first to a half-strength solution, then to full strength, and then back to half strength before returning it to the aquarium.

In some rare cases the protuberant eye arises from a pathogenic variation of the microscopic organism *Pseudomonas punctata* in the vitreous humor. It is a sign of incipient Dropsy, ascites, diagnosed by the scales standing out from the body. Such a fish should be painlessly destroyed (see footnote page 27). Good results have been obtained with injections of chloromycetin and streptomycin, but this is work outside the capacity of most aquarists.

It is much the same when a female fish is spawn bound. If the fish is a large one, the professional fish-breeder can release the eggs with the help of a bone knitting-needle. The ordinary aquarist should not attempt the operation and, in any case, it is virtually impossible to perform with success on a small aquarium fish. A fish that is spawn bound becomes very swollen, loses its balance and refuses food. The best that can be done is to raise the temperature of the water a few degrees, and gently massage the fish towards the vent, while holding it under water in a net.

From time to time fishes are injured in a fight or by knocking themselves against a stone. Small injuries may be left to look after themselves, but severe ones should be dressed by touching them with a camel's hair brush, or a wad of cottonwool, that has been dipped in a mild antiseptic such as a ten per cent solution of neo-silvol, or four drops of Condy's fluid in ½ pint of water. The same treatment may be given to external ulcers.

A fish that has been badly battered in a fight, or frightened by being chased with a net, or by some other unusual disturbance, may show all the signs of nervous shock: paling of the colours, irregular breathing and, in extreme cases, turning over on its side. A fish in such a distressed state is best left in peace and quiet, undisturbed. Feeding should be withheld until it shows signs of recovery, when it may be offered living food.

Of recent years much work has been done on treating fish diseases with antibiotics, but it is possible that some aquarists would find difficulty in handling them properly, even if they could obtain them without the prescription of a doctor or veterinary surgeon. Pet shops and aquarium dealers offer a large number of preparations for the treatment of fish diseases, and some of them contain antibiotics. One has to be suspicious of any preparation for which the claim is made that it is a cure for most or every disease (there is no universal panacea), and one has to accept the fact that some are harmless, but no more, if they are used in accordance with the instructions given. A few are excellent, however, and to be recommended with confidence.

The quiddities of the fishes

Few people, even those who keep fishes in aquaria, know much about fishes, how they move, eat, breathe and so forth. To begin, therefore, in spite of the evidence provided by our eyes, fishes do not drink. All the water that is taken in at the mouth immediately passes over the gills and out through the gill openings at the back of the head. No water reaches the stomach of the fish because the gullet is kept so tightly closed that water cannot enter it. When, however, a particle of solid matter, such as a morsel of food, touches the closed gullet, no matter how lightly, the muscles relax and the solid matter is pressed down the alimentary canal and into the stomach. No water goes with it, or if it does, only a negligible quantity, because the gullet clasps the solid matter too tightly to permit it. Finally, to lessen the risk of a piece of solid matter passing over the gills and so injuring them, they are protected by stiff fibres (known as gill rakers, although they do not rake the gills) whose function it is to strain the water before it reaches the delicate gills.

The gills are so constructed that as the water passes over them and the blood through them, the blood extracts oxygen from the water and releases carbon dioxide into it. After the exchange of gases has been made, the oxygenated blood is carried by the arteries to all parts of the body, where eventually it combines with elements of digested food for the production of energy and growth. The end products of this combination are largely carbon dioxide (which, as we have seen, passes out of the body through the gills) and nitrogenous wastes which are excreted by way of the kidneys.

It is particularly important for the aquarist to remember that the blood temperature of a fish, unlike that of the mammals and birds, but like that of the reptiles and amphibians, is not regulated to remain constant irrespective of that of the surrounding medium. It is not altogether true to say that a fish is a cold-blooded animal; it is properly true to say that it is a poikilotherm, that is an animal whose blood temperature varies with that of the surrounding medium. The blood temperature of a fish is always more or less the same as that of the surrounding water, and it is for this reason that fishes are more active at higher temperatures than lower ones; and that they become more hungry as the temperature rises, because energy is being used up.

From this it follows that every time that there is a change in the temperature of the water the fish has to undergo a major functional change. It must be given time to adapt itself to the change, and if it is not (for example if it is plunged into water several degrees higher or lower than the water in which it has been living) it will at worst be killed and at best suffer a severe functional derangement that may result in premature death. It is not quite true to say that the fish receives a chill because a chill can be contracted only by an animal that has a fixed body temperature. It amounts to much the same thing in the end, however, because the result of submitting a fish to changes of water at a lower temperature to that in which it has been living is much the same as subjecting a human being, heated by exertion, to an ice-cold bath. In both cases death supervenes if it is done too often.

The blood of freshwater fishes contains a higher proportion of salts than in the surrounding water. As, by what is known as osmosis, the tissues absorb water and dilute the blood, the fish's kidneys have to get rid of much excess water in order to protect the blood. The aquarist has to exercise care when topping up an aquarium or making a partial change of water, because changes in the salt content of the water react on the fish. Some species are more sensitive to osmotic changes than others and may be seriously harmed, if not killed, if they are kept for too long in a hard water.

Anglers have been heard to say that fishes, being

cold-blooded animals (in itself a mere half-truth), do not feel pain. It may serve to excuse the sport but it is not a scientific fact. The fish has a well-organized nervous system and there is little doubt that, in common with other animals, it can and does feel pain, if perhaps not to the same degree as the higher vertebrates. The nervous system of the fish represents the general plan from which that of the higher animals has been elaborated. It has good eyesight but water is too dense a medium to permit of distant vision, and from the position in which the eyes are situated it seems doubtful that they can ever be focused on the same object. The sense of smell, coupled with taste, is good, but the ear does not appear to be a very effective organ of hearing and seems to be concerned primarily with balance.

Along the side of the body, however, there is a series of very sensitive organs, made visible as a row of perforated scales from head to tail. Generally known as the lateral line system, but more properly as the acustico-lateralis system, it enables the fish to detect pressure changes and vibrations in the water. As the lateral line and the ear develop from the same rudiment, and both are supplied by the same nerve, it may be said that the inner ear is probably a modified part of the system.

There is also the air bladder, sometimes called the swim bladder, which has evolved from the lungs of the ancestral fishes which were partly air breathers. In some species the air bladder is connected with the gullet and is, in fact, an accessory breathing organ: in most it serves as a hydrostatic organ. It is kept filled with gases, derived from the blood, and by muscular compression on the walls the fish varies its specific gravity to match the depth at which it is swimming and remain there without effort.

Most fishes have seven fins. The dorsal or back fin, which is sometimes in two parts, the caudal or tail fin, and the anal fin, which is situated under the tail proper. These three fins are all single and situated in the middle line of the body. The pectoral or breast fins are paired, supported by shoulder bones and situated just behind the skull; the pelvic or ventral fins are also paired; they are situated under the abdomen. All these seven fins may be opened or folded, fanwise, because they consist of rays joined by membrane and sometimes supported by one or more comparatively strong spines. The number of spines and rays in the several fins is a guide to the identity of a species. In some species there is also a small fin, known as the adipose fin, situated in the middle line of the

back and behind the dorsal fin. It lacks spines and rays and consists of fatty tissue.

Swimming is accomplished mainly by flexion of the lateral muscles of the body, particularly by the tail giving the caudal fin a side-to-side sweep. The action may be compared to propelling a boat by means of a flexible stern oar. Apart from the caudal fin, the fins play very little part in driving a fish forward. The dorsal and anal fins serve as stabilizers, and the pelvics act in much the same way as the elevators of an aeroplane. The pectorals serve as steering organs and brakes: a fish turns to the right or left by raising the appropriate pectoral fin, and if it needs to stop quickly it spreads both forward to offer the maximum amount of resistance to the water.

The body of the fish is covered with scales which overlap like the tiles on a roof. The number of scales on the body of a fish remains constant from birth to death. That they do is a matter of some importance to the ichthyologist, because a count of the scales helps towards the identification of a species. As the number of scales remains constant it is clear that the scales must grow with the fish. Growth of the scale is accomplished by addition at the edges, and as fishes grow more rapidly in spring and summer (when food is plentiful) than at other times of the year, the concentric lines of growth on the scales are wider and more numerous at this time. It is, therefore, possible to determine the age of a fish by counting the zones of slow and rapid growth on a scale. However, this method applies only to those taken from the wild; fishes kept in aquaria are fed all the year round so that their growth is constant.

The scales are formed of a horny substance produced by activity of the skin and are themselves transparent. The colour of the fish is due to pigment cells, properly called chromatophores, in the dermis underneath. They are disposed in two layers: an outer and an inner, or deeper, layer. They are of different kinds, according to the colouring matter that they contain, and the combination of different kinds produces a variety of effects. In addition, the skin of the fish contains a large number of opaque plates (iridocytes) which reflect the light, and are therefore responsible for the bright metallic sheen that is so much admired.

If we know how fishes are coloured, we cannot be certain why they are. It is a widely accepted belief that, for the most part, the purpose of colour in fishes is to help conceal them from their enemies, that in fact, the fish blends with its surroundings. It may be the reason in some cases. There is not the slightest doubt that the dark vertical bars on the sides of the Angelfish (*Pterophyllum*) and the waving fins give it concealment among the swaying reeds of its natural haunts. It is not always so easy to find an explanation because in many cases fishes that are highly coloured live against a colourless background, and observers report that they stand out in conspicuous contrast to their surroundings. That the markings on the fish are no more than recognition marks, a livery so to speak, to enable a fish to identify members of its own species, would carry more weight if it could be explained how a fish, that cannot turn its head, knows the colour and markings on its own body. It seems probable that the skin pigment of fishes may represent excretion and serve no purpose at all. Expressed another way, that the rich coloration just happened and that although in some cases a fish is able to use its particular coloration and markings to adapt itself to its surroundings, in others it has no need, being adequately protected from its enemies by its speed and proximity to a safe retreat. If its colours serve any purpose they may well be flash colours to convey a warning signal. There is a quick flip of caudal fins, a flash of blue, yellow, green, red, and indeed of all the colours of the rainbow. The predator is temporarily dazzled by a sudden and unexpected display of colour, and before he has time to recover from his surprise, a whole shoal of fish has disappeared behind a rock or among a convenient bed of reeds; there to remain, demurely waiting until the danger has passed. When we see an isolated specimen in an aquarium, we may wonder how such a conspicuous object can ever elude discovery. But when we remember how we ourselves are temporarily blinded when a photographer releases his flash and opens the shutter of his camera, we begin to appreciate how the bright colours and bizarre markings that we see on many aquarium fishes may help them to escape capture.

To most aquarists breeding fishes is more or less synonymous with keeping them. It is, therefore, proper that we should end this section with some easy observations on the breeding of fishes in general, reserving the detail for mention, more appropriately, in the second part of this book.

In the minds of most people, the act of reproduction is associated with the pairing of a male and female of a species, followed by a union between the two. In fishes this is the exception rather than the rule. In all vertebrate animals the act of reproduction begins by the male fertilizing the ova of the female, but whereas in the higher vertebrates the male fertilizes the ova while they are still in the body of the female, in fishes there is rarely copulation; the female lays the eggs and the male then fertilizes them. The act of spawning is conducted in various ways.

Many fishes allow their eggs to drift at a depth to match their specific gravity. The practice is very common among marine fishes, and indeed occurs among all our food fishes with the exception of the Herring. Among tropical aquarium fishes it is practised by the Climbing Perch (*Anabas*) from south-east Asia and some other species, but never by any river fish because the eggs would be carried to the sea and destroyed by the change from fresh to salt water.

The Herring deposits its eggs on the bottom. It is a practice that is by no means uncommon among aquarium fishes. Our native Minnow is a typical example; among tropical fishes it is practised by many of the cichlids, and among subtropical fishes by the Black-banded Sunfish (*Mesogonistius*) from the United States.

Some fishes, notably members of the salmon family, bury their eggs. It is rarely practised by aquarium fishes, but the Argentine Pearlfish (*Cynolebias*) and the related *Nothobranchius* species from tropical Africa are among the exceptions. These fishes live in areas where the pools dry up in the hot weather and the fishes with them. To ensure the continuation of the species, the fishes bury their eggs in the mud, and as they are drought resistant the young hatch out when the rains come and refill the pools.

Many fishes build nests. The Stickleback (*Gasterosteus*) of our native ponds, and the Pygmy Sunfish (*Elassoma*) from the Everglades of Florida, use pieces of water plants to build nests in the manner of birds. Many of the anabantids build a nest by blowing bubbles of air and sticky mucus, which cling together to form a mushroom-like floating mass of foam on the surface of the water.

Some fishes carry their eggs with them. *Haplochromis* and *Tilapia*, from Africa, carry them in their mouths, a practice that is popularly known as mouth-breeding but more properly as buccal incubation. It is the practice of some South American catfishes (for example *Bunocephalus*) for the female to attach the eggs to the spongy integument of her belly by pressing against them with her pelvic fins.

An even more remarkable method of spawning is practised by the little Bitterling (*Rhodeus*) from central Europe. At the breeding season the female develops an ovipositor by means of which she places the eggs between the shells of a mussel; the sperms of the male are carried into the mussel, through the breathing apparatus, there to fertilize the eggs.

Almost as unusual in its method of spawning is *Copeina arnoldi* from the Amazon basin. The male and female leap together out of the water and cling for a few seconds to an overhanging leaf, there to deposit and fertilize the eggs.

These methods of spawning, however, are more the exceptions than the rule, and most aquarium fishes scatter their eggs among water plants. The eggs are demersal and adhesive. As a result, as they gravitate to the bottom they attach themselves to the leaves and stems of the plants, to stones, and when the fish are bred in domestication, to the glass of the aquarium. This method of spawning is very common among the cyprinids and characins. It is a very satisfactory method for fishes that have a large number of enemies because the eggs, attached to plants, are given camouflage, cannot be carried away by water movement and are situated where they receive the maximum amount of oxygen that is necessary for the development of the embryo.

The sex organs, or gonads, of fishes are ovaries (hard roe) in the female and testes or milt (soft roe) in the male. The ovaries are pinkish or yellowish in colour, granular in texture, elongated in shape, paired, and more or less intimately associated with the kidneys. The testes occupy much the same position in the male as do the ovaries in the female; they are, however, paler in colour and have a creamy rather than a granular texture.

The act of reproduction is very simple. Primarily the gametes (germ cells) are fragments of protoplasm containing nuclei that develop into ova in the ovaries and into spermatozoa in the testes. The nucleus, usually spherical or ovoid in shape with a firm superficial membrane, is composed of separate parts, called chromosomes, and the number of chromosomes is constant for each species. Every Guppy, for example, has forty-six chromosomes, every Siamese Fighting Fish forty-two, and so on. When a species has the same number of chromosomes as another, hybridization is made much easier. It is for this reason that, other things being equal, some species are much easier to cross than others. The chromosomes are a mixture of proteins, called chromatin, and lodged in the chromatin and arranged in a linear series along the chromosomes, are the genes. The gene is the factor in the transmission of acquired characteristics from parents to their offspring.

When the gametes are ripe the fishes are said to be in breeding condition. Their colours improve, they become exuberant, and the well-known drive begins.

The eggs pass from the ovary, by way of a passage called the oviduct, and out of the body by an aperture which in most species is shared with the excretory duct, but in some (for example the Pike) by a special aperture.

The number of eggs that a species deposits varies very greatly, and there is a very wide range within the same species. Much depends on the size and age of the fish and, of course, its condition. In general, it may be said that those species that protect their eggs (for example nest-builders) deposit many fewer eggs than those that take no interest in their eggs once they have been scattered and fertilized (for example barbs). This, of course, is only in the natural order of events. On the whole, aquarium fishes deposit very few eggs: they may be counted by the hundred. Among marine species the eggs are to be counted by the thousand, even by the million; the cod deposits anything from six to ten million eggs, a ling has been found to contain 160 million eggs and a large sunfish no less than 300 million.

It is rather remarkable that, despite this vast number of eggs, comparatively few remain unfertilized. It is probable, therefore, that the fertilization of the egg is not the outcome of blind chance, but that there exists some chemical attraction between the egg and the sperm. At all events, this does not mean that every fertile egg will hatch and the larva reach the adult stage. Far from it. The eggs and larvae of fishes have so many enemies in nature that it is a fair estimate that, in the case of the cod, less than one egg in every million ever becomes an adult fish.

The eggs of fishes, when cast into the water, are quite small. The majority vary in size from about 1 to 2 millimetres in diameter. Larger eggs are deposited by members of the salmon family: by contrary, the eggs of *Chanda* (the glassfishes of the aquarium) are no bigger than grains of sand. As soon as the egg comes into contact with the water, however, it swells by virtue of the osmotic uptake of water.

An unfertilized egg, as shed into the water, consists of living protoplasm and deutoplasm (yolk) encased in a protective vitelline membrane. The yolk (non-living foodstuff) accumulates at one end of the egg, called the vegetative pole; the protoplasm collects at the other end, called the animal pole. Since the egg of the fish is nearly all

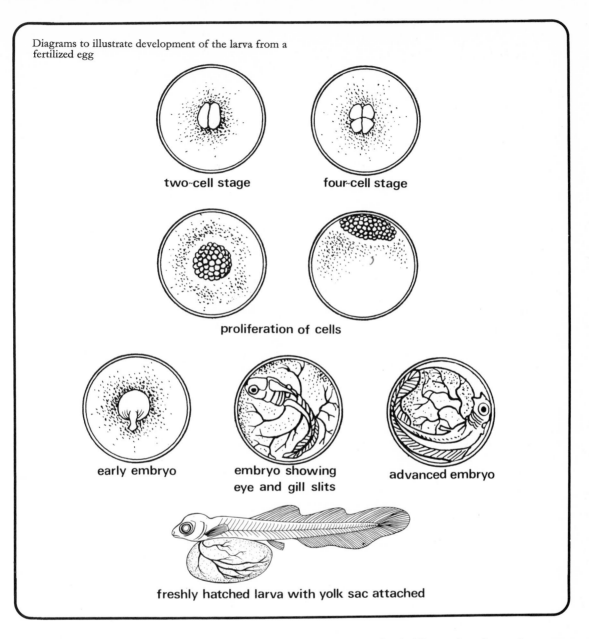

Diagrams to illustrate development of the larva from a fertilized egg

two-cell stage

four-cell stage

proliferation of cells

early embryo

embryo showing
eye and gill slits

advanced embryo

freshly hatched larva with yolk sac attached

yolk, the animal pole is virtually reduced to a small cap. An egg of this type is called telolecithal, as opposed to the microlecithal egg of the eutherian mammals, which is largely protoplasm and contains only a minute quantity of yolk.

The fertilization of the egg is performed by the male spermatozoon. Outwardly a sperm varies in appearance according to the species, but fundamentally its structure is the same in every vertebrate animal. It consists of a head, a middle-piece, and a tail or flagellum. The head contains the nucleus (with the same number of chromosomes as

the female nucleus). The nucleus forms the greater part of this region since it is merely invested with a thin layer of cytoplasm which is continued forwards into a pointed projection, called the acrosome. In the slender middle-piece are minute semi-solid bodies known as the centrosomes and mitochondria, and from it extends the tail whose undulations drive the sperm forward to come into contact with the egg.

The moment a sperm touches an egg the acrosome penetrates the vitelline membrane. The tail is cast off, and the head and middle-piece rotate (so that the middle-piece precedes the head) and are drawn deeply into the cytoplasm of the egg. As the male nucleus approaches the female nucleus, the haploid number of chromosomes appear in each of the nuclei, and the nuclear membranes break down. A star-shaped structure called an aster forms about the centrosome, which is released from the middle-piece, and a typical spindle appears. (A spindle is formed from threads of cytoplasm arranged along the length of the fertilized egg.) The male and female chromosomes become distinct and arrange themselves on the spindle. In this way the diploid number of chromosomes is restored and the egg, having received both paternal and maternal chromosomes, is now said to be fertilized and known to the embryologist as a zygote. At the same time, a chemical change in the cytoplasm renders the egg incapable of penetrations by supernumerary sperms.

Development of the embryo begins by a process of cleavage. In a matter of minutes the protoplasm divides into two, the two halves again divide into two, and so on, until many thousands of cells (blastomeres) are formed. Division is not particularly rapid. Observation kept on the eggs of a Zebra Killie (*Fundulus heteroclitus*) showed that after five hours there had been eight cleavages forming 256 cells. This process, however, does not take very long to build up many thousands of cells; for at the next cleavage there are 512 cells, at the next 1024, at the next 2048, at the next 4096, and so on. Cell division, of course, continues throughout life, but the process of cleavage is arbitrarily held to end with the completion of the embryonic stage, called the blastula. In its simplest form the blastula is a hollow sphere built up of a single layer of blastomeres, enclosing a central cavity known as the blastocoele.

The next stage of development is known as gastrulation. By complex cell movement, the blastomeres move from their largely superficial position in the blastula to their approximately definitive position in the embryo. One might say that the blastula is converted into a double-walled cup of blastomeres. It is known as the gastrula and its central cavity, called the archenteron, is the beginning of the alimentary canal.

Specialization or organization (what the embryologists call organogeny) now begins. The subject is altogether too deep and involved to be discussed here; it must suffice to say that the process implies the laying down of the organs and systems of the body, step by step, until the adult stage is reached. The period of incubation may be anything from twenty-four hours to a fortnight or more, depending on the species and the temperature of the water.

When an egg hatches the young fish emerges as a larva. In general appearance it resembles a tadpole for, to the superficial observer, the most prominent feature is the yolk-sac carried abdominally. A notochord (to be replaced in the adult by the vertebral column or backbone) is present.

At this stage, as every fish-breeder knows, the larvae hang at rest (occasionally labouring for short distances) some to the aquatic plants, others to the sides of the aquarium and stones, still others at the surface of the water.

For a few days the larva exists by absorbing the remainder of the yolk-sac. The period largely depends on the temperature of the water. The higher the temperature, the quicker the yolk-sac is absorbed.

Once the yolk-sac has been absorbed, however, the fish (now called a post-larva) has developed a pair of pectoral fins, an air bladder and an alimentary canal, also a median fin that eventually divides into the dorsal, caudal and anal fins. It is now able to swim and eat, and strikes out in search of the minute organisms that form its first food.

Henceforward, growth is determined as much from without as from within. That is to say, if the post-larva is to reach the adult stage, it must obtain the right food in enough quantity, and under the artificial conditions of aquarium-life the food has to be supplied by the breeder.

There is a large group of fishes known as live-bearing, or viviparous, fishes, so called because the female brings forth the young alive. The group is represented to aquarists mainly by the family Poeciliidae, characterized by the male having the third, fourth and fifth rays of the anal fin modified into a gonopodium or intromittent organ.

When Guppies and other live-bearers were first introduced into England observation was kept on them in order to try to find out how the copulatory act took place. No-one ever saw it and it was deduced, therefore, that true copulation did not take place, but that the male, when chasing the female, extended his gonopodium and fired the sperm packets at her. These were drawn into her genital orifice by a sucking action.

Later research in America has proved that this is not the case. While working with the late Dr Myron Gordon, whose main work was cancer in fishes, Dr Eugenie Clark kept observation for many months on platies, recording every action of the fishes. During her observations she noticed an unusual contact between male and female. It happened very rarely and usually when the fishes were placed together after having been isolated for several hours. The male chased the female, and suddenly the two fishes seemed glued together, side by side, for a period that lasted up to five seconds. The details need not concern us but, in brief, by using a set of virgin females each placed with a male for ten minutes, and observing all that happened, and then by means of artificial insemination, Dr Clark proved that this was the true copulatory act. The long-held belief that the male fired the sperms at the female from a distance was a fallacy.

Subsequent experiments with guppies and other live-bearers showed that they too had a similar, rare copulatory act.

The eggs are fertilized while still in the ovisacs of the ovaries, or within the cavity of the ovary itself, and may undergo development in either position. As in the case of the oviparous species, the embryos are nourished by the yolk contained originally in the ova, but the oxygen necessary for respiration is supplied by the blood of the mother. Although the fishes are generally known as viviparous species, in point of fact the more correct term is ovoviviparous, for in true viviparity there is no interposition of any egg-membranes.

Among the poeciliids one fertilization serves for a number of successive broods delivered in a year. In the closely related family Goodeidae (represented to aquarists by *Neotoca bilineata*) the female has to be fertilized for every brood.

Another peculiarity among live-bearers is to be found in the rarely seen *Jenynsia lineata*, for here the gonopodium can be moved either to the right (dextral) or to the left (sinistral) but never to both sides. The urogenital opening of the female is covered by a large scale (known as the foricula) which is attached to one side or the other, and in consequence opens only to the left or to the right. The result of these curious anatomical features is that a dextral male can mate only with a sinistral female, and vice versa. The aquarist whose aim it is to breed the species, however, need not be overconcerned about obtaining the necessary matched pair; for by a dispensation of nature dextral males and sinistral females are very much in the majority.

Parental care is largely unknown among fishes. Most eat their eggs as soon as they have been deposited and the larvae as soon as they have hatched out. There are, of course, exceptions, and parental care usually takes the form of constructing some sort of a nest for the reception of the eggs.

As we have already seen, among the North American freshwater sunfishes, the male *Elassoma* builds a nest of fine-leaved plants, and the male *Mesogonistius* scoops out a shallow, basin-like depression at the bottom, carefully removes all pebbles, and lines it with sand. After the eggs have been deposited he guards them carefully, keeps the nest clear of sediment, and remains on guard until the young are free swimming. Much the same practice is found among some of the cichlids. Many of the anabantids build a bubble nest and buccal incubation (mouth-breeding) which, as we have seen, is practised among the aquarium fishes *Haplochromis* and *Tilapia*, is a particularly interesting form of parental care. The eggs, and later the fry, are carried in the mouth of the parent fish, usually the female but sometimes by the male, and sometimes indifferently by either. It is altogether a remarkable sight. The eggs are carried for from fifteen to eighteen days and during this period the parent fish takes no food, and so becomes very emaciated. Three or four days after hatching, the young fish are let free but at the least sign of danger they retreat to the protecting mouth.

What purpose these several forms of parental care serve is not altogether certain. Some aquarists, with more sentiment than scientific accuracy, have been known to clap their hands and speak of mother love. It seems a shame to destroy the illusions of those who are impressed by the apparently human behaviour of a mere fish, but the plain truth is, of course, that it is idle to explain animal behaviour in the same terms as human behaviour. Any suggestion that these precautions are concerned with the protection of the young for the continuance of the species is largely ruled out by the fact that, among the majority of fishes, as soon as the young become free swimming the parents will eat them if given the opportunity.

Numerous theories have been advanced but it must be clearly understood that they can only be theories, by reason of the fact that no-one is wise enough to be certain that he knows the truth about animals. On the whole, the generally accepted theory is that a fish, in common with all animals, has some sense of possession. Later, however, comes that irresistible urge, again common to all animals, to hunt something smaller than itself and especially when it is on the move. In support of this theory, and once again we must stress that it is only a theory, we know from observation that if the fry do not move about much the parents leave them alone. Dog does not eat dog but the fact that fish will eat fish may be accounted for by the fact that it is a primitive animal whose behaviour is always the result of reflex actions and never of conscious thought. Cannibalism is a permanent institution among fishes for a fish lacks the capacity to make a distinction between families, genera, or even species.

At the breeding season fishes are largely promiscuous. It may be true that some of the cichlids are rather choosy (an old male that has lost its mate will not always take to a new one), and there is some evidence to show that the Chinese Snakehead (*Channa asiatica*), and perhaps others of the genus, are monogamous. But true monogamy among fishes, if it exists, cannot be proved, and the general run of fishes are not very particular in their sexual relationship. Some practice communal breeding, and it is no uncommon thing for a female to mate with several males. There is nothing that can be described as personal affection between two fishes, and no jealousy. Even courtship, in the true sense of the word, hardly exists. The nearest approach to a definite courtship occurs in a few species in which the male gives an elaborate display before pairing. The classic example is the male Siamese Fighting Fish (*Betta*) with his dramatic nuptial display. But even this, together with a battle royal for the favour of the female if another male comes on the scene, is very largely fugitive. It lasts only for the mating period, or at best, for one season.

Finally, to the question: how long do fishes live? There is no one answer and no one answer would suffice. The data are lacking. We know that some like the Guppy rarely exceed two years, and others like the cichlids may live for twenty or more. For the many other species no records are available, and if they were could hardly be relied on. Keeping small fishes at too high or too low a temperature, pollution and improper feeding, are only a few of the reasons why many aquarium fishes fail to reach their allotted span of life.

From time to time a fish in an aquarium will be seen to spiral to the bottom and be dead when it gets there. A post-mortem reveals nothing. We must assume that such fishes have died of natural causes, that nature has done with them.

In all animals, including man, decline sets in as sexual activities cease. In civilized communities the old may be looked after. In the wild there is no Welfare State. We rarely see an old animal in nature. With the stagnation of activities and increasing feebleness, the procurement of food becomes a difficult problem, and a violent death from rivals or enemies soon follows. In captivity animals may live a little longer, protected as they are by man. Sooner or later, however, the delicate machine breaks down. Once it has ceased to reproduce, Nature, ever ruthless, cares nothing for the individual. Mammal and bird, reptile, amphibian and fish, death comes to all: the race goes on.

Part 2
The Fishes

In the days when science was a much younger study, the classification of animals and plants was empirical and arbitrary. It was usual for a naturalist to describe some new animal or plant with a noun and a string of adjectives, all of course in Latin as the language of science. As an example, in 1686 Lister described a fish as *piscis triangularis capite cornutus; cui e media cauda cutacea aculeus longus erigitur*.

Obviously such a method was very unsatisfactory and gave rise to much confusion, because very often an animal would be described by two different workers in very different words, and later workers were not to know that they were the same animal. Just over 200 years ago, however, Carl von Linné, the famous Swedish naturalist, conceived what we now know as the binomial system of nomenclature. He gave to every plant and every animal two, and only two, names. In the case of plants he used it for the first time in his *Species Plantarum*, published in 1753, and in the case of animals, in the tenth edition of his *Systema Naturae*, published in 1758. Today the system is universal and Lister's description has been reduced to *Ostracion tricorne* (Cowfish), known by this name to every ichthyologist from California to Cathay. The first name, known as the generic name, denotes the genus to which the animal or plant belongs; the second name, known to botanists as the specific epithet and to zoologists as the trivial name, is peculiar to the new species.

The rules that govern nomenclature need not concern us. It is enough to say that those who have difficulty in understanding systems of classification fail to appreciate that a system of classification is not something that is as rigid and immutable as the Laws of the Medes and Persians. Fundamentally a system of classification is no more than a convenient method of filing each animal and each plant in accordance with its resemblance to, and differences from, others. As a result, just as two businessmen will differ about the best way to file their correspondence and documents, so two taxonomists will differ on the best way to classify animals and plants. Furthermore, a system of classification can never be rigid because as more and more is learnt about animals and plants, and about their pedigrees, so modifications have to be made in the method of classifying them.

In all systems of classification, the lowest taxon is known as the species. In a wide sense, a species may be defined as a group of individuals able to breed among themselves (postulating that one disregards geographical separation), but not with organisms of other groups. It is a practical definition, to the extent that it embraces the great majority of animals and many plants. It is not an ideal definition, however, because it is not fully comprehensive: reproductive isolation admits of degrees, and in the case of some organisms is no criterion at all; while there is the further problem that it is not always known whether two kinds of organisms are not in fact able to breed together in natural conditions.

For all general purposes, however, the definition will serve, and the next higher taxon is the genus, which is defined as a group of species (sometimes only one species) which closely agree together in all essential characteristics.

Next above the genus is the family, which may be defined as a number of genera (sometimes only one genus) that bear resemblances to each other.

We need go no further; for in the pages that follow the fishes are arranged by families in ascending order. That is to say, so far as it is possible to do so, as revealed by the study of fossils, the most primitive families are placed first, and the most recent (determined by their advancing degree of structure) last. Within the families we have rejected the usual practice of describing every species in detail because most members of a genus are very similar in appearance to each other. Instead, in the main, we have discussed the genera, and mentioned those species that are most suited to life in an aquarium.

Family POLYPTERIDAE

The family Polypteridae is a small one that is native to Africa, from the Sahara southwards to the Congo. It is represented to aquarists by two genera *Polypterus* the bichirs, and *Calamoichthys* the reedfishes. In the wild they inhabit the flooded margins of rivers, where they lie concealed for most of the day and search for food at night. Worms, insect larvae, crustaceans and small fishes, are readily taken by them and swallowed whole. In general they tend to quarrel among themselves but may be kept with other species provided the size is right.

Of the genus *Polypterus* the species usually available to aquarists are *P. ornatipinnis* from the Upper and Middle Congo, and *P. palmas* from Sierra Leone, Liberia and the Congo. Both are elongated in shape, grey to greyish green in colour, fading to yellowish on the belly. In the wild they reach a length of about 12 to 14 inches, but growth is slow. A temperature range of 22 to 28°C is recommended. A third species, *P. bichir* from the

Nile and lakes Rudolf and Chad, has been introduced into the aquarium. It is, however, a less satisfactory aquarium fish than *P. ornatipinnis* or *P. palmas* because it grows to a length of 2 feet, and has the reputation of being quarrelsome.

The genus *Calamoichthys* is represented to aquarists by the single species *C. calabaricus* from the delta of the Niger and Cameroun. Its requirements are much the same as those of *Polypterus* but it needs a much larger aquarium as it grows up to 3 feet in length. It is a handsome fish, olive-green on the back shading through pale green on the side to yellow on the belly. In shape it is serpentine, or eel-like, with no pelvic fins. It is timid and peaceful.

Family OSTEOGLOSSIDAE
It is of particular interest to zoogeographers that the family Osteoglossidae ranges across equatorial South America, Africa, Indonesia and Australia; for it helps to support Wegener's Theory of Continental Drift (see page 127). The family is represented to aquarists by the species *Osteoglossum bicirrhosum*, popularly known as the Arowana, from Guyana and the Amazon basin. It is a very handsome fish of a greyish-silver to greenish-yellow colour with a rainbow iridescence and an orange throat. A striking feature is a pair of forked barbels pointed stiffly forwards from the lower jaw.

The aquarium should be thinly planted, kept covered, and retained at a temperature of about 25°C. It is a very predatory fish as is only to be expected from the large gape of the mouth, and living food, to include small fishes and houseflies, is more or less essential. Some specimens will learn to take strips of meat or fish from between finger and thumb. For the aquarium only young specimens should be chosen because growth is fairly rapid and in the wild a fully grown specimen will reach 40 inches and more. Nothing certain is known of its breeding habits but it is thought to be a mouth-breeder, and its congener *Sceleropages* from Indonesia certainly is.

O. bicirrhosum shares the same range as *Arapaima gigas*, a game fish and one of the world's largest freshwater fishes that reaches a length of 15 or 16 feet and a weight of about 450 pounds.

Family PANTODONTIDAE
The family Pantodontidae is native to the western coast of Africa, from the Niger to the Upper Zambezi. It is a very small family represented, in fact, by only one species *Pantodon buchholzi*, commonly known as the Butterfly Fish because its pectoral fins are large, set low, and attached to the body by membranes. By spreading them, the fish is able to glide above the surface of the water, and the first specimens were taken in the net of an entomologist searching for rare butterflies.

It is a small fish that reaches a length of only about 4 or 5 inches at most, olivaceous or greenish brown in colour, and characterized by a large mouth with small sharp teeth, and similar teeth on the palate and tongue.

Although it is quite hardy and thrives at a temperature of 24 to 27°C, it is not altogether an ideal fish for the home aquarium, and is more usually to be seen in public aquaria. Its natural diet is small insects, and although it will take all the regular living foods, feeding must be at the surface; for it will ignore any food that has fallen below the level of its eyes. The aquarium must be kept covered at all times. The fish has been known to breed in captivity but the fry rarely live for more than a few weeks owing to the difficulty of supplying them with suitable food. Sexing, however, is a very easy matter; for the anal fin of the female is fan-shaped with twelve to fourteen rays, whereas that of the male has nine rays and among them a genital tube.

Family NOTOPTERIDAE
Popularly known as knifefishes, the family Notopteridae, that embraces the two genera *Notopterus* and *Xenomystus*, is native to tropical Africa and India, through Malaysia, to Indonesia. Members of this family may be recognized by the anal fin, which extends from just behind the pectorals and runs the length of the body to unite with the caudal fin. The dorsal fin is quite small and, in fact, is lacking in *Xenomystus*.

The essential requirements of these fishes are a temperature range of 24 to 28°C, living or frozen food, and a shaded aquarium with ample hiding-places in which they can swim freely; by nature they are nocturnal. They are not aggressive but they are best kept with fishes about their own size and never with those whose habit it is to nip the fins of others. The long rippling anal-caudal fin invariably attracts fishes with this tendency.

Xenomystus nigri from the upper tributaries of the Nile, westwards across Africa to Liberia, is the species most frequently seen in aquaria. In colour it varies from a uniform dark grey to a reddish brown, paler on the belly. It reaches a length of about 8 inches, and as yet, has not bred in captivity.

Family MORMYRIDAE

Members of the family Mormyridae are confined to Africa. They are found throughout the continent, excluding the Mediterranean coast, the Sahara and Malagasy. Known to German aquarists as parrotfishes (*papageifische*) they are not difficult to identify on account of a finger-shaped process on the jaw that serves as a feeler, and which in some species is prolonged into a proboscis. Mormyrids are very intelligent, and without doubt, the most intelligent of all aquarium fishes. Indeed, the weight of their brain in proportion to that of their body is greater than it is in man.

The family embraces a number of genera but for the aquarium, the most satisfactory species are those of the genus *Gnathonemus*. Members of this genus are peaceful and settle down well in the aquarium, but as they are nocturnal by nature and therefore shy, the aquarium must be well planted with ample hiding-places for them. Small living food, particularly worms, and a temperature range of 24 to 28 °C are recommended.

G. petersi from the Congo and Cameroun northwards to the Niger, is the species usually offered for sale. Of a uniform dark brown it occurs in some lights as violet-brown. The dorsal fin is set well back over the anal fin, and the area between is prettily marked with transverse bars. It reaches a length of about 9 inches.

G. moori from Cameroun and Congo, that reaches a length of 8 inches, and *G. schilthuisi* from the Middle Congo, that reaches only 4 inches, are two other attractive members of this interesting genus. None has yet bred in captivity.

Family UMBRIDAE

The family Umbridae contains only one genus *Umbra*, with two species in the United States and one in Europe. Distribution is local. The American species are found only in the eastern states from the neighbourhood of the Great Lakes to Georgia; the European species is found only in the middle and lower systems of the Danube and Lower Dniester rivers. In America these little fishes (they grow to no more than about 4 or 5 inches) are known as mud-minnows. In England they are known as dogfishes (not to be confused with the marine dogfish which is a small shark), a translation of the Austrian *hundfisch*, a name given to them because the pectoral and pelvic fins are moved alternately, in the manner of the legs of a running dog. In the wild they inhabit still waters (muddy pools) and, as a result, are admirably suited to life in a well-planted aquarium

at room temperature. They eat all the regular living foods, as well as such substitutes for them as scrapings of raw meat and the like.

U. krameri is the European species; *U. limi* and *U. pygmaea* the American. Males (said to be rare) may be distinguished from the females by the fact that they are at least 2 inches smaller. They will spawn readily in captivity if the aquarium is thickly planted and the water is soft and acid. All three species are reasonably peaceful and should not be placed with fishes inclined to bully. As they are very active fishes that jump freely, the aquarium should be kept covered at all times.

Family CHARACIDAE

The family Characidae* is one of the largest among the freshwater fishes, and over 100 species are known to aquarists. In the Old World it is confined to Africa, in the Nile valley, and south of the Sahara, excluding Malagasy and the Cape. In the New World it is found in Central America, excluding the West Indies, and through South America as far south as latitude 40°, excluding Chile.

The characins are very closely related to the cyprinids. They may be distinguished by the fact that, with some exceptions, they have teeth in the jaws and an adipose fin. Usually both features are present, but sometimes one and sometimes the other, rarely neither.

Feeding characins is not difficult. Most are omnivorous. Only a few are strictly carnivorous and fewer still are herbivorous. Most, therefore, will take dried food, especially if it contains meat, fish and the like, and all the regular living foods and suitable substitutes for them.

The majority are small fishes quite suitable for a community aquarium; indeed, *Hemigrammus* and *Hyphessobrycon* species are probably the most popular of all aquarium fishes. Some of the larger species (for example, *Serrasalmus*) are too dangerous to be trusted in an aquarium with other fishes, and *Exodon paradoxus*, when up to about 2 inches in length, will fight anything from that size upwards. All characins need a heated aquarium.

Members of this family are oviparous but, with

---

* We are aware that taxonomists have removed from this family a number of groups and referred them to the families, Hemiodontidae, Citharinidae and Gasteropelecidae. Aquarists, however, are notoriously conservative, and in order to avoid creating more confusion than is necessary, we are retaining the older classification until such time as the distinguishing features of the families are more generally known.

some exceptions, not very easy to breed. In most the eggs are adhesive or semi-adhesive. The aquarium should be thickly planted with fine-leaved plants, the water soft, shallow, acid, and at a temperature of about 27 °C. Most species scatter their eggs at random and eat them if given the chance. Some species (for example *Pyrrhulina rachoviana*) attach their eggs to plants and protect them; others (for example *Copeina guttata*) deposit their eggs in a depression in the planting medium; remarkably *Copeina arnoldi* deposits its eggs on a leaf overhanging the water.

In general males are smaller and slimmer than females but in some species there are secondary sexual differences, such as coloration of body or fins or length of fins. Some of the smaller species have the well-known characin hook, a tiny hook that develops at the tip of the rays of the anal fin (less frequently of the caudal and pelvic fins) of the male. The hooks cannot be seen with the un-aided eye but sexing can be accomplished by catching the fish in a very fine-meshed net (silk or nylon is ideal) and promptly tipping it out. As the female fish has no hooks she drops off the net immediately, but the male, by virtue of the hooks, clings to the net for a few seconds. It is a practical method of sexing fishes although not always reliable because the hooks of some species are more liable to catch in the net than those of others, and much depends on how vigorously a caught fish struggles to escape.

The genus *Alestes* is represented to aquarists by the species: *A. chaperi*, *A. longipinnis* and *A. nurse*, once referred to the genus *Brycinus*. They are native to tropical Africa. All three are handsome fishes of a yellowish-green colour and active swimmers. In domestication they tend to be shy. *A. chaperi* is probably the most satisfactory species for an aquarium because it reaches a length of only about 3 or 4 inches; *A. longipinnis*, the Long-finned Characin, reaches about 5 inches; *A. nurse* reaches about 9 inches and is altogether a bigger fish than its congeners. Nothing appears to be known about their breeding habits. Living food should be given to them.

In translation *Anoptichthys* means the fish without eyes, and *A. jordani* is the well-known Blind Cavefish from Mexico. It is a translucent pink in colour with a lavender sheen and hyaline fins.

A number of blind fishes are known. They inhabit underground caves and as no light reaches them their eyes have degenerated. As a rule, these fishes are bottom feeders that have found their way into caves and become trapped. Most have some sensory organs which enabled them to find food and survive. *Anoptichthys*, however, is remarkable, because it is believed to descend from *Astyanax mexicanus*, a fish unlikely to be trapped in the first place, and once trapped, unlikely to survive. In a community aquarium blind fishes do no harm and come to none; they are in no way handicapped by their lack of eyes. They eat anything.

Aphyocharax rubripinnis is a small fish that reaches about 3 inches in the wild but rarely more than 2 inches in captivity. It is well known to aquarists under the name of the Bloodfin, so called because all the fins, with the exception of the pectorals, are blood-red in colour. The body is a greenish silver.

Spawning is pretty to watch. An aquarium at least 2 feet long should be filled to a depth of about 6 inches with well-aerated water and stocked with fine-leaved plants. Two males and one female should be introduced. The fish jump clear of the water, come together in mid-air, and as they fall back to the surface, the female scatters a large number of transparent eggs in all directions. On completion, the brood fish should be removed. At a temperature of about 24 °C the eggs incubate in about thirty hours. The fry are not difficult to raise on infusoria, followed by screened daphnids, microworms and powder-fine dried food. The difficulty is to get the fish to breed. Mass-breeding has proved very successful. A native of the Argentine this little fish is able to withstand a temperature as low as 17 or 18 °C, but anything below 21 °C is ill advised.

The genus *Arnoldichthys* is represented to aquarists by the species *A. spilopterus* from western Africa. It is a small, peaceful fish that reaches little more than 2 inches in length, and is not particular about its food. It is characterized by a red eye, from which derives the popular name of Red-eyed Characin. As yet it has not bred in captivity.

The genus *Astyanax* is native to the New World from Texas southwards to Buenos Aires. It is represented to aquarists by three species: *A. bimaculatus*, *A. fasciatus* and *A. mexicanus*. As aquarium fishes they are very satisfactory, for they eat almost anything, breed readily and are peaceful.

Breeding presents no difficulties. The best results have been obtained in large aquaria with water at about 24 °C. Strong and healthy broods have been raised, fed with fine dried foods from the start. Males are slimmer and more colourful than females.

Carnegiella species are native to the north of

South America. They are popularly called hatchet-fishes because the body is laterally compressed, short and deep, so that the fish is shaped not unlike a hatchet. Flying characins is another, and perhaps better, common name that has been given to them. In the wild they swim at the surface of the water searching for small insects, and when disturbed skim the surface for considerable distances, some even rising clear of the water.

The genus is represented to aquarists by three species: *C. marthae* the Black-winged Hatchetfish, *C. strigata* the Marbled Hatchetfish, and *C. vesca*. All are quite small, reaching a length of under 3 inches.

Other genera in this group are *Gasteropelecus* and *Thoracocharax*. All three genera are much alike but *Carnegiella* may be set apart by the absence of an adipose fin.

None is really a satisfactory fish for the aquarium, and they are more for the aquarist seeking a novelty than for anyone else. It is by no means easy to supply them with their natural food and although they will take daphnids, fruit flies, and even dried foods, it must be offered to them near the surface. They are not long lived and to be able to keep one for a year is very creditable. Very few, if any, live longer than eighteen months and only then if the conditions are perfect. Clear water is essential, and it is hardly necessary to add that the aquarium must be kept covered at all times. Breeding them is a rare feat.

The genus *Characidium* is widely distributed through eastern South America, from the Orinoco to the La Plata rivers. It is represented to aquarists by the two species *C. fasciatum* and *C. rachovi*. They are not altogether ideal aquarium fishes, because by nature they are bottom livers, and in the aquarium spend much time hiding among the plants and stones. Apart from this, however, they are well suited to aquarium life. They reach no more than 2 or 3 inches, are peaceful, flourish well in a temperature range of 18 to 22°C, and eat all the regular living, as well as dried, foods.

Sexing is not difficult. The dorsal and anal fins of the male are more elongated and the colour markings more distinct than those of the female. For breeding, the water should be shallow and at a temperature of about 25°C. The aquarium should be thickly planted with bottom plants, such as Willow Moss, because spawning takes place in the lower part of the aquarium. The period of incubation is about two days, and the young fish must be given plenty of small living food if they are to succeed.

Charax gibbosus is native to the Amazon basin and northwards to the Guianas. Of a brownish-amber colour, in a good light the side reflects opalescent tints of pink, blue, green and lavender. It reaches a length of about 4 or 5 inches, is peaceful, hardy and eats anything. Characteristically it swims in a head-downwards position but the head itself remains more or less horizontal. Together with a humped nape, it has the appearance of being deformed, and this has earned for it the popular name of the Humpbacked Headstander. It is sometimes called the Glass Headstander. An exceptionally long anal fin does nothing to improve its looks.

Cheirodon axelrodi is a small fish, barely 2 inches long, found in the forest pools of the Upper Rio Negro. It is almost identical with *Hyphessobrycon innesi*, the well-known Neon Tetra of the aquarists and, in fact, was given the name of *Hyphessobrycon cardinalis*. Later it was brought to light that the day before publication another worker had placed it in the genus *Cheirodon*, and given it the trivial name of *axelrodi*. This name, therefore, takes priority, but the popular name of Cardinal Tetra remains.

In reality, *C. axelrodi* is rather slimmer than *H. innesi*, and the brilliant red under the iridescent blue-green longitudinal stripe is considerably brighter and extends to the tip of the snout.

The genus *Copeina* is native to South America, from Colombia and the Guianas to the Amazon. It is very closely related to *Pyrrhulina* and, indeed, differs from it only in dentition. There is no adipose fin and no lateral line.

The genus is represented to aquarists by three species: *C. arnoldi*, *C. callolepis* and *C. guttata*. They are all small fishes that reach a length of 2 or 3 inches, and are peaceful, easily fed and hardy. They flourish well at a temperature of 22 to 26°C, and *C. guttata* is hardy enough to tolerate a range of from 15 to 32°C.

To aquarists the main interest in the genus is that all three species breed in a different way. *C. arnoldi* deposits its eggs out of the water on an overhanging leaf. In the aquarium a small piece of frosted glass, painted green and hung at an angle a few inches above the surface, makes a good substitute. In the wild the male and female leap together out of the water and cling for a moment or two to the leaf. During this period the female deposits a few eggs and the male fertilizes them. When spawning is over, the male takes up a position not far from the eggs and, from time to time, sprays them with water by lashing his tail violently from side to side. *C. callolepis* spawns in the normal way of characins. The eggs are adhesive and deposited on the leaves of broad-leaved submerged plants such as *Cryptocoryne* species. *C. guttata* digs a depression in the planting medium and the female deposits anything up to 1,000 eggs in it. Here they are fertilized by the male, who guards them and aerates them by fanning them with his fins.

Corynopoma riisei is popularly known as the Swordtail Characin, because the fins of the male, particularly the lower lobe of the caudal fin, are much elongated. The most characteristic feature, however, is an extension of the gill plate of the male. It takes the form of a long process of bone, the extremity flattened into a paddle. Normally it is held close to the body but at breeding time the male circles round the female, occasionally extending one of his paddles towards her and curving his anal fin in her direction. The sperms of the male are contained in a capsule (spermatophore) and transferred to the oviduct of the female. They are retained there to fertilize the eggs, which are usually attached to a large-leaved plant. At a temperature of about 24°C the eggs incubate in about two days and the fry are free swimming about two days later. They are not difficult to raise to maturity. Once mated the ·female will spawn many times without the presence of a male.

C. riisei is native to Venezuela and Trinidad. It is peaceful, eats most things, is sufficiently hardy to withstand a temperature range of 20 to 29°C, and reaches a length of only about 2 inches.

Creagrutus beni the Gold-striped Characin, from the north-east of South America, is a small fish that reaches a length of about 2 or 3 inches. It is hardy, omnivorous and altogether a very satisfactory fish for the community aquarium. As in *Corynopoma riisei* and other related species, fertilization is internal.

The genus *Creatochanes* is native to South America from the Guianas to Paraguay. It is represented to aquarists by the two species *C. affinis* and *C. caudomaculatus*, the Tail-spot Tetra. Both are very similar in shape and coloration. *C. affinis*, popularly known as the Orange-finned Characin, is the species usually offered for sale. It is not a very satisfactory aquarium fish because it grows to the fairly large size of 6 inches and is very pugnacious; it fights even with its own kind. It must, therefore, be kept by itself. Its breeding habits are not known.

Crenuchus spilurus from the Amazon basin, is popularly known as the Sail-fin Characin because

the dorsal and anal fins of the male are large and sail-like. Full development, however, does not occur until the fish is in its second or third year. It is by no means a bad-looking fish. The general colour is olive-brown, greenish below, the two colour areas separated by a golden band that extends from the gill cover to the tail. It reaches a length of about 3 inches, and it is safe with fishes about its own size, it is best kept away from small fishes as it has a large mouth and eats most things that come its way. Little is known about its breeding habits.

Ctenobrycon spilurus is a small 3-inch fish native to the coastal areas of northern South America. It is peaceful, omnivorous and prolific. As many as 800 eggs have been deposited in one spawning, although between 200 and 300 is more usual. It breeds in the regular way of characins, and at a temperature of 25°C, the period of incubation is about three days. Although not strictly an herbivorous species, the adult fish enjoy alga and other green food. The young should be started off on plenty of infusorians and green water, and should be ready for screened daphnids at the age of three weeks.

Exodon paradoxus is native to South America from the north coast to the Amazon basin. It is a small 3-inch fish but what it loses in size it gains in coloration. Its grey-green colour with red and violet tints and silvery reflections and two large round brown spots – one on the shoulder girdle and one on the caudal peduncle – make it one of the most handsome of the characins: all the more so as it is an exceptionally active fish. Unfortunately it tends to be pugnacious, and specimens no more than 2 inches long will take on anything the same size as themselves and upwards. It breeds in the regular way of characins but the young are not easy to raise. Living food is strongly recommended.

The genus *Gasteropelecus*, or hatchetfishes, is native to the north of South America. In general appearance representatives of this genus are very similar to *Carnegiella* and *Thoracocharax* species but may be distinguished from the former by the presence of an adipose fin, and from the latter by a less pronounced belly. The genus is represented to aquarists by three species: *G. levis* the Silver Hatchetfish, *G. maculatus* the Spotted Hatchetfish, and *G. sternicla* the Common Hatchetfish. As their habits and requirements are the same as *Carnegiella* they need not be repeated.

The genus *Gephyrocharax* is native to Panama and Venezuela. It is represented to aquarists by

43

Gasteropelecus levis

three species: *G. atracaudata* popularly called the Platinum Tetra, from Panama, *G. caucanus* from the River Cauca in Colombia, and *G. valencia* from Lake Valencia in Venezuela. All are small fishes that reach a length of about 2 or 3 inches, and are quite long lived for fishes so small. Hardy, peaceful and omnivorous they are easy to keep in an aquarium and easy enough to sex, because in the male the outer margin of the anal fin is convex and wavy, whereas in the female it is straight. Breeding, however, is not so easy. As in *Corynopoma riisei* and other related species, fertilization is internal. At 25°C the eggs incubate in about twenty-four hours, and the fry must be given the smallest infusorians for their first food.

Gymnocorymbus ternetzi is native to Paraguay. It is well known to aquarists under the popular name of the Black Widow, so called because posteriorly the body, including the dorsal, anal and adipose fins, is jet-black. At its best it is a very

handsome fish but unfortunately it is not very often seen at its best because light, change of living conditions and other considerations result in the fish losing its characteristic black markings, which also fade with age. Beyond this, however, it is a very satisfactory aquarium fish; it is small, hardy, omnivorous and quite peaceful. It breeds in the regular way of characins. A variety with longer fins than the type has been developed by aquarists.

The genus *Hemigrammus* is native to South America, from the Orinoco to Paraguay and the Rio Grande do Sul. Altogether some thirty species have been identified, of which the best known as aquarium fishes are *H. caudovittatus* the Buenos Aires Tetra, from the La Plata basin, *H. gracilis* the Glowlight Tetra from Guyana, *H. marginatus* from Venezuela to the Argentine, *H. ocellifer* the Beacon or Head-and-tail-light Fish, from Guyana to the Amazon basin, *H. pulcher* the Pretty Tetra, from the Upper Amazon, *H. rhodostomus* the Red-nose

Tetra, from the Lower Amazon, *H. rodwayi* from Guyana to the Upper Amazon, and *H. unilineatus* the Feather Fin or One-line Tetra, from Trinidad and the north of South America.

All are small fishes that reach a length of only about 2 or 3 inches, peaceful enough to be kept in a community aquarium, hardy and omnivorous, thriving best on living food or suitable substitutes. Colourful and active they have the further virtue of being quite long lived for their size. If kept under good conditions their average life-span is from five to seven years.

They breed in the regular way of characins. The main requirements are a large, well-planted aquarium with water about 10 inches deep and at a temperature of about 25°C. The period of incubation is two or three days. It is best to use two males with one female but, as is only to be expected from a genus with such a wide geographical range, some species breed more readily than others, and some have refused to breed in captivity.

Hemigrammus species are closely related to *Hyphessobrycon* species but may be distinguished by the fact that in *Hemigrammus* the base of the caudal fin is scaled, in *Hyphessobrycon* it is scaleless.

Hemiodus semitaeniatus from Guyana and the Amazon basin, is a rather large, slim fish of a silvery colour, that reaches a length of about 8 inches. As a result it needs a large aquarium because it is very lively and fast on the fin. It is, however, peaceful, eats anything (including the plants) and is hardy. It has not yet bred in captivity.

Its congener *H. gracilis* which reaches a length of about 5 or 6 inches and is slimmer in the body, is rarely seen in aquaria.

Hyphessobrycon species are very similar to *Hemigrammus* species but may be distinguished from them by the fact that the base of the caudal fin is scaleless; in *Hemigrammus* it is scaled. Both genera share the same geographical range.

About forty species of *Hyphessobrycon* are known but only a dozen or so are regularly introduced into the aquarium: *H. bifasciatus* the Yellow Tetra, with two grey vertical bars on the shoulder and a number of V-shaped bars along a faint silvery lateral stripe; *H. eos* the Dawn Tetra, with a rather faint spot on the shoulder, a horizontal stripe along a golden side and a conspicuous dark spot on the lower part of the caudal peduncle; *H. erythrurus* the Red-tailed Tetra, with a silvery stripe that extends from a dusky shoulder-spot to a black spot on the caudal peduncle; *H. flammeus* the well-known

Flamefish or Red Tetra from Rio, with two dark vertical spots on the shoulder and usually a fainter spot just behind the gill plate; *H. herbert-axelrodi* the Black Neon, with a broad black band, accompanied by a green-blue line from behind the gill plate to the caudal fin; *H. hetero-rhabdus* the Flag Tetra, with a three-coloured horizontal stripe – red, yellowish to white and blue-black – from gill plate to caudal fin; *H. innesi* the Neon Tetra, with a glowing blue line (that appears green under artificial light) from the snout, through the eye to the adipose fin, and a splash of rich red from the base of the pelvic to the root of the caudal fin; *H. metae* the Loreto Characin, with a wide black band that extends from the eyes to the caudal peduncle; *H. minimus* the Pygmy Tetra, with a dark line, accompanied by a blue metallic band, from the gill cover to a round black spot on the base of the caudal fin; *H. pulchripinnis* the Lemon Tetra, with a dark triangular spot on the caudal peduncle; *H. rosaceus* the Rosy Tetra, very similar in appearance to *H. serpae* but with no shoulder-spot; *H. rubrostigma* the Bleeding-heart Tetra, with a large blood-red spot below the origin of the dorsal fin; *H. scholzei* the Black-line Tetra, with a dark horizontal line, edged above with a metallic line, from the eye to the root of the caudal fin; *H. serpae* very similar in appearance to *H. rosaceus* but with a dark spot on the shoulder.

Like *Hemigrammus* species, all are small fishes, about 2 or 3 inches long, and *H. minimus* is a mere 1 inch in length, sometimes less. Their requirements, care and breeding (when they perform) are the same as for *Hemigrammus*. *H. innesi*, named for William T. Innes, the well-known American aquarist who died in 1969, is very similar to *Cheirodon axelrodi* and is generally considered one of the most beautiful of aquarium fishes.

Megalamphodus megalopterus from Brazil, is popularly known as the Black Phantom Tetra. It is a small fish that reaches a length of about 1½ inches, greyish olive to black on the back, shading to silvery white on the belly. It is peaceful and eats anything. The male has a larger dorsal fin than the female, and the female has a red adipose fin.

The genus *Metynnis* embraces some twenty-two species native to South America, from the Orinoco to the La Plata rivers. It is represented to aquarists by three species: *M. maculatus* from Guyana to the Parana River; and *M. roosevelti* and *M. schreit-muelleri* from the Amazon basin. They are not difficult to identify; the body is deep and laterally compressed, the belly from throat to anal fin serrated, and the base of the adipose fin more than

Metynnis schreitmuelleri

half the length of the base of the dorsal fin. They reach a length of 6 or 7 inches and this, coupled with a protruding jaw, suggests pugnacity; in fact they are quite peaceful fishes that may be introduced into a community aquarium so long as no very small fishes are kept there.

Metynnis species are quite easy to keep in a temperature range of 21 to 26°C, and require plenty of green matter in their diet because they are very largely herbivorous. Large fishes will soon destroy the plants in an aquarium.

M. roosevelti and *M. schreitmuelleri* have bred in captivity. Spawning occurs in the regular way of characins. Slightly acid water is favoured, and at a temperature of 26°C the period of incubation is about four days; the fry are free swimming four or five days later. They feed on small water fleas or brine shrimps from the start and make rapid growth.

The genus *Mimagoniates* is native to south-east Brazil and Paraguay. It is represented to aquarists by three species: *M. barberi*, *M. inequalis* the Croaking Tetra, once referred to the genus *Glandulocauda*, and *M. microlepis* the Blue Tetra. They are small fishes suitable for the community aquarium, but rather sensitive about the oxygen content and temperature of the water, which should not be allowed to fall much below 19°C nor rise above 23°C. Their natural food is small water insects, daphnids and the like, but in captivity they will take dried food provided it is near the surface or in mid-water. The structure of the mouth makes it hard for them to pick up anything from the bottom.

In general sexing is easy because in the male the dorsal fin is pointed; in the female it is rounded. Breeding, however, is not so easy; they are not a prolific species and fertilization is internal, as in *Corynopoma riisei* and similar species. The main requirements are a large aquarium well stocked with plants, and shallow water at a temperature of about 25°C. The eggs incubate in two or three days and the fry need very small infusorians for their first food.

M. inequalis makes an interesting pet because, unusually in a characin, it has a supplementary breathing apparatus similar to but not so highly developed as that of the anabantid fishes. Occasionally it comes to the surface of the water, takes a gulp of air with a faint chirruping noise, and expels the de-oxygenated air through the gills in the form of tiny bubbles.

The genus *Moenkhausia* is native to South America from the north coast, through Brazil, to Paraguay. It is represented to aquarists by four small species: *M. dichouri* from Paraguay, that reaches a length of about 3 inches; *M. oligolepis* the Glass Tetra, from Guyana and the Amazon basin, that reaches a length of about 4 or 5 inches; *M. pittieri* from Lake Valencia in Venezuela, that reaches only 2 or 3 inches; and *M. sanctae-filomenae* from the La Plata basin, that reaches a length of about 2 to 3 inches. Hardy, peaceful and omnivorous, they are well suited to a community aquarium, although once *M. oligolepis* has reached maturity it is not altogether to be trusted with other fishes. All have a tendency to eat the plants.

The sexes may be distinguished by the dorsal, anal and pelvic fins, which are larger and more pointed in the male than in the female. Breeding occurs in the regular way of characins but in captivity none breeds readily.

Mylossoma argenteum is native to the Amazon basin. The general colour is silvery and the body unmarked except for a large dark spot on the gill plate. It is very similar in appearance to *Metynnis* species but may be distinguished by the smaller adipose fin, and the anal fin which is concave and not straight. The serrated belly is very pronounced.

This species flourishes at a temperature range of 21 to 26°C and is a suitable species for a community aquarium as long as no small fishes are also kept. It grows to a length of about 8 inches and eats most things, including the plants. Its breeding habits are not known.

Nannaethiops unitaeniatus is native to equatorial Africa, from the Nile to the Niger and Congo. It is commonly known as the African Tetra. It is a handsome fish, dark brown to reddish brown on the back, shading to golden brown on the side and yellowish white on the belly. The side is marked with a horizontal stripe that extends from the snout, through the eye, to the caudal fin. It is, however, a rather shy fish and displays its colours only when conditions are right for it. It reaches a length of about 3 inches (the male is rather smaller than the female) is peaceful and hardy, omnivorous and a ready breeder.

Breeding is conducted in the regular way of characins. A large number of eggs are deposited among thickets of fine-leaved plants. At a temperature of about 26°C the period of incubation is two days and the fry are easily raised on infusoria, followed by screened daphnids, newly hatched brine shrimps and the like. The brood fish should be removed as soon as spawning is completed.

The genus *Nannostomus** is native to the Guianas and the Amazon basin. It contains a number of small fishes that reach a length of only about 2 inches, very closely related to *Poecilobrycon* species even if, as some think, they are not identical. They are represented to aquarists by five species: *N. anomalus* from the Amazon to the Rio Negro; *N. aripirangensis* from the island of Aripiranga in the Lower Amazon; *N. beckfordi* from the Guianas to northern Brazil; *N. marginatus* from the Guianas and the Amazon; and *N. trifasciatus* from the Amazon basin. It is characteristic of these species, as well as of others and *Poecilobrycon* species, that in the dusk of evening and when frightened, the horizontal stripes on their sides fade and their place is taken by broad, sloping bars.

They are peaceful fishes that flourish at a temperature of 24°C with a range of a degree or two either way. Although they are omnivorous feeding is something of a problem because they have very small mouths and all food – living or dried – has to be specially graded. Even medium-sized daphnids are too big; they can manage only the smallest.

Nannostomus species breed in the regular way of characins but not very readily. The aquarium should be large, the water slightly acid and, as the male is a hard driver, it is best to mate two females with one male. At 24°C the period of incubation is about two days, and if the fry are to survive they must be given the smallest infusorians for their first food.

Nematobrycon palmeri commonly known as the Emperor Tetra, is a small 2-inch fish native to the Pacific slope of Colombia. It is attractively marked: brownish on the back shading to blue, separated from a yellow-gold belly by a broad black stripe.

It is a peaceful fish that eats anything and flourishes in a temperature range of 22 to 24°C. As it tends to be shy it is best kept in a well-planted aquarium away from boisterous fishes. It breeds at about 26°C in the regular characin way.

The genus *Neolebias* is native to tropical western Africa. It is represented to aquarists by *N. ansorgei* which some ichthyologists refer to the genus *Nannaethiops*. It is a small fish reaching little more than 1½ inches in length at most, peaceful but too shy to make a good community fish,

omnivorous but with a liking for *Tubifex* and gnat larvae. It favours the rather high temperature of 27°C (a temperature below 23°C is to be avoided) and well-matured, soft and acid water. It breeds in the usual characin manner but only rarely in captivity.

Phenacogrammus interruptus the Rainbow Characin or Congo Tetra, is a small 3-inch fish native to the River Congo and its tributaries. It is a very handsome fish with a bluish back, a broad gold stripe along the side, and the rest of the body green. A peculiarity is a black, feathery extension from the bifurcation of the caudal fin, more pronounced in the male than in the female. This grows, and on reaching a particular size falls off and grows again. It is a peaceful fish that eats most things and flourishes at the normal temperature range of 22 to 25°C. It breeds in captivity, but not very readily. The fry take small daphnids from the start.

The species is not to be confused with *Alesto-petersius caudalis*, once referred to the genus *Petersius*, which shares the same geographical range. The two species are very much alike but *A. caudalis* is a translucent yellow to yellowish grey with an almost white belly. It is commonly known as the Yellow Congo Characin.

Phoxinopsis broccae is native to the neighbourhood of Rio de Janeiro. It is an attractive little fish, rarely more than just over an inch in length, dull yellowish brown on the back, silvery below, the caudal peduncle marked with a golden ring. It is peaceful to the extent of meekness, and is best kept in isolation because in a community aquarium it gets pushed away from food. It is omnivorous but the mouth is small and food must be graded to suit it. In captivity it breeds readily. In the male the front part of the anal fin is convex. Soft water and fine-leaved plants are essential. The fry are difficult to raise.

Piaractus nigripinnis native to the Amazon, was once referred to the genus *Colossoma*. It grows to about 8 or 9 inches and is rather too large for the community aquarium. Young fishes are silvery with large brown spots on the side. In adult fishes the spots are absent. Living foods and suitable substitutes for them are necessary if it is to be kept in health.

Poecilobrycon species popularly known as pencil-fishes, are very similar to *Nannostomus* species and some taxonomists regard the two genera as one. They share the same geographical range and their requirements, care and culture are the same.

P. eques the Knightly Pencilfish, and *P. uni-*

---

* According to some taxonomists *Nannostomus* species and *Poecilobrycon* species are identical. As, however, their findings are not universally accepted, we have retained the two genera separate: *Nannostomus* without an adipose fin and *Poecilobrycon* with one.

fasciatum, are the species usually to be seen in aquaria. *P. unifasciatum*, but not *P. eques*, swims head-upwards, the body at an angle.

Prionobrama filigera from the Upper Amazon, is popularly known as the Translucent Bloodfin. The body is translucent (but in a good light appears a light blue) and the fish itself is very similar in appearance to the well-known Bloodfin *Aphyocharax rubripinnis*. Care and culture are the same for both species.

Pristella riddlei from Venezuela, the Guianas and the Amazon basin, is well known to aquarists as the X-ray Fish, so called because the lower part of the body is almost transparent. This makes sexing easy. If a strong light is placed behind the fishes the air bladder can be seen through the body wall: in the male it is pointed, in the female it is rounded and situated rather higher in the body. Breeding, however, is not so easy. It occurs in the regular way of characins, but the brood fish should be matched; both should be about the same size and well over a year old.

This is a small fish that reaches a bare 2 inches in length. Peaceful and omnivorous it makes a good community fish but it needs clear water, a good light, more living than dried food, and a temperature range of 24 to 27°C. It is unwise to allow the temperature to fall below 21°C. An albino form is known.

The genus *Pseudocorynopoma* is native to southern Brazil and Paraguay. It is represented to aquarists by two species: *P. doriae* and *P. heterandria*. Both are fairly small fishes, reaching about 3 or 4 inches in length, peaceful, omnivorous (but with a preference for living food), and undemanding in their requirements. Their breeding habits are the same as those of *Corynopoma riisei*. *P. doriae* is commonly known as the Dragon Fin because the dorsal, anal and pelvic fins of the male are greatly enlarged, the forward rays of the dorsal and anal prolonged.

The genus *Pyrrhulina*, native to South America, is very closely related to the genus *Copeina*. It is represented to aquarists by four species: *P. laeta* from Guyana, Colombia and the Amazon basin; *P. nattereri* and *P. vittata* from the Amazon basin; and *P. rachoviana* from La Plata and Argentina. All are small fishes that reach a length of about 2 or 3 inches, peaceful, omnivorous and hardy. They are characterized by scales rather on the large size, and the upper lobe of the caudal fin (especially in the male) larger than the lower one. *P. rachoviana* is a ready breeder, the other three are not.

Roeboides microlepis the Small-scaled Glass Characin, is native to eastern Brazil, Paraguay and Argentina. It reaches a length of about 4 inches, is peaceful, and breeds in the regular way of characins. It swims in a head-downwards position, and usually keeps near the bottom.

The genus *Serrasalmus*, popularly called piranhas, is native to the Orinoco, through the Guianas, and southwards to Paraguay. It is represented to aquarists by three species: *S. nattereri* the Red-bellied Piranha; *S. rhombeus* the Spotted Piranha; and *S. spilopleura* the Dark-banded Piranha. All are large fishes. In the wild, *S. nattereri* reaches a length of about 12 inches, *S. rhombeus* about 14 inches and *S. spilopleura* about 10 inches. They are, in fact, game fishes and give good sport but small specimens are sometimes offered for sale to aquarists. They are essentially for the specialist. They must be kept in isolation and handled with care for even a small fish can inflict a nasty bite on a careless hand. Dark tales are told of their feeding habits but, in truth, they are not fussy feeders, and may be fed with large earthworms, strips of raw meat, pieces of fish and the like. The practice of feeding them with living fishes of a fair size is deplorable and cruel.

Thayeria obliqua the well-known Penguin of the aquarists, is a small 3- to 4-inch fish from the Amazon basin. It is peaceful, hardy, omnivorous, and requires nothing special except a large aquarium kept covered at all times; it is an active swimmer and a first-class jumper. When at rest it holds itself head-upwards, the body at an angle.

The side is marked with a broad black band that extends from behind the gill plate to the tip of the lower lobe of the caudal fin. In the allied species *T. sanctae-mariae* the lateral band begins at the hinder end of the dorsal fin. In all other respects the two species are very similar.

Breeding occurs in the regular way of characins. The eggs are deposited on the leaves of plants near the bottom, and the brood fish should be removed as soon as spawning is over. At a temperature of about 27°C the period of incubation is from thirty-six to forty-eight hours.

The genus *Thoracocharax*, or hatchetfishes, is native to the north of South America. It is represented to aquarists by the two small species *T. securis* and *T. stellatus*, which reach a length of about 3 or 4 inches. They are very similar in appearance to *Carnegiella* and *Gasteropelecus* species but may be distinguished from the former by having an adipose fin, and from the latter by their more pronounced belly. Their care, habits and requirements are the same as for *Carnegiella*, but

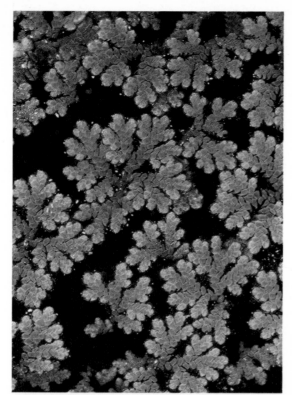

Opposite page
Above left *Synnema triflorum*
Above right *Eleocharis acicularis*
Below *Echinodorus paniculatus*

Left *Azolla caroliniana*
Below *Salvinia natans*

Serrasalmus rhombeus

T. stellatus has a geographical range from central Brazil, through Paraguay, to the Argentine, and specimens imported from the Argentine should not be kept at too high a temperature.

Family ANOSTOMIDAE

The family Anostomidae is native to Central America, including the West Indies, and South America as far south as Buenos Aires. It is represented to aquarists by half a dozen genera, the members of which are well suited to an aquarium. In the wild they inhabit sluggish waters and spend most of the time in a head-downwards position seeking for food on the bottom. Most are omnivorous but some are herbivorous, and even those that are omnivorous need plenty of vegetable matter in their diet. All need a heated aquarium.

The genus *Abramites* is represented to aquarists by two species: *A. hypselonotus* from the Upper Amazon; and *A. microcephalus* from the Lower Amazon. Both reach a length of about 5 inches

and although small specimens are peaceful enough, larger ones are inclined to be quarrelsome: *A. hypselonotus* particularly so and it should never be introduced into an aquarium where smaller fishes are living. *A. hypselonotus* is grey marked with eight dark bars; *A. microcephalus* is variable, grey to brown, with seven very dark vertical bars on the side. It is popularly known as the Head-stander or Head-standing Fish. Neither is very often seen in aquaria because even in the wild they are rather rare, and although *A. microcephalus* has bred once or twice in captivity, there is no record of *A. hypselonotus* ever having done so.

The genus *Anostomus* is native to the northern countries of South America and is represented to aquarists by four species: *A. anostomus*; *A. fasciolatus*; *A. taeniatus*; and *A. trimaculatus*. As aquarium fishes they are not very popular for little, if anything, is known about their breeding habits and, with the exception of *A. anostomus* that reaches about 4 or 5 inches, they reach the fairly large size

Chilodus punctatus

of 8 or 9 inches. They are, however, curiously marked fishes, and in this way are of interest to aquarists. On the whole they may be said to be peaceful but some bullying is to be expected from a large fish that has teeth in its jaws. They flourish best in soft acid water and on a mixed diet.

Chilodus punctatus is commonly known as the Spotted Headstander, or Head-standing Fish. It is native to the north of South America. A small fish that reaches a length of about 3 inches, it is peaceful and eats almost anything. From all accounts it needs a large aquarium with a dark bottom, sparsely planted and a patchy cover of floating plants. The water should be soft, slightly acid, and at a temperature of 25 to 27°C. Living food, as well as green food, is an essential part of its diet. Breeding is a rare event because the conditions must be perfect.

The genus *Curimatopsis* is native to Argentina. It is represented to aquarists by the species *C. saladensis* from the Salado River system. It is a quiet little fish that reaches a length of about 3 inches and likes to shoal with its own kind and keep itself to itself. It is a first-class scavenger that searches the bottom for food (but does not grub for it) and enjoys alga and other vegetable matter. It is hardy enough to withstand a temperature as low as 18°C, and at a temperature of about 25 or 26°C, breeds readily in the regular way of oviparous species. In general appearance it is very similar to *Barbus* species but is easily set apart from them by the presence of an adipose fin.

The genus *Leporinus* is native to South America east of the Andes. It is represented to aquarists by some six or seven species but only four are regularly introduced into the aquarium: *L. fasciatus* from the Orinoco, through Brazil, to the La Plata; *L. fredirici* from Guyana to the Amazon; *L. melanopleura* from western Brazil; and *L. striatus* from the Matto Grosso and other districts. All are rather showy fishes, in particular *L. fasciatus* the Black-banded Leporinus. Young

Right   *Pantodon buchholzi*
Below right   *Anoptichthys jordani*
Below   *Gymnocorymbus ternetzi*

Opposite page
Above   *Exodon paradoxus*
Below   *Xenomystus nigri*

Leporinus striatus

fishes are metallic yellow, adults orange, the body encircled by a number of jet-black bands. Young fishes usually exhibit five bands but as the fish grows they divide into two, and an adult fish will end up with ten or more.

Leporinus species reach the large size of 10 or 12 inches but they are peaceful fishes, and small specimens are quite suitable for a community aquarium. They eat most things but are largely herbivorous and must have access to alga and other vegetable matter. Like most of the family they spend much of their time hanging head-downwards in the water. They are by no means sluggish fishes, however, and should be given a large aquarium, kept covered at all times because they are excellent jumpers. There is no record of these species ever having bred in captivity.

The genus *Prochilodus* is native to South America, from Ecuador, Peru and the Guianas in the north, through Brazil, to La Plata in the south. It is represented to aquarists by the two species *P. insignis* and *P. taeniurus* from Guyana and the Amazon basin. Both are large fishes that in the wild reach 1 foot or more in length and are

Europe, Africa (excluding Malagasy), most of Asia, and respects Wallace's Line.* In the New World it is confined to North America from approximately latitude 60° N. to 20° N.

Externally the Cyprinidae bear a close resemblance to the Characidae but may be distinguished by the absence of an adipose fin and a toothless mouth. In the cyprinids the dentition is restricted to teeth in the throat; they are attached to the pharyngeal bones and bite against a horny pad on the base of the skull. Many cyprinid fishes have barbels which are always lacking in characins. The barbels, however, are never more than two pairs (a rostral and a maxillary) whose function it is to help the fish in its search for food and perhaps warn it of an obstruction. In some species the barbels are large and fleshy, in others they are rudimentary, in still others so fine and hair-like that they escape notice unless looked for.

Cyprinid fishes are very diverse in size. They range from the 1-inch *Rasbora maculata* of Malacca, to the 6-foot *Barbus tor* the Mahseer of India, with scales as large as the palm of a man's hand. In between, the family embraces a number of small fishes particularly suited to life in an aquarium, and much favoured by aquarists because they are undemanding in their requirements and most are easy to breed. Sexing, however, is by no means easy and calls for some experience in the handling of fishes. In the main the sexes can be distinguished only because the male is slimmer and more brightly coloured than the female. In some of the European and North American species the male shows nuptial tubercles at spawning time.

All are omnivorous and feed largely on daphnids, worms, insect larvae, and the like, together with suitable substitutes, dried food and vegetable matter. Although a few of the larger species may develop a tendency to bully smaller fishes, on the whole they are peaceful and do no harm. All are oviparous and although it was long thought that *Barbus viviparus* from Natal was a live-bearer, it has since been found that the case for viviparity rested on the discovery of the fry of a cichlid in the gut. With the notable exception of *Rhodeus sericeus* that deposits its eggs between the shells of a mussel, most scatter their eggs in thickets of submerged plants. The eggs are demersal and adhesive. As they gravitate to the bottom they stick to the leaves and stems of the plants, to the stones and,

esteemed as food. Young, small specimens are suitable for the aquarium as they are peaceful, colourful and herbivorous. A temperature range of 22 to 24°C suits them well.

Family CYPRINIDAE
The family Cyprinidae, sometimes popularly called the carp family and sometimes the minnow family, is the largest of all the freshwater fish families. It embraces about 1,500 species with a geographical range that is almost cosmopolitan. In the Old World it is represented throughout

---

* A biological boundary line passing between the islands of Java and Bali and Borneo and Celebes, to the west of which the flora and fauna is Asian in character, to the east and south Australian.

Opposite page
Above left *Hyphessobrycon rosaceus* and *H. rubrostigma*
Above right *Serrasalmus nattereri*
Below *Hyphessobrycon innesi*

Above *Nannostomus marginatus*
Below *Hyphessobrycon serpae*

in domestication, to the glass of the aquarium. After the eggs have been fertilized by the male, the brood fish should be removed for they are ready eaters of their own spawn. Although most species favour fine-leaved plants such as *Myriophyllum* and *Cabomba*, some species (for example *Rasbora*) prefer broad-leaved plants such as *Cryptocoryne*. As a general rule most favour water that is soft and slightly acid but some (for example *Tanichthys albonubes* whose habitat is mountain streams) prefer water that is rather hard.

Alburnus alburnus the Bleak, is native to the whole of Europe (including Britain) north of the Alps. In the wild it grows to a length of about 8 inches but aquarium specimens rarely exceed 6 or 7 inches.

It is an active and rather handsome fish with bright glittering scales that at one time, if no longer, were used in the manufacture of artificial pearls. It flourishes in an aquarium at room temperature but although hardy it will not tolerate sudden changes of temperature. It eats most things including dried food, and in the wild its normal diet is flies, gnats, midges, and the like. The eggs are deposited on stones.

Aphyocypris pooni from the neighbourhood of Canton in China, is very similar to *Tanichthys albonubes* from the same locality, and much confusion has arisen because both have been imported under the same popular name of Mountain Minnow. There is, however, a difference in the dentition, and externally the two species may be distinguished by the dorsal fin which in *A. pooni* is red at the base and tipped blue. It may be kept and cared for in the same way as *T. albonubes*.

Balantiocheilus melanopterus native to Thailand, Borneo and Sumatra, grows to a length of about 14 inches in the wild, but small specimens are quite suitable for an aquarium at a temperature range of about 23 to 26°C. It is popularly known as the Silver or Bala Shark although why is not clear to us because it is by no means shark-like either in appearance or behaviour. In appearance it is a typical cyprinid, and a remarkably handsome one with a silvery to yellowish silver body, the belly paler, and the fins a deep yellow with black margins. It is omnivorous and as well as living foods will eat dried food and vegetable matter. Its breeding habits are not known.

The genus *Barbus* embraces a large number of species. The precise number, however, cannot be stated because some taxonomists refer them to the genus *Puntius* and others to the genera *Barbodes* and *Capoeta*. The truth appears to be that some barbs (more correctly barbels although not all species have them) should be referred to the genus *Barbus* and others to the genus *Puntius*, but until further research has been made to determine the limits of the two genera, it is convenient to refer them to the well-known *Barbus* genus. Meanwhile those who refer them to the genera *Puntius*, *Barbodes* or *Capoeta*, are exchanging a known name for an unknown one and are no more correct.

Barbus species have a wide geographical range and some reach a very large size. Here, however, we list only the smaller species that are native to Africa, India and south-east Asia. They are quite easy to identify because in body shape and fin formation they are very similar to the well-known Goldfish of the garden pond, and like it they are seldom still. It is for these reasons, as well as the fact that they are peaceful, eat most things, and flourish in a moderate temperature of 22°C with a range of a couple of degrees either way, that they are so very popular with aquarists.

Breeding occurs in the regular way of cyprinids and presents no difficulty. Admittedly, some species (for example *B. everetti*) do not breed readily in captivity but most do, and some (for example *B. conchonius*) can be spawned more or less to order.

Among aquarists there is not the least doubt that the Asian barbs are better known than the African. From a very early date *B. conchonius* has been a great favourite. First described by Hamilton-Buchanan in 1822 it was introduced to the aquarium in 1903 and has held its place ever since. Native to northern India, Bengal and Assam, in the wild it reaches a length of 5 or 6 inches but in captivity it rarely exceeds 3 or 4 inches. The general colour is greenish brown, shading to light olive on the side and silvery on the belly. At breeding time, however, and at other times when stimulated by good conditions, the male but not the female, assumes a fiery-red colour. It is for this reason that it is popularly known as the Rosy Barb.

B. everetti the Clown Barb from Malaysia, reaches a length of about 4 or 5 inches. It is not a ready breeder and it is essential to separate the male and female for two or three weeks before spawning time, and feed them well with living foods.

B. lateristriga from Malaysia and Indonesia is rather on the large size. In the wild it reaches about 8 inches although aquarium specimens rarely, if ever, exceed 5 inches. It is a voracious feeder with a preference for daphnids and gnat larvae, and rather sensitive to sudden changes of temperature. It is popularly known as the Spanner Barb because the markings on its side bear a strong resemblance to what we call an adjustable spanner, and our American friends a monkey wrench.

B. nigrofasciatus is found in the streams of southern Ceylon. Popularly known as the Nigger Barb it makes a colourful and active addition to the community aquarium. It reaches a length of about 2 inches.

B. titteya the Cherry Barb, is so called because its body is flushed with a reddish tint that, under good conditions, is almost scarlet. Native to Ceylon, it too rarely exceeds 2 inches in length.

B. pentazona from Malaysia, and *B. tetrazona* from Thailand, Borneo and Sumatra, together with a number of subspecies, are popularly known as

tiger barbs because in general colour they are yellowish silver and marked with blue-black vertical stripes. They reach a length of about 2 inches and breed readily.

B. arulius, B. filamentosus the Black-spot Barb, *B. melanamphyx* the Ember Barb, *B. orphoides,* and *B. schwanenfeldi* the Tinfoil Barb, are newcomers to the aquarium. All have been introduced since 1950. *B. arulius* from south-east India, reaches a length of about 5 inches. It is of a delicate brown colour with a pattern of dark blotches on the side. The rays of the dorsal fin of the adult male are elongated. It is a rather boisterous fish with the further disadvantage that in captivity it does not breed readily. *B. filamentosus* from south-west India, reaches a length of about 6 inches. Mature specimens are silvery to greenish silver, with a large

Barbus schwanenfeldi

Right *Anostomus anostomus*
Below *Chilodus punctatus*

Opposite page
Above *Barbus nigrofasciatus*
Below *Prochilodus insignis*

dark blotch above the anal fin. Young fish are highly coloured with broad black vertical bars on the side. It is a ready breeder. *B. melanamphyx* from India, reaches a length of about 4 inches. A yellowy silver in colour, flushed pink to fiery red, it is marked with a dark, horizontal lozenge behind the gill plate and another on the caudal peduncle. A black bar extends from the dorsal fin, over the head and across the eye. *B. orphoides* from Thailand and Indonesia, is a large fish that in the wild reaches a length of about 10 inches. The general colour is silvery, the side an iridescent blue, the gill plate marked with a red blotch. *B. schwanenfeldi* also from Thailand and Indonesia, is even larger than the foregoing species. In the wild it reaches a length of 13 or 14 inches. For the aquarium, therefore, only young specimens should be chosen, and the aquarium must be a large one because it grows rapidly. It is quite a showy fish, with a deep body of a shining silvery colour, and overtones of brilliant yellow. The dorsal and caudal fins are red.

Other Asian species are: *B. binotatus* the Spotted Barb, from Malaysia and Indonesia, that reaches 5 or 6 inches; *B. chola* the Swamp Barb, from India and Burma, that reaches 4 or 5 inches; *B. cummingi* from Ceylon, that reaches about 2 inches but usually less; *B. dorsimaculatus* from Sumatra, that reaches little more than 1 inch; *B. dunckeri* from Malaysia, that reaches 4 or 5 inches; *B. fasciatus* the Striped Barb, from Malaysia and Indonesia, that reaches about 5 inches; *B. gelius* the Gold Barb, from Orissa, Bengal and Assam, that reaches little more than 1 inch and 2 inches at most; *B. lineatus* the Lined Barb, from Malaysia, that reaches about 4 inches; *B. oligolepis* the Checker Barb, from Sumatra, that reaches about 2 inches; *B. phutunio* the Pygmy Barb, from Orissa through Bengal to Burma, that reaches rather less than 1 inch and is the smallest of the genus; *B. semifasciolatus* the Half-striped Barb, from south China, that reaches 2 or 3 inches;* *B. sophore* from India and Burma, that reaches about 5 inches; *B. stoliczanus* from Burma, that reaches about 2 inches; *B. terio* from Orissa, Bengal and the Punjab, that reaches about 3 inches; and *B. ticto* the Two-spot Barb, from southern India and Ceylon, that reaches about 3 inches.

Although taxonomists have classified more barbs from Africa than Asia, less than a dozen of them are represented in the aquarium.

B. callensis from Algeria and Morocco, and perhaps southern Spain, is one of the larger species that in the wild reaches a length of about 8 inches. As it has been found in hot springs, it should be given the fairly high temperature of 27°C.

B. callipterus and *B. trispilus* the Three-spot

Barbus oligolepis

---

* The fish sold under the name of *Barbus schuberti* is a golden variety of this species.

Barb, are native to western Africa from Liberia to the Congo; further south *B. fasciolatus* the African Banded Barb, is native to Angola. All three reach a length of 2 or 3 inches, and need a temperature of not less than 22°C.

B. camptacanthus from tropical western Africa, is silvery yellow to pinkish in colour, and as the fins of the male are a brilliant red it has become known as the African Red-finned Barb. A full-grown specimen reaches a length of 5 or 6 inches and tends to bully. Small specimens are peaceful and quite suitable for the community aquarium.

B. hulstaerti from the Lower Congo is a newcomer to the aquarium. It was, in fact, introduced only as recently as 1956, and given the popular name of the Butterfly Barb on account of its brilliant and pleasingly contrasted coloration, small size and activity.

B. lineomaculatus the Seven-spot Barb, and *B. usambarae*, are native to Tanzania and Zambia, and *B. unitaeniatus* the Slender Barb, ranges across the continent from Angola to Natal. All three reach a length of 2 or 3 inches and are peaceful.

B. wöhlerti comes from Mozambique. It is a small fish that reaches little more than 1 inch in length, of a light brown colour with a reddish-violet stripe that extends from the gill plate to the root of the caudal fin. It is popularly known as the Sickle Barb as in the male the anal fin is sickle-shaped.

B. werneri is a more northerly species that ranges from Egypt, through the Sudan, to Lake Victoria. It is olive-green to yellowish on the back, shading to white on the belly, the side is marked with three to eight black spots. It breeds readily and is resistant to a low temperature which, during the winter months, should be reduced to a range of 12 to 15°C.

The genus *Barilius* ranges from Japan and China, through southern Asia, to Africa. It is represented to aquarists by two species: *B. christyi* from the Congo, and *B. neglectus* from Japan. Both flourish in a temperature of about 24°C but *B. neglectus* should be wintered in a temperature range of 15 to 18°C. Both are peaceful and omnivorous but they have a preference for living food, especially flies, gnat larvae, and the like.

B. christyi reaches a length of about 5 inches. The general colour is dark olive with a bluish-green reflection. There is a striking red-gold blotch on the snout from which the popular name of the Coppernose has been derived. It has not yet bred in captivity.

B. neglectus reaches a length of about 3 inches and is very unassuming in coloration. The back is brownish, shading to yellowish on the side with a longitudinal stripe. It breeds readily over a pebbly bottom.

The genus *Brachydanio* is represented to aquarists by a few small species that are native to India, Malaysia and beyond. Like all cyprinids they are oviparous but the eggs are non-adhesive and, therefore, do not stick to the plants but gravitate to the bottom. As the brood fish are greedy eaters of their spawn, in captivity the aquarist is faced with the problem of protecting the eggs before he has had time to remove the brood fish from the aquarium. A number of ingenious devices have been suggested. One, probably the best, is to tie a number of round glass or plastic rods loosely together with lead wire. This is known as a spawning mat, and if it is made the same length and width as the aquarium, and raised about 2 inches above the bottom, the eggs will fall between the rods where the fish cannot follow them. The water should be not more than 5 or 6 inches deep (to give the fish less time to grab the eggs as they gravitate downwards), with a neutral reaction, and at a temperature of 24 to 27°C. At the higher temperature the period of incubation is from thirty-six to forty-eight hours.

The aquarium should be a large one because *Brachydanio* species grow rapidly: they are sexually mature when a year old, and few live for more than three years.

They hybridize well and a number of crosses have been made by experimental aquarists. The results, however, have never been very satisfactory: the offspring are not particularly attractive and many are sterile.

B. albolineatus is native to Burma and Indonesia. It reaches a length of about 2 inches. The general colour is a glowing blue suffused with shell-pink to a delicate green. It is popularly known as the Pearl Danio because, when seen against the light, it appears to be made of mother-of-pearl. It is at its best in a temperature range of 23 to 29°C. A golden variety is known.

B. frankei from India is a newcomer to the aquarium. It was introduced as recently as 1963. It has been given the popular name of the Leopard Danio, because the general colour is yellowish, heavily speckled black to blue-black. It reaches a length of 2 or 3 inches.

B. nigrofasciatus the Spotted Danio, is native to Burma. It reaches little more than an inch in length, and although it breeds in the same way as other members of the genus, spawning is more difficult. The general colour is a warm brown and two stripes extend from the gill plate to the caudal fin.

B. rerio is native to eastern India, from Bengal to the Coromandel Coast. It reaches little more than 1 or 2 inches in length but is exceptionally hardy. It appears to be resistant to white spot (see page 28) and has been known to tolerate temperatures as low as 15 and as high as 40°C. It is popularly known as the Zebra Fish because the sides are striped with alternate bands of royal blue and yellow that extend from the snout to the extremity of the caudal fin.

The genus *Carassius* is represented by two species: *C. auratus* particularly well known as the Goldfish; and *C. carassius* the Crucian or Bronze Carp, and a natural variant of the latter, distinguished from it by a slimmer body and a caudal fin that is more forked, known as the Gibel or Prussian Carp. All three are suitable for a large unheated aquarium.

C. auratus is native to China. In the wild it is a dull greenish-olive-coloured fish that is sold in most markets as a food fish. The handsome deep red or gold-coloured fish kept as a pet, is a domesticated variety of the wild fish, whose colour has been obtained and has to be retained, by selective breeding.

Strictly speaking the Goldfish is a pond fish more than an aquarium fish, and for the aquarium the more suitable fishes are the fancy breeds that have been developed by breeders (mainly Oriental) over the centuries. A very large number is known but only a few are regularly offered for sale. The Shubunkin, the Comet, the Fantail, the Veiltail, the Telescope, the Moor, the Celestial, the Lionhead and the Oranda, are the best known. With the exception of the Shubunkin and the Comet, these fancy fishes are rather more delicate than the common Goldfish, and the temperature of their water should not be allowed to fall much below 15°C. All are peaceful, omnivorous and breed in the regular manner of cyprinids, although considerable experience is necessary if first-class specimens are to be bred and brought to maturity. The common Goldfish reaches a length of from 10 to 12 inches but the fancy breeds never grow so big.

C. carassius is native to central Europe north of the Alps and Pyrenees. It is also found in the Thames valley and East Anglia. The general colour is olive or greenish brown to dull bronze and is, in fact, very similar to the wild Goldfish. It may be distinguished from it by a deeper body and by the dorsal fin, the upper margin of which is convex and in the Goldfish is either straight or concave. It usually reaches a length of about 6 to 10 inches although much larger specimens have been known to occur.

Chrosomus erythrogaster is native to southern Canada, southwards to the central United States. It is particularly populous in the freshwater streams of the Mississippi valley.

The back is olive-brown, the belly a brilliant red from which it has been given the popular

name of the Red-bellied Dace. It reaches a maximum length of about 3 inches. It needs well-oxygenated water at a temperature range of 20 to 23°C. A temperature as high as 26°C is critical for it.

The genus *Cyprinus* is represented by the species *C. carpio* the Common Carp, and a number of varieties that have been developed from it by selective breeding. All are suitable for a large and unheated aquarium.

C. carpio, originally native to China and central Asia and westwards to the Black Sea, is now widespread across the Northern Hemisphere in the New World as well as the Old.

In general appearance it is very similar to *Carassius* species, but may be distinguished from them by the presence of four barbels on the upper lip. The back varies in colour from blue-green to a dark bluish green, the sides from bluish green to golden yellow. It is a large fish and specimens up to 40 inches long have been found in the wild. More usually, however, it reaches a length of about 12 to 15 inches, sometimes even less.

The Mirror Carp, sometimes called the King Carp, is a variety which is scaleless except for a few large scales with a metallic lustre at the base of the fins and along the lateral line. The Leather Carp is a variety that is almost scaleless. The Red or Golden Carp is a variety extensively found in China, and bred in Japan for ornamental ponds under the name of *higoi*. It comes in a number of different colours. Another variety, known as the *koi*, appears to be a genus hybrid of *Cyprinus* × *Carassius*. It has been the subject of much crossing and back-crossing. As a result some specimens are scaled, some partly scaled, and some scaleless. Furthermore, some have barbels and some do not. Inevitably, therefore, the pedigree of the fish is hard (if not impossible) to determine, and one can be certain of nothing about it except that in an aquarium it is a very handsome ornament.

Like *C. carpio* from which they have been developed, these four varieties reach a large size. Only small specimens should be chosen for the aquarium, therefore, and they should be kept with fishes about the same size as themselves; all are omnivorous and will take a small fish as readily as a big worm.

Danio species are very similar to *Brachydanio* species but may be set apart by the larger dorsal fin and size. Two species are represented to aquarists: *D. devario* from northern India; and *D. malabaricus* the Giant Danio, from the coastal fresh waters of Malabar and Ceylon. Their requirements

Above *Cyprinus carpio* var. Golden or Red Carp (*higoi*)
Below *Cyprinus carpio*

are the same as for *Brachydanio* species but their eggs are adhesive and they breed in the regular way of cyprinids.

D. devario is a greenish silver in colour, paler on the underparts, the front part of the body suffused with blue. Three blue stripes extend from below the dorsal fin to the caudal peduncle and continue as a broad band on the upper lobe of the caudal fin. It reaches a length of about 4 inches.

D. malabaricus is a metallic blue to olive-grey on the back, white with a rose tint on the belly. The side is horizontally striped with light blue and yellow. In the wild it reaches about 6 inches but aquarium specimens rarely exceed 4 inches.

The genus *Epalzeorhynchus* is native to Thailand and Indonesia. It is represented by two species: *E. kallopterus* and *E. siamensis*. Both are peaceful fishes and an asset in an aquarium because they do some scavenging. The mouth is situated on the underside and the upper lip is furnished with a strong, horny fringe adapted for scraping algae off stones. They spend most of their time browsing among the stones and roots of the plants, but as they are capable of a considerable turn of speed, they should be kept in a large aquarium. Beyond this they are undemanding fishes and their main requirements are soft water at a temperature range of 23 to 26°C, and living food. In the wild both reach a length of about 6 inches, but in the aquarium rarely more than 3 or 4 inches. They are characterized by a black stripe that extends from the snout, through the eye, to the bifurcation of the caudal fin. *E. kallopterus* is dark olive on the

Below *Cyprinus carpio* var. Mirror Carp

Cyprinus carpio var. *koi*

back, yellow to white on the belly: *E. siamensis* is a heavier-built fish of a golden or honey colour, and some specimens have green flecks on the side.

E. siamensis is a newcomer to the aquarium and has not yet been given a popular name. *E. kallopterus* has been given the popular names of the Selimang, the Flying Fox and the Pal: the first is the most desirable.

The genus *Esomus* is native to India, Ceylon and Malaysia. It is represented to aquarists by two species: *E. danricus* the Flying Barb; and *E. malayensis* the Malayan Flying Barb.* They are peaceful fishes, undemanding in their requirements, but they need a large aquarium kept covered at all times, and a temperature range of about 22 to 24°C. They will take dried food but must have some living food in their diet if they are to remain in good health.

Spawning occurs at a temperature of 26°C. The act is conducted among the floating plants but the eggs are only partly adhesive and gravitate to the bottom, so that a spawning mat as recommended

for *Brachydanio* species (see page 66) should be used. The period of incubation is about forty-eight hours but the fry are not easy to raise: a constant and liberal supply of small living food must be given to them.

E. danricus is native to Burma, northern India, Ceylon and the Nicobar islands. The general colour is olive-green to light brown on the back, silvery with a violet sheen on the belly. It reaches a length of 4 or 5 inches. Two pairs of barbels are present, the maxillary pair sweep back to the middle of the body.

E. malayensis is native to Malaysia and southern Vietnam. It is very similar to the above but smaller (it reaches only about 3 inches) and shows a black spot at the base of the anal fin.

Most members of the genus *Garra* (once *Discognathus*) are native to Africa but one species is found in Borneo, and several in India and beyond. They are characterized by a sucking disc behind the ventrally situated mouth, enabling them to cling to a stone against the fast-flowing waters of the streams and rapids in which they live.

G. taeniata from Thailand, popularly called the Siamese Stone-lapper, is the only species known to aquarists. The back is a brownish red, the belly

---

* The fish known as *E. lineatus* from the mouth of the Ganges, is probably a variant of *E. danricus*; *E. goddardi* from Thailand is rarely, if ever, imported.

Gobio gobio

white. A dark brown to black stripe extends from the gill plate to the root of the caudal fin. It reaches a length of about 6 inches, is peaceful, and eats dried as well as living food and the algal growths found on stones.

Gobio gobio commonly known as the Gudgeon, ranges across the Old World from Europe (excluding southern Italy, Scotland and Norway) eastwards across Asia to China. It reaches the fair size of about 6 inches and in some countries, notably France, is esteemed as a table delicacy (*une friture de goujons*). Doctors once recommended it, swallowed alive, as a cure for consumption.

The Gudgeon makes a satisfactory fish for an unheated aquarium, but as in the wild it is found in the shallows of lakes or on the beds of fast-flowing rivers, the water should be shallow, clear and well aerated. The bottom should be layered with pebbles for the Gudgeon is a bottom feeder and does a lot of rooting. It should be kept only

with fishes about the same size as itself, and fed with worms, pieces of raw meat, and the like.

Idus idus is distributed across Europe north of the Alps and Pyrenees (excluding Great Britain) to western Siberia. It is a large fish that in the wild reaches as much as 30 inches, but small specimens are suitable for an unheated aquarium, provided it is a large one. The back is olive-brown to very dark brown, the side silvery with a bluish sheen. It is commonly known as the Orfe or, more correctly, the Silver Orfe to distinguish it from a golden-coloured variety known as the Golden Orfe that occurs in natural waters and is extensively cultivated for aquaria and ornamental ponds. It is believed to have been introduced into England from Austria, where it has replaced the Goldfish in ornamental waters. Both forms are fast swimmers and will eat most things although their natural food is surface insects, small crustaceans, and the like.

Idus idus

The genus *Labeo* is native to Africa and southeast Asia. It is represented to aquarists by a handful of species of which *L. bicolor* from Thailand, introduced to British aquarists in 1953, is the best known and most popular. It is a remarkably handsome fish with a velvety all-black body and a blood-red caudal fin. Commonly called the Redtailed Black Shark, this is very much a misnomer for it is, in fact, a timid fish and in a community aquarium should be provided with suitable places in which to hide. It reaches a length of about 5 inches, flourishes in a temperature range of 24 to 27 °C and feeds on living food, suitable substitutes, and by scraping off stones.

L. erythrurus also from Thailand, *L. frenatus* from northern Thailand, *L. forskali* from the Nile basin and *L. wecksi* from the Congo, are other members of the genus whose introduction to the aquarium has been made comparatively recently. Their care and requirements are the same as for *L. bicolor*, and although all *Labeo* species are suitable for the community aquarium they have a tendency to quarrel among themselves; *L. bicolor* in particular.

Leuciscus leuciscus the Dace, is widespread through Europe north of the Alps and Pyrenees. In the wild it reaches a length of about 12 inches, but in the aquarium rarely more than 8 or 9 inches.

Young specimens make satisfactory fishes for the unheated aquarium but it must be a large one, and kept covered at all times, because Dace are fast swimmers and very active. They feed mainly on water insects, crustaceans, and the like, but dried food is readily taken. Breeding takes place

Above *Labeo bicolor*
Below *Leuciscus leuciscus*

from March to May and the eggs are deposited on water plants.

The genus *Morulius* is very close to the genus *Labeo*. It is represented to aquarists by the species *M. chrysophekadion*, commonly known as the Black Shark, from Thailand and Indonesia. It calls for the same care as *L. bicolor* and like it is a velvety all-black fish, but each scale on the side is marked with a yellow to reddish spot, and all the fins are black. The dorsal fin is sail-like. It is a much larger and more peaceful fish than *L. bicolor*. In the wild it reaches a length of about 24 inches and even aquarium specimens will grow to 10 inches.

The genus *Notropis* is a large one that embraces something like 100 species. They are native to the streams and rivers of North America east of the Rockies.

Only one species, *N. hypselopterus* from Alabama, Georgia and Florida, is represented to British aquarists. It is a well-coloured little fish that reaches a length of about 2 inches, and is at its best in a temperature range of 18 to 21°C, reduced in winter to 16 to 18°C. The general colour is a coppery brown with an olive sheen on the back, the light-coloured belly is sometimes yellow. The side is marked with a metallic blue-black stripe, bordered above and below by red-gold, that extends from the gill plate to the base of the caudal fin. It is peaceful, omnivorous, and needs plenty of swimming space. In captivity it seldom, if ever, breeds.

The genus *Osteocheilus* is native to Malaysia and Indonesia. It is represented to aquarists by two species: *O. hasselti* the Bony-lipped Barb from Thailand and Indonesia; and *O. vittatus* from the Sunda islands. They are large fishes that reach a length of from 10 to 12 inches and for the aquarium only young specimens should be chosen. Their main requirements are a large aquarium with water at a temperature range of 22 to 25°C, living food and plant matter. Both species are olive-green in colour, shading to light silver on the side and belly, *O. vittatus* with a dense black stripe that extends to the bifurcation of the caudal fin.

Phoxinus phoxinus the Minnow, well known to schoolboys everywhere as the Tiddler and by many

Phoxinus phoxinus

other names, is widespread throughout Europe with the exception of southern Spain and Iceland. It is a small fish that rarely exceeds a length of about 3 inches, peaceful and well suited to an unheated aquarium, although in the wild Minnows are usually to be found in fast-flowing water.

The colour is very variable but a good fish usually has an olive-green to grey-green back shading to a metallic yellow-green on the side and to yellowish white on the belly. During the breeding season (April to July) the male wears a red chest.

Spawning is fairly simple. The water should not be more than 6 inches deep, crystal clear and well aerated. The eggs are deposited on stones and the young hatch out in about six days.

A Minnow will eat almost anything that is offered to it. In the wild it feeds mainly on insect larvae and small crustaceans. It is partial to worms.

The genus *Rasbora* embraces about thirty species and subspecies but only about a dozen of them are regularly introduced into aquaria. All are native to Malaysia and through Indonesia to the Celebes and Philippines.

In their natural habitat they inhabit shallow waters with a strongly acid reaction. They swim in shoals and spawn among clumps of broad-leaved plants such as *Cryptocoryne* species. In captivity they spawn rarely and from what is known of their habits it is generally thought that they are community breeders.

Rasbora species are colourful fishes, peaceful and hardy, although they will not tolerate a temperature below 21°C. Like all cyprinids they are omnivorous but if they are to be kept in health, their diet must contain some living food or suitable substitutes.

R. argyrotaenia the Silver Rasbora, is yellowish brown on the back to orange on the side. A light orange stripe with a silvery sheen extends from the snout to the base of the caudal fin. In the wild it reaches a length of 6 or 7 inches but in the aquarium only 3 or 4 inches.

R. caudimaculata is steel-blue to blue-green in colour with a violet to pinkish sheen. It is popularly known as the Greater Scissorstail because it

Rasbora heteromorpha

Rhodeus sericeus

reaches a length of anything up to 8 inches, and Scissorstail has long been one of the popular names attached to R. *trilineata*.

R. *daniconius* the Slender Rasbora, is olive with a pink and green sheen on the back, silvery on the belly. A blue-black metallic stripe, edged yellow above and below, extends from the snout to the root of the caudal fin. It reaches a length of 3 or 4 inches in an aquarium but as much as 8 inches in the wild.

R. *einthoveni* the Brilliant Rasbora, is light grey, the edges of the scales dark grey to black. A bold black stripe extends from the tip of the lower jaw to the base of the caudal fin. It reaches a length of about 3 inches.

R. *elegans* the Yellow Rasbora, is yellow to olive-brown on the back, the side marked with one dark spot below the dorsal fin and another on the caudal peduncle. It reaches about 5 inches.

R. *hengeli* is very similar to R. *heteromorpha* but paler in colour and smaller; it reaches a length of little more than 1 inch.

R. *heteromorpha* the Harlequin Fish, is well known to aquarists on account of a striking wedge-shaped blue-black blotch on the hinder part of the body. The general colour is brownish green suffused with pink to coppery tones. It reaches a length of about 2 inches.

R. *kalochroma* the Clown Rasbora, is yellowish red to red, the side marked with a blue-black spot

Scardinius erythrophthalmus

behind the gill plate and another above the anal fin. It reaches 3 or 4 inches.

R. *leptosoma* is light brown shading to silvery on the belly. A red, gold and black stripe extends from the snout, through the eye, to the base of the caudal fin. It reaches a length of 2 or 3 inches.

R. *maculata* the Spotted Rasbora, is sometimes called the Pygmy Rasbora because it reaches 1 inch at most and is the smallest member of the genus. The general colour is a golden olive with a soft pink to purple sheen. The belly is greenish white. The side is marked with several blue-black dots surrounded by red.

R. *pauciperforata* the Red-striped Rasbora, is a transparent silver with a sea-green tinge on the side. A narrow metallic stripe, copper to red, accompanied by a fine dark line, extends from the head to the root of the caudal fin. It reaches a length of about 3 inches.

R. *taeniata* is olive-brown to green with a light green to silvery-blue sheen. A blue-black stripe, edged above with gold, extends from the eye to the caudal fin. It reaches a length of about 3 inches.

R. *trilineata* the Scissorstail, is dark olive-yellow to green on the back, silvery on the side, whitish on the belly. A dark brown stripe extends along the side to a spot on the caudal peduncle,

and beyond to the bifurcation of the caudal fin; another, and darker, line extends from just in front of the anal fin to the base of the lower lobe of the caudal. In the wild it reaches a length of 6 or 7 inches, and specimens up to 9 inches have been found; aquarium specimens rarely exceed 3 inches.

Rhodeus sericeus the Bitterling or Bitter Carp, is a small 3-inch fish native to central and eastern Europe, Asia Minor, and perhaps Great Britain because in recent years garden escapes have established themselves in some rivers in southern Yorkshire. The back is greyish green, the sides silvery with blue-green iridescent streaks. It lives quite happily in an aquarium at a temperature that does not exceed 22°C and is omnivorous with a preference for bloodworms and similar living food.

Spawning takes place about April. It is an interesting performance. By means of a long ovipositor the female deposits the eggs between the open shells of a mussel, preferably of the genus *Anodontina* the so-called Swan Mussel. The male ejects milt over the mussel and it is drawn into the mollusc through the respiratory apparatus, there to fertilize the eggs. Incubation takes place within the mussel and, in fact, only when the young fish are able to fend for themselves – a

Gyrinocheilus aymonieri with two *Barbus nigrofasciatus*

matter of about four or five weeks – do they leave the mussel.

Scardinius erythrophthalmus the Rudd or Red Eye, is widespread throughout Europe, with the exception of the Iberian peninsula, southern Italy, Scotland and parts of Scandinavia, and eastwards into Asia Minor. It is a large fish that may grow to a length of 15 or 16 inches, but usually less, and young specimens are quite suitable for an unheated aquarium. The back is olive-green shading to a metallic yellow on the side and white on the belly. In size and general appearance it is very similar to the Roach (*Rutilus*) but may be distinguished from it by the dorsal fin, which in the Roach is immediately above the pelvics, but in the Rudd set back from them. There is a golden variety of a metallic golden-yellow colour, with a reddish tinge. Both forms are omnivorous and particularly partial to surface insects. Breeding occurs in April to June in the regular manner of cyprinids.

Tanichthys albonubes popularly known as the White Cloud Mountain Minnow, is so called because in the wild it is found in the waters of the White Cloud Mountains near Canton. It is a small fish less than 2 inches in length and is similar in size and appearance to *Aphyocypris pooni*.

The general colour is brownish green. It is at its best at the age of two or three months, and then shows a flashing blue-green stripe from the eye to the root of the caudal fin. With advancing age the stripe loses much of its brilliance.

Omnivorous, peaceful and hardy, it does best in hard water at the temperature range of 20 to 22°C, reduced in winter to 16 to 18°C. It is likely to die if kept for a prolonged period in too high a temperature.

It breeds readily either in an unplanted aquarium, with a spawning mat as recommended for *Brachydanio* species (see page 66) or in the regular way of cyprinids on dense clumps of fine-leaved plants such as *Myriophyllum*. The fry are not difficult to raise and, under good conditions, grow rapidly and reach maturity in about six months.

Botia lohachata

Tinca tinca the Tench, is widely distributed throughout Europe including the British Isles, although it is absent from northern Scotland. It is a very large fish that in the wild has been known to reach 2 feet and more, but as normally it is found on the beds of sluggish ponds with thick plant growth, small specimens are very much at home in an unheated aquarium. The general colour is a dark olive-green; the scales are small and a golden glint gives the fish a most attractive burnished appearance.

An even more attractive golden form has a rich bronze colour that rivals the Goldfish for coloration. It is not found in the wild (other than as an occasional mutant) but is bred by pisciculturists for stocking ornamental waters. Both forms are peaceful, omnivorous, and spawn in the regular way of cyprinids.

Family GYRINOCHEILIDAE

The family Gyrinocheilidae is native to south-east Asia. It is a small family that consists of only one genus *Gyrinocheilus*, with three species. They are characterized by a mouth situated on the underside. It is surrounded by well-developed lips to form a sucking organ and is furnished with rasp-like folds. This specialization makes these fishes excellent destroyers of algae.

G. aymonieri from Thailand, is the only species represented to aquarists. It is a uniform grey-brown in colour with dark blotches on the back, a large dorsal fin, and a dark stripe along the side usually broken up into blotches. Like the other members of the genus it eats large quantities of algae which it scrapes off stones and well-established plants without damaging them; in consequence it has been given the popular name of the Algae Eater.

In the wild it grows to a length of about 10 inches, although in the aquarium considerably less, and so it needs plenty of room in which to move, and adequate aeration. Young fish are peaceful but advancing age brings pugnacity. Its breeding habits are not known.

Family COBITIDAE

The Cobitidae or loach family is native to the fresh waters of Europe and Asia. A few species have extended into Ethiopia but none is found in the New World, and like the Cyprinidae to which they are closely related, they respect Wallace's Line.

Loaches may be distinguished from cyprinids by the elongated, oblong, compressed or cylindrical, but never depressed, body; by a mouth surrounded by from six to twelve barbels; by the soft-rayed and short dorsal and anal fins; and by the rudimentary, or lack of, scales.

As a general rule loaches are to be found in shallow, fast-flowing water over a gravel bed. They are bottom livers that spend most of their time lying on the stones or among the crowns of the plants. In captivity, therefore, they should be supplied with well-aerated water that is not too deep. Some species, however, are able to use the intestine as a supplementary breathing organ. If the water becomes saturated with carbon dioxide, they will be seen to rise to the surface, take in at the mouth a gulp of atmospheric air, which passes out at the vent as a bubble. In a community aquarium such a fish is very useful, because it gives a warning when the water is polluted. On the whole, however, loaches are not ideal fishes for the community aquarium. They do a lot of rooting and some of the larger species not only uproot small plants, but stir up so much sediment that the water becomes cloudy. As scavengers their place in the aquarium has long been taken by the more gentle *Corydoras* species.

Most loaches are very sensitive to changes of atmospheric conditions. Before a storm they become very active and swim in a way which suggests an attempt to leave the water. At one time, the peasants of central and eastern Europe kept specimens of *Misgurnus fossilis* in bowls as living barometers. No more need be said than that although this fish does presage a storm, it is very doubtful that it gives warning of one as much as twenty-four hours ahead as has been claimed.

In the wild loaches feed on the larvae of water insects, daphnids, worms, and the like. In the aquarium their diet may be augmented with dried food and some will eat decomposing plant matter.

All loaches are oviparous but their breeding habits are not known. Only *Acanthophthalmus* species, *Cobitis taenia* and *Misgurnus anguillicaudatus* have spawned in captivity, but rarely.

The genus *Acanthophthalmus* is native to south-east Asia. Altogether some six or seven species and subspecies are represented to aquarists, but only four are regularly introduced into the aquarium. All are very much alike. They are slim little fishes that reach a length of some 2 or 3 inches, worm-like in shape and locomotion. There are six barbels in the form of a stubby moustache on the upper lip, and a short spine in front of each eye. The general colour is pinkish yellow, crossed by a number of dark brown, vertical bands, that in some species extend to the belly. Albino forms are known.

All are peaceful, good scavengers and flourish at a temperature range of 24 to 28°C; some have spawned in captivity but their breeding behaviour is not yet properly understood.

A. kuhlii kuhlii the Coolie Loach or Leopard Eel, is native to Sumatra and Java; it has fifteen to twenty vertical brown bars, the first three on the head. *A.k. sumatranus* is native to Sumatra; it has twelve to fifteen vertical dark bars, the first three on the head. *A. semicinctus* the Half-banded Coolie Loach, is native to Malaysia; it has twelve to sixteen vertical dark bars, the first three on the head and, with the exception of the three on the head and the one at the root of the caudal fin, they extend only to the middle line of the body. *A. shelfordi* is native to Borneo; the vertical dark bars are interrupted to form a pattern of dark patches.

Acanthopsis choirhynchus popularly called the Horse-faced or Long-nosed Loach, is native to south-east Asia. It is a fairly large fish whose coloration and markings are very variable. In the wild it reaches a length of about 7 inches but young fishes are quite suitable for an aquarium at a temperature range of 25 to 28°C. It is peaceful and may be introduced into a community aquarium, although it is largely a fish for the specialist because it eats only living food and is active only during the hours of darkness: at other times it remains buried in the planting medium. Nothing is known of its breeding habits.

The genus *Botia* is native to south-east Asia, from Pakistan, through India and Malaysia, to Indonesia. It is represented to aquarists by about ten species: *B. beauforti* from Thailand; *B. berdmorei* from Burma and Thailand; *B. horae* the Cream Loach, from Thailand; *B. hymenophysa* the Banded Loach, from Thailand, Malaysia and Indonesia; *B. lecontei* from Thailand; *B. lohachata* the Gandak, from Pakistan; *B. macracantha* the Clown Loach, from Thailand, through Malaysia, to Java; *B. modesta* the Orange-finned Loach, from Thailand, Malaysia and Vietnam; and *B. sidthimunki* the Pygmy Loach, from Thailand. The species sometimes marketed under the name of *B. lucas-bahi* from the Tachin River in Thailand is probably a subspecies of *B. hymenophysa*.

With the exception of *B. sidthimunki*, which reaches a length of little more than 1 inch, most *Botia* species reach a length of 3 or 4 inches, and in the wild *B. beauforti*, *B. berdmorei*, *B. hymenophysa* and *B. macracantha* reach a length of from 8 to 12 inches, although usually remaining smaller in the aquarium. They flourish at a temperature of about 25°C, eat anything and, like most loaches, make good scavengers. They are quite peaceful. *B. lohachata* will sometimes swim alongside another fish and nuzzle at its side: it is thought that it sucks the mucus from the body of the fish. If it does, it appears to do no harm, although we have known some fishes become rather frightened at the unusual treatment to which they are subjected.

B. macracantha is probably the most popular member of the genus; it is certainly the most highly coloured. The body is light orange, crossed by three blue-black, wedge-shaped bars: one over the head through the eye to the gill plate, another in front of the dorsal fin to the belly, the third behind the dorsal fin to the anal fin.

Cobitis taenia commonly called the Spined Loach, is found throughout Europe (including Great Britain) southwards to North Africa and eastwards across northern Asia to Japan. The colour is variable, buff to sandy, spotted dark brown, the side marked with a regular row of large, brown blotches.

The Spined Loach reaches the fair size of 4 or 5 inches and should be kept in a large aquarium at a temperature range of 15 to 18°C. The bottom should be layered with a sandy soil, never gravel, as it likes to bury itself with only its head exposed. In the wild it feeds largely on worms and by sifting the bottom-soil.

Breeding occurs from April to June. Nothing is known of the practice, however, except that a large number of reddish eggs are scattered indiscriminately and gravitate to the bottom. At a temperature of 15°C they incubate in about a week. As the young fish obtain most of their food from the debris that collects on the bottom, they are not difficult to raise to maturity.

Lepidocephalus thermalis from India and Ceylon, is not unlike *Cobitis taenia* but may be distinguished from it by the presence of eight barbels (*Cobitis* has only six) and smaller spots on the side. A temperature of 24°C suits it and it is not faddy about its food. Its breeding habits are not known.

Acanthophthalmus semicinctus

Above *Cobitis taenia*
Below *Noemacheilus barbatulus*

Hypopomus artedi

The genus *Misgurnus* is represented in the aquarium by two species: *M. anguillicaudatus* the Japanese Weatherfish from China and Japan, and *M. fossilis* the Common Weatherfish, from central and eastern Europe. Both are hardy and may be kept under the same conditions as *Cobitis taenia*. They are, however, much larger fishes: in the wild *M. anguillicaudatus* reaches a length of about 10 inches and *M. fossilis* about 15 inches; in captivity they do not grow so big and become quite tame.

The genus *Noemacheilus* is represented to aquarists by *N. barbatulus* the Stone Loach, found throughout Europe (including Great Britain) and eastwards across Siberia to Korea, and *N. fasciatus* from Indonesia.

N. barbatulus grows to a length of 4 or 5 inches, and should be kept and cared for in the same way

as *Cobitis taenia*. *N. fasciatus* reaches a length of 3 or 4 inches, and needs an aquarium at a temperature of about 24°C. The back is olive-green to brown in colour, the side lemon shading to primrose on the belly. From ten to twenty brownish-red bars taper vertically from the back to the middle line of the side.

Family GYMNOTIDAE
The family Gymnotidae is native to the southern countries of Central America (including the West Indies) and to South America (excluding the Atlantic coast) as far south as La Plata.

Family RHAMPHICHTHYIDAE
The family Rhamphichthyidae is native to South America (excluding the Atlantic coast) as far south as La Plata.

Family STERNARCHIDAE

The family Sternarchidae is native to South America (including the Atlantic coast, but excluding Colombia north of the Magdalena River) as far south as La Plata.

Members of these three families are very much alike: all are rather eel-like in appearance and locomotion. The dorsal fin is absent or reduced to an adipose strip, and the caudal fin, if present, is reduced to a mere bunch of rays. The anal fin is very long. It extends from below and just behind the head, to the tip of the tail, and is often as thin as the blade of a knife. Locomotion is effected by undulating movements of the anal fin; and by reversing them, the fish can swim backwards as easily as forwards.

The families are represented in the aquarium by six species. They are fishes for the specialist more than for the ordinary aquarist; for all members of these families are large fishes, strictly carnivorous and nocturnal, or at least crepuscular. Nothing is known of their breeding habits. It is in their favour, however, that they are quite hardy and will tolerate a temperature range of 23 to 28°C, and most are peaceful (although it is a wise precaution to keep them with fishes about the same size as themselves) but tend to quarrel with their own species.

Gymnotus carapo (fam. Gymnotidae) is native to the West Indies, Guatemala and southwards through South America to La Plata. It is popularly known as the Banded Knifefish. In the wild it reaches a length of 24 inches, and under good conditions, an aquarium specimen will reach about 12 inches in two or three years. The general colour varies from pale yellow to brown, with about twenty dark yellow, backward-sloping bars on the side.

Eigenmannia virescens (fam. Rhamphichthyidae) is found throughout the geographical range of the family. It is popularly known as the Green Knifefish because in a direct light the flesh colour of the body shows greenish reflections. It reaches a length of 18 inches in the wild.

Hypopomus artedi (fam. Rhamphichthyidae) is native to eastern Guyana. It is popularly known as the Spotted or Speckled Knifefish and is the smallest of the group, reaching a length of only about 7 inches. The general colour is grey-green with black dots.

Steatogenes elegans (fam. Rhamphichthyidae) is native to the Amazon basin. It reaches a length of about 8 inches. The general colour is yellowish brown to ochre, darker on the back than on the side. The belly is yellowish white to white. Some twelve to twenty irregular dark brown, vertical bars extend from the back to about the middle line of the side.

Sternarchella schotti (fam. Sternarchidae) is native to central Brazil. It is characterized by a long filamentous dorsal fin that can be depressed into a groove along the middle of the back. The general colour is brownish with a large number of black dots. It reaches a length of about 9 inches.

Sternarchus albifrons (fam. Sternarchidae) is native to Surinam and the Amazon. It is popularly known as the Black Ghost because the body and fins are a uniform velvety black. A white line extends along the back, from the snout to about the middle of the body, and two white bars surround the caudal peduncle. In the wild it reaches a length of 20 inches.

Family DORADIDAE

The family Doradidae is native to South America north of La Plata. It contains a number of genera but only two species of the genus *Doras* are regularly introduced into the aquarium. They are hardy enough to tolerate a temperature range of 20 to 26°C and although they are good scavengers (with a preference for meaty food), they are not altogether satisfactory community fishes for they grow to a fairly large size, will eat small fishes, and are crepuscular. Not much is known about their breeding behaviour but some species are said to be nest-builders and both sexes are said to tend the eggs.

An interesting characteristic of some species is the emission of a grunting noise, both in and out of the water. No vocal chord is present. The sound arises by a special mechanism of the air bladder and the processes of the vertebrae above it, combined with the movements of the pectoral spine grinding in the glenoid cavity.

D. asterifrons once referred to the genus *Astrodoras*, is native to central and eastern Brazil. The general colour is dark grey, shading to dirty white on the belly. It reaches a length of 4 or 5 inches.

D. spinosissimus once referred to the genus *Acanthodoras*, is native to Brazil. It is popularly known as the Talking Catfish. The general colour is dark brown blotched with white on the back; the side a lighter brown with white bands. It reaches a length of 6 inches.

Family SILURIDAE

At one time all catfishes were included in the family Siluridae. Today the family embraces only

Kryptopterus bicirrhis

those catfishes that range across the Northern Hemisphere from central Europe eastwards to China and Japan.

The family includes many very large species, notably *Ompok pabda* from northern India and beyond, a food fish that reaches a length of about 5 feet, and the even larger *Silurus glanis* commonly called the Wels, the only catfish found wild in Europe, that grows up to 9 and 10 feet in length. Dark stories are told by anglers, who claim to have found ducks, geese, dogs and even children in the stomachs of their catches. We know what anglers are, but after making every allowance for exaggeration, and the discovery in the stomachs of the fishes of parts of the corpses of the drowned, it is essential to stress that only very small specimens should be chosen for the aquarium. Such fishes flourish quite well in an unheated aquarium, but they must be kept by themselves for clearly they

will eat anything that comes their way and which is small enough for them to swallow.

In the heated aquarium the family is represented by a number of genera, of which the best known is *Kryptopterus*. The two species regularly offered for sale to aquarists are *K. bicirrhis* and *K. macrocephalus*; both are from Malaysia and beyond and both call for the same care and living conditions. A large aquarium (because they are active fishes) is required, the water not too deep and at a temperature range of 20 to 25°C, together with small living food. Several of the same species should be kept together as solitary specimens tend to mope.

K. bicirrhis is popularly known as the Glass Catfish because the body is transparent; the internal organs may clearly be seen crowded into a small space immediately behind the head. In reality the general colour of the body is yellowish, that, by reflected light, displays a wealth of

Mystus vittatus

prismatic colours. It reaches a length of 4 inches.

K. *macrocephalus* is a translucent yellowish or greenish with a bluish sheen when seen by reflected light. It reaches a length of 5 inches.

Family BAGRIDAE

The family Bagridae is native to the Nile valley and Africa (excluding Malagasy) south of the Sahara, and from India and China eastwards to Japan and Indonesia.

Most members of the family are large fishes that reach a length of 18 inches and more; only a few are less than 7 or 8 inches long. For the aquarium, therefore, young specimens should always be chosen. They may be kept at a temperature range of 20 to 26°C and fed on living food of all kinds and suitable substitutes. Most species are voracious feeders and, of course, must be kept away from small fishes. For this reason, as well as for the fact that they are nocturnal, they are not ideal for a community aquarium.

Numerous genera are known but only *Leiocassis* represented by L. *siamensis*, and *Mystus* represented by M. *tengera* and M. *vittatus*, are regularly offered for sale to aquarists. All are comparatively small fishes that reach a length of about 6 or 7 inches. Their breeding habits are unknown.

L. *siamensis* from Thailand, popularly called the Barred Siamese Catfish, varies in colour from a dark coffee, blue-black or grey-blue; the underparts from pale yellow to whitish. The side is strikingly marked with four irregular, light-coloured, transverse bars.

M. *tengera* from northern India, is greenish to yellow, the back pale brown, the belly white. The side is marked with four or five wavy, dark brown, longitudinal bands that taper from the gill plate to the caudal peduncle.

M. *vittatus* from India, Burma and Thailand, is very similar to the above but may be distinguished from it by the fact that the upper lobe of the caudal fin is larger than the lower one. The colour varies from a greyish silver to golden, and the longitudinal bars on the side vary in colour from pale blue to dark brown or black.

Family AMEIURIDAE

In the Old World the family Ameiuridae is native to eastern China, from Hong Kong to Peking: the majority of genera, however, are to be found in

86

shallow depressions on the bottom: they do not breed in aquaria.

Family SCHILBEIDAE

The family Schilbeidae is native to the Nile valley and Africa (excluding Malagasy) south of the Sahara. In Asia it is found in India, Burma and beyond.

A number of species are known but *Etropiella debauwi* from the Congo, and *Pangasius sutchi* from south-east Asia, are the only two regularly offered for sale to aquarists. Unusually for catfishes both swim in the middle to upper strata of water.

E. debauwi is translucent with a silvery-white throat and belly, and three steel-blue horizontal stripes on the side that darken with age to blue-black. It needs the fairly high temperature range of 24 to 27°C and living food. As it is a very active fish that likes to shoal it is best when kept with its own species, although it is peaceful enough and small enough (it reaches a length of about 3 inches) for a community aquarium.

P. sutchi is a translucent yellow with a greenish sheen on the side and two or three very dark horizontal stripes. The eyes are large. A temperature range of 20 to 25°C suits it. As it eats most things and even in the aquarium grows to 6 inches and more, it should be kept apart from small fishes.

Family CLARIIDAE

The family Clariidae is found throughout Africa (including Malagasy) and northwards into Lebanon. Further east it is widespread in India, Pakistan and beyond.

Three or four genera are known to aquarists but only one genus, *Clarias*, is regularly offered for sale to aquarists. Members of this genus are large fishes and only young specimens, therefore, should be introduced into the home aquarium. A soft, sandy planting medium and a temperature range of 20 to 25°C are the main requirements. The aquarium must always be kept covered as all members of this family have an accessory breathing organ that enables them not only to live in poorly oxygenated water but also to remain out of it for quite long spells. In the wild they frequently leave the water at night to search for food. All members of the genus are actively predacious and should be kept by themselves and fed on living food, such as worms and snails, and suitable substitutes. Most are greedy enough to eat anything that is offered to them.

Altogether about half a dozen species are known.

the New World where they are confined to the Great Lakes of the United States and the Mississippi basin.

The family is represented to aquarists by a handful of species, all from the United States: *Ameiurus melas* the Black Bullhead, *A. natalis* the Yellow Bullhead, *A. nebulosus nebulosus* the Brown Bullhead, *A. n. marmoratus* the Marbled Bullhead, and *Ictalurus punctatus* the Spotted Cat, which may be set apart from *Ameiurus* species by its deeply forked caudal fin. All five species, however, are more or less tadpole-shaped, of varying coloration, and in the wild grow to a large size. *Ameiurus* species reach a length of from 12 to 18 inches, and *I. punctatus* is a food fish that commonly reaches 30 inches and has been known to reach about 4 feet.

For an unheated aquarium small specimens must be chosen and kept either on their own or with fishes no smaller than themselves, because they are actively predacious and their natural food is small animals and other fishes. They will not take dried foods and in captivity must be given living food such as earthworms, slugs and snails.

In the wild and in garden ponds they breed in

Malapterurus electricus

C. angolensis from tropical western and Central Africa, and *C. batrachus* from Ceylon, through eastern India to Malaysia, Indonesia and beyond, are probably the two best known to aquarists.

C. angolensis is coffee to black with a bronze sheen with light-coloured blotches and spots on the side. The belly varies from beige or pale brown to white. It reaches a length of 24 inches.

C. batrachus is greyish blue with a bronze sheen on the back. The belly varies from pale blue to pink. The side is marked with whitish spots. It reaches a length of 20 inches. In this form it is rather rare and those specimens offered for sale are more usually white.

Family MOCHOKIDAE

The family Mochokidae is native to Africa (excluding Malagasy) south of the Sahara, and northwards through the Nile basin.

It is represented to aquarists by the genus *Syno-dontis*, the so-called upside-down catfishes, as some species swim on their backs, a practice that has resulted in a reversal of the usual colour pattern; the back is light coloured and the belly dark. *Synodontis* species are very peaceful and make good community fishes, although some fishes resent the incessant movements of their long barbels. They are, however, crepuscular and need a large aquarium dimly lit. A temperature range of

species that swims on its back to be introduced to aquarists. As a result, it was given the popular name of the Upside-down Catfish. The back is pale grey to cream with dark brown to black blotches. The belly is black. It reaches a length of 3 or 4 inches. The reversal of the colour pattern may also be noted in *S. batensoda* from the Nile basin and Senegal, another species that swims on its back. It is a much bigger fish than *S. nigriventris* and reaches a length of about 9 inches.

S. robbianus from the Niger, is of a nut-brown colour and darkly spotted. It reaches a length of about 5 inches.

Family PIMELODIDAE

The family Pimelodidae is native to the West Indies, Mexico, Central America and South America east of the Andes as far south as latitude 40°.

Members of this family are closely related to the Bagridae of the Old World, but may be distinguished from all other catfishes by the large adipose fin and the very long barbels which, in some species, are almost as long as the fish itself.

The family is a large one but only five species are regularly seen in the home aquarium, mainly because pimelodid fishes are crepuscular. They do not take kindly to life in an aquarium unless respect is paid to the fact that in the wild they lie hidden most of the day and only become active in search of food when it becomes dark. A temperature range of 20 to 26°C is recommended, and though omnivorous they show a marked preference for living food and suitable substitutes.

Microglanis parahybae popularly known as the Harlequin Catfish, is native to south-east Brazil and the hinterlands of Paraguay and Argentina. It is a small fish that reaches about 3 inches, peaceful and undemanding in its requirements. The colour varies from yellowish brown to chocolate, the head and body are marked with numerous blotches.

The genus *Pimelodella* is represented to aquarists by two species: *P. gracilis* from the Orinoco to the La Plata rivers, and *P. vittata* from south-east Brazil. Both are brownish in colour, *P. gracilis* with a dark stripe that extends from the gill plate broadening to the root of the caudal fin, *P. vittata* with a narrow black stripe from the snout to the root of the caudal fin. Both are peaceful and not overlarge: *P. gracilis* reaches a length of about 5 inches, *P. vittata* about 3 inches.

Pimelodus clarias is widespread throughout the geographical range of the family. It is a large fish

22 to 26°C is suitable, and feeding should consist of living food and plenty of algal growth or lettuce.

S. alberti from the Congo, is blue-grey to olive-brown, the back and sides marked with large dark blotches. It reaches a length of 5 or 6 inches.

S. angelicus from tropical western Africa and the Congo, is grey to dark violet with reddish-yellow to brownish-red blotches. It reaches a length of about 8 inches.

S. decorus from tropical western Africa, is whitish, the sides and fins blotched and banded black. It reaches a length of about 7 inches.

S. nigriventris from the Congo, was the first

Corydoras agassizi

that in the wild reaches a length of 12 inches, but aquarium specimens rarely exceed 4 inches. The general colour is light gold, shading to white on the belly. Young fish show numerous dark brown spots on the back, side and fins that disappear with advancing age, and in some specimens never develop.

Sorubim lima the Spatula Catfish, sometimes called the Shovel-nose Catfish, is so called because the snout is spatulate. The general colour is greyish green, sometimes flecked with a darker colour. A broad, deep black stripe extends from the snout, broadening posteriorly to cover almost the whole of the lower lobe of the caudal fin. Specimens in aquaria reach a length of about 8 inches; in the wild considerably more. They should not be kept with fishes smaller than themselves, especially slow-moving ones.

Family BUNOCEPHALIDAE

The Bunocephalidae is a small family of catfishes native to the upper and middle course of the Amazon basin and the Guianas. They are popularly called banjo fishes for, seen from above, they bear a marked similarity in shape to the well-known musical instrument.

The family is represented by the genus *Bunocephalus* of which only two species: *B. coracoideus* (*bicolor*) the Two-coloured Catfish, and *B. kneri* are known to aquarists. Both are native to the western Amazon and Ecuador and both are small fishes that reach a length of 5 or 6 inches. They are good scavengers that will eat almost anything, and peaceful. In common with other catfishes, however, they are crepuscular or nocturnal and spend their days half-buried in the planting medium. It is, therefore, best to keep them with their own kind in a sparsely planted aquarium, rather than in a well-planted community aquarium, with a soft, sandy bed and plenty of sediment. A temperature range of 20 to 25°C is advised.

B. coracoideus is dark brown marked with dark bands and blotches, and small light-coloured spots.

B. kneri is greyish brown marbled pale and dark, sometimes with rows of dark blotches.

Family MALAPTERURIDAE

The family Malapteruridae contains only one species, *Malapterurus electricus* the Electric Catfish, so called because it is able to deliver an electric shock strong enough to make a man jump. It is found in the Nile basin and south of the Sahara to the Zambezi, with the exception of Lake Victoria and the rivers of eastern Africa.

In general colour it is a medium grey, flecked with a number of irregular dark spots. A young fish has a light-coloured ring round the caudal peduncle. Only a young fish should be chosen for the home aquarium and it should be kept by itself, for Electric Catfishes are very quarrelsome and predatory, and even in captivity generally reach a length of 6 or 7 inches. A temperature range of 23 to 30°C is recommended and living food, particularly earthworms, is essential.

Hypostomus plecostomus

Its breeding habits are unknown although it is said that the eggs are deposited in a depression and incubated in the mouth.

Family CALLICHTHYIDAE

The family Callichthyidae is native to tropical South America. Members of this family are commonly known as mailed catfishes, because the body is armoured with two rows of overlapping plates, each beset at the hinder edge with movable denticles. By virtue of an accessory breathing apparatus they are able to live in foul water: air is gulped at the surface, and the oxygen absorbed into the blood through the thin walls of numerous small blood vessels in the lining of the gut.

The family is represented to aquarists by four genera. The best known is *Corydoras* but all are very satisfactory aquarium fishes for they tolerate a temperature range of 18 to 26°C, are omnivorous to the point of making excellent scavengers and, with the exception of *Callichthys callichthys* and *Hoplosternum* species that reach a length of some 7 or 8 inches, all are small fishes that range in size from little more than 1 inch to 4 inches at most.

Brochis coeruleus the Short-bodied Catfish, is native to the Upper Amazon. The top of the head is brown with a green tinge; the lower part of the head and the side are bright green shading to yellow.

Callichthys callichthys sometimes called the Hassar but more usually the Armoured Catfish, is native to eastern Brazil southwards to La Plata. The body varies in colour from dark grey to dark olive with a delicate blue or violet sheen on the side. The belly is bluish grey to brown.

A bubble nest is blown by the male on the underside of *Riccia* or a broad-leaved plant. About 120 to 150 eggs are deposited in the nest and, at a temperature of about 27°C, incubate in about four days.

Among catfishes, species of the genus *Corydoras* are the best known to aquarists and certainly the most popular. They are very pleasing little fishes, peaceful, omnivorous and excellent scavengers. They have the further advantages that they are hardy enough to tolerate a wide temperature range, are small (none exceeds 4 inches and most vary in size from about 2 to 3 inches) and long-lived.

Altogether some two dozen species are known. About half this number is mentioned below; they are regularly imported for sale, and although they do not breed readily in captivity, at some time or another most have done so.

The male is rather smaller than the female and has longer and more pointed pelvic fins. Two or three males should be placed with one female and brought into condition by feeding with earthworms, bloodworms, gnat larvae, and a reliable dried food. The water should be alkaline (pH 7·2) and alkaline stones may be introduced into the aquarium to counteract the tendency of the water to become acid. As soon as the female shows signs

Loricaria parva

of spawning, the temperature of the water should be raised to about 27°C, a plentiful amount of living food should be offered and overnight the temperature of the water should slowly be reduced to about 18°C or even to as low as 15°C. This supplies a stimulus. The eggs are deposited on fixed objects and incubate in three or four days. It is best to remove the brood fish because, if given a chance, they will eat the fry.

C. aeneus the Bronze Catfish, is found from Venezuela to La Plata. It is a shiny olive-green to brass, with a golden stripe that curves from the nape to below the adipose fin.

C. agassizi is widely distributed in western Brazil. It is pale brown to clay, the body and vertical fins marked with irregular dark blotches.

C. arcuatus the Arched Catfish, is found in the Upper Amazon basin. It is ivory-white with a mauve sheen, and a dark stripe that curves from the eye to the base of the caudal fin.

C. hastatus the Pygmy Catfish, is found in the Amazon basin. It is light brown, with a jet-black stripe that extends from above the pectorals to a large arrow-shaped spot at the base of the caudal fin.

C. julii (*leopardus*) the Leopard Catfish, is found in the coastal district between Rio de Janeiro and Pernambuco. The general colour is grey, the head and upper half of the body peppered with numerous irregular dark markings.

C. macropterus is found in southern Brazil. The general colour is yellowish brown shading to yellowish on the belly. The side is marked with an irregular dark band and dark blotches alternate above and below it.

C. melanistius the Blue-spotted Catfish, is found in the Orinoco basin. The general colour is pale grey suffused salmon-pink. The body and head are peppered with small black spots. A black band extends from the top of the head over the eye.

C. myersi is found in the Amazon basin. The body is bright orange-red, the side marked with a very broad dark brown band from the front of the dorsal fin to the root of the caudal.

C. nattereri the Blue Catfish, is found in central and eastern Brazil. It is light brown with a silvery-blue sheen, and a dark stripe that extends from the gill cover to the base of the caudal fin.

C. paleatus the Peppered Catfish, is found in south-eastern Brazil and the La Plata basin. It is green to brown, with large dark blue-black spots on the side and similar, but smaller, spots on the back.

C. punctatus the Spotted Catfish, is found in Guyana and the northern tributaries of the Amazon. It is light brown in colour, with blackish brown spots on the side.

C. reticulatus the Reticulated Catfish, is found in the Amazon basin. The back is olive with metallic reflections. The side is white with a net-like pattern of intense black.

C. treitli the Long-nosed Catfish, is found in eastern Brazil. The general colour is brownish yellow, the side paler with a yellowish reflection, and marked with an irregular dark band that extends from the gill cover to the root of the caudal fin.

The genus *Hoplosternum* is very similar to the genus *Callichthys*. It is represented to aquarists by two species: *H. littorale* from Trinidad, Guyana and Brazil as far south as the Parana; and *H. thoracoratum* from Trinidad, Guyana and the Amazon basin. Both are fairly large fishes that in the wild reach a length of about 8 inches, and both are omnivorous. Little is known of their breeding habits but it is said that they spawn under surface plants and that the male cares for the young.

Family LORICARIIDAE

The Loricariidae is a family of armoured catfishes native to northern and central South America, and northwards into Central America to Nicaragua.

Some seven genera, embracing about twenty species, are known to aquarists but only about nine species are regularly offered for sale. All are omnivorous and make good scavengers. Earthworms and bloodworms are readily eaten but they must be supplemented with large quantities of soft alga, or a suitable substitute such as chopped lettuce, if the fishes are to survive. They are peaceful and harmless fishes, quite suitable for a community aquarium, although their habit of rooting among the plants is rather against them if the appearance of the aquarium is a matter of consideration. A soft to medium-hard rather than a hard water is to be recommended, at a temperature range of 21 to 25°C.

Spawning in captivity is rare and *Loricaria parva*, *Otocinclus affinis* and *Xenocara dolichoptera* are probably the only three members of this family that have spawned in aquaria.

The genus *Farlowella* is native to southern Brazil and La Plata. Members of the genus are very similar in appearance to *Loricaria* species but may be distinguished by a slimmer and more elongated body, and by the dorsal fin being set well back and immediately above the anal fin.

F. acus popularly called the Needlefish, is

olive-green to yellowish brown, the belly yellowish. It reaches a length of about 6 inches.

F. gracilis is a rather large species that will grow up to 8 inches. The body is grey marked with indistinct blotches: the belly is grey to yellowish.

Members of the genus *Hypostomus* were once referred to the genus *Plecostomus*. They are native to south-east Brazil and La Plata. *H. plecostomus* popularly known as the Sucker-mouth Catfish, is the species usually seen in aquaria. The general colour is greyish brown, the side marked with longitudinal rows of dark brown spots. It is a large fish that in the wild grows to a length of 16 inches. For the aquarium, therefore, only small specimens should be chosen but *H. rachowi*, from the neighbourhood of Rio de Janeiro, is a smaller and more suitable fish which reaches only 5 or 6 inches. It is a cloudy grey in colour marked with yellow-brown spots.

Loricaria parva is very similar in appearance to *Farlowella* species but may be distinguished by the position of the dorsal fin. It is popularly known as the Whip-tail because the uppermost and lowermost rays of the caudal fin are considerably lengthened. The general colour is a lemon-yellow to yellow-grey with a number of dark bars and spots on the side. It reaches a length of 4 or 5 inches.

The genus *Otocinclus* is native to north-east Brazil. About six species are known but *O. affinis* the Sucking Catfish, that reaches a length of little more than an inch, *O. flexilis* (*arnoldi*) and *O. vittatus* that reach a length of 2 or 3 inches, are the best-known species. They are excellent aquarium fish for provided they have access to alga and other vegetable matter in sufficient quantity, they do no damage to even the most delicate plants. They are not particular about water conditions and will tolerate a temperature as low as 20°C.

Xenocara dolichoptera the Blue Chin, is native to the Amazon basin. The general colour is dark brown to greenish brown with a blue-black sheen and a sprinkling of small white spots. The belly is bluish grey with white spots. It reaches a length of 4 or 5 inches.

Family ORYZIATIDAE

The family Oryziatidae is a small one that contains only one genus, *Oryzias*, native to south-east Asia, from India and Ceylon, through Malaysia and Indonesia, to Japan.

At one time *Oryzias* species were referred to the family Cyprinodontidae but they may be distinguished from all members of this family by the non-protrusible upper jaw. The pectoral fins are set high up and the base of the anal fin is long.

The genus contains seven species but only four are represented to aquarists: *O. celebensis* from Celebes; *O. javanicus* from Java and Malaysia; *O. latipes* from Japan; and *O. melastigma* from India and Ceylon. All are small fishes that reach a length of 2 inches at most and they are popularly known as medakas or rice fishes, because they are found in large numbers in the flooded paddy-fields. They are harmless little creatures that in the wild live on daphnids, small water insects, and the like. In the aquarium they will take dried food readily and flourish well in a temperature range of 20 to 24°C.

Breeding is not difficult. The aquarium should be stocked with fine-leaved and floating plants and situated where it will receive plenty of sunlight. The eggs are amber tinted and hang from the vent of the female until fertilized and brushed off on to the plants. The period of incubation is about fourteen days at 24°C and the young fishes may be raised on infusoria and dust-fine dried food. Provided that the brood fish are well fed and there are plenty of plants in the aquarium, most of the fry will reach maturity in the same aquarium as their parents.

Family CYPRINODONTIDAE

The Cyprinodontidae (tooth-carps, top-minnows or killifishes) is a large family of oviparous fishes, found in the Old World throughout Africa (including Malagasy but excluding the Cape) and extending across southern Europe and Asia, from Lisbon, through Asia Minor, India and Malaysia, to China, Korea and Japan; and in the New World from Quebec and Ontario in the north, through the United States, Central America (including the West Indies) and South America east of the Andes, to Buenos Aires in the south.

Most are small fishes with an oblong to elongated body; in general depressed anteriorly and compressed posteriorly. The dorsal and anal fins are set well back on the body. On the whole they are not active fishes; in the wild they inhabit stagnant ponds and slow-moving waters over muddy bottoms. Most spend their time idling at the surface or in mid-water (the head up and the body held at an angle) but they can move very quickly if necessary, and the aquarium should be kept covered at all times as they are excellent jumpers.

To be kept in good health they should be fed on living food and suitable substitutes. A few are partly herbivorous and need to be supplied with algae, duckweed, or cooked and minced green vegetables from the kitchen. Most are peaceful and may be kept in a community aquarium although some fin nipping is to be expected from them, and those species that have big mouths may, and sometimes do, swallow small fishes whole.

With some exceptions they breed readily in captivity. The water should be about 7 inches deep and at a temperature of 24 to 27°C. The eggs of most species are adhesive and are deposited among the floating and submerged plants, either singly or in batches, over a period of several days. The best results are obtained if the eggs are given some shade during the period of incubation. The period of incubation varies with the species and, of course, with the temperature of the water. At about 25°C it may be anything from a week to a fortnight, and nothing more precise is to be said because as the eggs are deposited over a period of several days, the eggs from one spawning do not all hatch on the same day. For the same reason the fry do not develop uniformly. As a result, frequent sortings must be made in order to prevent the larger fry from harassing the smaller.

Some species (for example *Leptolucania ommata*) will require infusorians for their first food. Most, however, are able to take bigger food such as newly hatched brine shrimps, finely screened daphnids and mashed whiteworms, from the start.

It is as well to remove the brood fish from the aquarium as soon as the eggs have been deposited and fertilized. The majority, however, do not appear to molest their young, and the fry will be fairly safe if the breeding aquarium is thickly planted.

Members of the genus *Aphanius* are found in the fresh and brackish waters of the Mediterranean basin, the Gulf of Persia, north-west India, the south-eastern states of the United States, Mexico and Cuba.

The genus is represented to aquarists by five species: *A. dispar*; *A. fasciatus*; *A. iberus*; *A. mento*; and *A. sophiae*. All are native to the Old World but are rarely imported. It is hard to understand why, because they are small fishes, colourful, peaceful, and easy to keep in a mixture of one part sea water to four parts fresh at a temperature range of 20 to 25°C; moreover they can be acclimatized to fresh water if it has an alkaline reaction (*p*H 7·4). Although carnivorous by nature most will take dried food but as they have rather small mouths the food offered to them, whether living or dried, must be small.

Two-year-old specimens are the best from which to breed. Spawning occurs in the regular way of cyprinodonts but, as the male is a very hard driver, the aquarium should be thickly stocked with submerged plants to furnish cover for the female before removal. At a temperature of 24 to 27°C the fry hatch out in about ten days. They are quite large and grow rapidly if given plenty of finely screened daphnids, mashed whiteworms, and the like.

Members of the genus *Aphyosemion* are popularly known as lyretails because in most species the caudal fin of the male is shaped like the musical instrument of antiquity. They are native to tropical Africa, from Gambia to Angola.

The genus is a fairly large one but only about fifteen species and subspecies are regularly introduced into the aquarium. They are very colourful fishes but should not be kept in a community aquarium. Some males are very quarrelsome towards other fishes and as they inhabit well-shaded pools in the wild, where the temperature is not so high as may be supposed, in captivity they need an aquarium with a peaty planting medium, not too bright a light, and a temperature about 22 and certainly not above 24°C.

Aphyosemion species are largely carnivorous, and although they will eat dried food, for lack of something better, daphnids, earthworms, whiteworms and insect larvae are the best foods for them.

Breeding presents some difficulties because some species deliver adhesive eggs that stick to the plants, and others spawn in the planting medium. As some specimens have been known to spawn either way, it may be assumed that there is no exact dividing line between the two groups, and that the fish is capable of adapting its spawning behaviour to given conditions.

Specimens about six to nine months old are the best breeders. The aquarium should be stocked with plenty of floating plants (*Riccia* is ideal) and large clumps of submerged plants such as *Vallisneria*, *Myriophyllum* and *Fontinalis*. The water should be well matured, clear, at a temperature of 23 or 24°C and not more than 7 inches deep.

Spawning begins by the male and female taking up a side-by-side position and trembling excitedly. While trembling, the female delivers a single egg, and the male fertilizes it. The spawning act is continued for a week or longer, until anything from sixty to a hundred or more eggs have been delivered. It is best to remove the fertilized eggs and incubate them in very shallow water, about 2 inches deep. The eggs may take anything from ten to twenty-one days or longer to incubate; those of the bottom spawners take several weeks, and exceptionally those of *A. sjoestedti* five to six months.*

The eggs are best incubated at 22°C and rather remarkably, the higher the temperature the longer the eggs take to hatch. It is as well, therefore, not to allow the temperature to rise much above 22°C because a prolonged period of incubation usually results in many embryos dying within the egg.

The water in the aquarium in which the eggs of the bottom spawners are incubated should be siphoned off and the soil allowed almost to dry out. After a resting period the aquarium should be carefully refilled with matured water at a temperature of 22°C.

The fry of *Aphyosemion* species are able to eat finely screened daphnids, newly hatched brine shrimps, and other small living food, from the start. They grow rapidly and reach maturity in about four or five months. If kept under good conditions they will live for three years or more and, with the exception of *A. sjoestedti* that reaches a length of 3 or 4 inches, and *A. gulare* that reaches about 5 inches, aquarium specimens rarely exceed 2 inches.

A. arnoldi is native to the delta of the Niger. The male is brownish red on the back, olive-green on the side, blue-green to indigo on the caudal peduncle. Irregular crimson lines and dots mark the head and body. The female is brownish olive to grey-brown. It is a bottom spawner.

A. australe from Gabon, is well known to aquarists as the Cape Lopez Lyretail. The male is a very beautiful fish; dark brown on the back shading to blue-green on the belly. The gill cover and shoulder are marked with bright red bands and irregular dots; the side with red dots in more or less horizontal rows. The female is brownish shading to green on the belly. The eggs are scattered among the plants.

A. bivittatum bivittatum is native to western Africa from the Niger to Gabon. It is popularly known as the Red Lyretail. The male is brown to reddish brown with crimson spots and two dark brown stripes along the side. The female is more soberly coloured and the stripes not so well defined. *A.b. hollyi* the Blue Lyretail, shares the same geographical range and is very similar to the foregoing, but the general colour of the male is more bluish. The female is light brown. Both species are bottom spawners.

A. calliurum calliurum the Red-chinned Lyretail, is native to western Africa from Liberia to Loanda. The general colour of the male is blue-green to red-brown, the throat light brown to pink. The female is light brown with red spots. *A.c. ahli* shares the same geographical range and is more or less identical with the foregoing, but the male is a deep blue, the head and body marked with blood-red bands and dots that form irregular horizontal stripes. The female is a greyish purple. Both species scatter their eggs among the plants.

A. cinnamoeum popularly known as the Cinnamon Killie, is native to western Cameroun. The male is cinnamon-brown with a greenish sheen. The caudal fin is rounded. The female is a uniform greyish brown. It is a bottom spawner.

A. christyi from the Congo is very variable in coloration, but usually the male is a reddish yellow to bluish green, marked with red spots. The eggs are scattered among the plants.

A. cognatum is native to the Lower Congo. The male is dark olive on the back shading to light green on the belly. The body is marked with numerous red spots that combine to form irregular horizontal bands. The female is grey to yellowish. It scatters eggs at the surface.

A. filamentosum the Plumed Lyretail, is native to western Africa, from Lagos to Cameroun. The male is dark olive-yellow on the back, green on the head and throat, bluish on the belly. The head and body are marked with numerous reddish streaks. The female is paler in colour and has less pronounced markings. It spawns indiscriminately at the surface, in mid-water and at the bottom.

A. gardneri is popularly known as the Steel-blue Lyretail. It shares the same geographical range as *A. filamentosum* and is very similar to it in appearance. The general colour of the male is steel-blue, the back olive, the belly whitish. It is marked with splashes and dots of crimson. The female is light brown, the markings paler. It is a bottom spawner.

A. gulare the Blue Gularis, is native to western Africa from the delta of the Niger to Cameroun. The colour is very variable but the male shows a predominantly blue side with red to purplish irregular markings. The female is a uniform reddish brown. It is a bottom spawner.

A. liberiensis from Liberia, is popularly and

---

* It is probable that the bottom-spawning species are what are known as annual fishes. In the wild they inhabit ponds that contain very little water and dry up during the rainless months. The eggs, however, are drought resistant. They are buried in the mud at the bottom of the pond, and incubate when the succeeding rainy season refills the pond. The parent fish die as the ponds dry up.

rather obviously known as the Liberian Killie. The male has a blue-green body marked with many red blotches and spots; the female is brown. Spawning occurs sometimes in mid-water and sometimes at the bottom.

A. meinkeni the Round-tailed Killie, is native to tropical western Africa. The general colour of the male is blue-green shading to grass-green, with irregular red lines and dots that form horizontal, broken lines from the gill cover to the root of the caudal fin. The female is light brown with a reddish gill plate. It spawns on plants near the bottom.

A. sjoestedti from Guinea to Cameroun, is commonly called the Golden Pheasant because the coloration of the male is similar to that of the ornamental fowl. The body is reddish brown with a brilliant light orange lateral stripe, irregularly marked with red. The caudal fin is rounded. The female is pale brown to grey-brown. It is essentially a bottom spawner.

Aplocheilichthys is a genus of fishes native to tropical Africa. It is represented to aquarists by a handful of species with all the qualifications they could want in a fish. They are colourful, peaceful, small (they reach a length of not much more than an inch) and may fairly be called hardy and prolific. Soft, acid water (*p*H 6·8) is the most suitable, and although they will tolerate a room temperature of 19°C, a range of 23 to 26°C is to be preferred. Their natural food is insects and their larvae. In the aquarium, therefore, they should be fed on small living food but most will manage on dried food if it contains shrimps, insects, and the like. They are very agile fishes and great jumpers; many losses will occur if the aquarium is not kept covered at all times.

They breed in the regular way of cyprinodonts but the female does not scatter the eggs: either they are produced singly or in small clusters that hang at the vent of the female until brushed off on the plants.

A. flavipinnis is native to Nigeria. The general colour is a greenish to yellowish grey, the belly lighter, with a green sheen.

A. katangae from the Congo basin, is pale yellow on the head and back; the throat and belly white. A broad stripe extends from head to caudal peduncle.

A. macrophthalmus from Lagos, is popularly known as the Lamp Eye or Lantern Eye because the eyes are exceptionally large compared with the size of the fish, and in a subdued light they reflect (they contain no luminous property) golden green,

like the domestic puss. The general colour is grey-green, lighter on the belly. The back is marked with a narrow dark stripe; the side with two light green ones.

A. myersi from the Congo, is olive-green to brownish with a blue-green sheen when seen by reflected light.

A. schoelleri is native to Egypt. The general colour is bluish grey to green, the scales finely edged with black.

The genus *Aplocheilus* is native to India, Malaysia and Indonesia. It is represented to aquarists by four species whose care, requirements and breeding habits are very similar to the related genus *Aplocheilichthys*.

In most species the dorsal and anal fins of the male are pointed; those of the female are rounded. Breeding is not difficult but the fry are on the small side and must be fed with rotifers and dust-fine dried food for the first week or ten days of their lives.

A. blocki is popularly called the Madras or Green Killifish because it is native to Madras and southern India (including Ceylon), and the general colour is dark green with a metallic sheen. The belly is purplish. The gill cover displays a light green spot. It reaches a length of about 2 inches.

A. dayi comes from Ceylon and is, therefore, commonly called the Ceylon Killifish. The back is golden, the side a metallic green, the belly blue to violet. The body is peppered with red spots. It reaches a length of about 3 inches.

A. lineatus is native to southern India and Ceylon and is popularly known as the Deccan Killifish. The general colour is olive-brown, shading from dark on the back to light on the belly. The side is marked with brilliant green-gold dots in longitudinal rows, and posteriorly a number of vertical bars. It reaches a length of about 4 inches.

A. panchax is widespread in south-east Asia, from India (including Ceylon) through Burma and Thailand, to Malaysia and Indonesia. The colour is exceptionally variable and may be anything from light olive-brown to dark olive-green. The scales are marked with blue-green dots from which the popular name of Blue Killifish derives. It reaches about 3 inches.

Chriopeops goodei from Florida, is well known to aquarists as the Blue Fin because those of the male are suffused with blue. It is a small species that rarely exceeds 2 inches, quiet and peaceful and well suited to a community aquarium. Indeed, kept by itself it is apt to become nervous. It is at its best in well-oxygenated water, at a temperature range

Opposite page
Above *Barbus tetrazona*
Below *Danio malabaricus*

Left *Barbus semifasciolatus*
Below *Brachydanio albolineatus*

of 20 to 22°C, and when fed on living food. Most specimens, however, will take dried food.

The back is dark grey to brown, the side grey shading to silvery on the belly. A dark stripe extends from the snout, through the eye, to a dark spot at the root of the caudal fin.

In captivity it breeds readily. The water should be neutral or slightly alkaline. Only a few eggs are deposited daily and the spawning period extends over four or five weeks. As the brood fish are very partial to eating their young, they or the eggs should be removed as soon as possible. At about 22°C the incubation period is a week. The fry will take dust-fine dried food from the start.

Cubanichthys cubensis the Cuban Killie, is a small peaceful fish that comes from western Cuba. It flourishes on the usual living foods and favours water at a temperature range of 22 to 25°C. The general colour is olive-green to loam; the side marked with blue-green dotted stripes that extend from the gill plate to the caudal peduncle. The fins are transparent but the dorsal and anal of the male are edged blue.

It breeds in the regular way of cyprinodonts but it is not a prolific species. The eggs are carried at the vent of the female until brushed off by the plants. At 24°C the period of incubation is about ten to twelve days, and the young have a very small yolk-sac and must be offered food from birth.

Cynolebias is a genus of fishes native to the southeast of South America. It is represented to aquarists by about five species. They should be fed on the usual living foods (gnat larvae and bloodworms for preference), kept at a temperature of 21 to 26°C, and are better by themselves than in a community aquarium, particularly *C. wolferstorffi* which is notoriously aggressive.

It is easy enough to distinguish the sexes because not only is there a difference of coloration, but the male has more rays than the female in the dorsal and anal fins. Breeding is far from easy because they are annual fishes. In the wild they live in ponds and ditches that for a part of the year contain very little water and sometimes dry up. The eggs are deposited in the mud where they remain until the next heavy fall of rain refills the pond. The eggs then hatch and the fry develop.

To reproduce these conditions in an aquarium is difficult and calls for experience. The aquarium should be given a peat bottom and the temperature of the water raised to about 26°C. The spawning period lasts for several weeks with periods of rest during which the brood fish show

Aplocheilus dayi

signs of being extremely hungry. They must be fed with living food. Once spawning is over the brood fish should be removed. The water in the aquarium should be siphoned off slowly and the soil allowed almost to dry out. After a resting period of two or three weeks the aquarium should be filled slowly with matured water and the eggs allowed to incubate. If all goes well the fry will hatch out in six to eight weeks after refilling the aquarium, and strike out in search of rotifers and the smallest of screened daphnids.

C. adloffi is turquoise-blue, the back darker. A dark stripe crosses the eye; the side displays nine to twelve dark, vertical bars. The female is a light grey-brown with indistinct bars on the side. It reaches a length of about 2 inches.

C. bellotti is the well-known Argentine Pearlfish or Blue Chromide. The body is deep blue, darker on the back. A dark stripe crosses the eye. Small light blue dots pepper the body and vertical fins. The female is loam coloured with a dark stripe across the eye. It reaches a length of about 3 inches.

C. nigripinnis is a uniform blue-black to black, the body and fins peppered with sea-green to pale blue spots. The female is light brown with irregular blotches on the side. It reaches a length of about 2 inches.

C. whitei is brown, the body and fins peppered with blue spots. The female is lighter in colour than the male with a bluish sheen on the side and a dark spot at the root of the caudal fin. It reaches a length of about 3 inches.

C. wolferstorffi is brownish blue, the back

Opposite page
Above left *Carassius auratus* var. Fantail Goldfish
Above right *Epalzeorhynchus kallopterus*
Below *Rasbora elegans*

Left *Rasbora kalochroma*
Below *Rasbora pauciperforata*

darker, the body and fins peppered with silvery-white spots. The female is yellowish with irregular spots and blotches. It reaches a length of about 4 inches.

Cynopoecilus is a genus of fishes native to southeast Brazil and represented to aquarists by the two species *C. ladigesi* and *C. melanotaenia*. They are closely related to *Cynolebias* and *C. ladigesi* is said to breed in the same way. *C. melanotaenia* probably breeds in the same way also but there are reports that it spawns on plants in mid-water.

The care of both species is the same. Soft and slightly acid water at a temperature range of 21 to 25°C, small living food and an aquarium to themselves are recommended.

C. ladigesi is a metallic emerald-green with dark wine-red stripes. The female is grey-green to brown. It reaches a length of little more than an inch.

C. melanotaenia is dark reddish brown, the belly yellowish. A red band extends from the lower jaw, through the eye, to the base of the caudal fin. The female is paler in colour. It reaches a length of about 2 inches.

Cyprinodon variegatus is native to the east coast of the United States, from New England to Florida and Texas. It is well known under the popular names of the Sheep's-head and the Pursy Minnow.

It is clear from its geographical range that the temperature should not be too high. About 19 to 21°C suits it admirably. As it is found in sea water as well as in brackish and fresh waters, it is best kept in a mixture of one part sea water to four parts fresh. It will eat dried food but living food is to be preferred if it is to remain in good health. It is very voracious but by no means quarrelsome.

The male is silvery grey, the throat, breast and belly light orange. The side is marked with dark, irregular vertical bars and metallic-blue spots. The female is pale olive.

The eggs are deposited sometimes on the plants, sometimes on the sides of the aquarium and sometimes on the bottom. They incubate in about six to twelve days and the young fish are able to take newly hatched brine shrimps and small screened daphnids from the start.

Members of the genus *Epiplatys* are small fishes that are found in the sluggish and stagnant waters of western tropical Africa. They are at their best when kept in soft to medium-hard, slightly acid (*p*H 6·5) water, at a temperature of 24 to 28°C. Feeding should consist mainly of insects and insect larvae. Some specimens, however, will take dried food.

They breed in the regular manner of cyprinodonts. The spawning lasts for a period of two or three weeks. A few eggs are deposited on the plants every day and these should be removed to another aquarium. The period of incubation is from one to three weeks.

Many species have been classified by taxonomists but only the eight listed below are regularly seen in aquaria. With the exception of *E. sexfasciatus* that reaches a length of about 4 inches, none reaches more than 2 inches.

E. annulatus the Clown Killie, is so called because the ground colour is yellow, with four broad, chocolate-coloured bands from behind the eye to the caudal peduncle. The female is less brightly coloured.

E. chaperi the Fire-mouth Killie, is dark olive-brown on the back shading to light brown on the side. The side is marked with four to six, usually five, vertical bars. The popular name is derived from the fact that the lower lip and throat are bright red. The female is less brightly coloured than the male and her throat is yellow.

E. dageti is greenish with shadowy dark bars and a reddish sheen on the side. The throat is red. The female is less colourful than the male.

E. fasciolatus the Striped or Banded Killie, is brownish on the back shading through green on the side to whitish on the belly. The side is marked with about ten dark brown, vertical bars and a horizontal stripe from gill cover to caudal peduncle. The female is light brown to olive-green with paler markings.

E. longiventralis is dark brown on the back shading to greenish brown on the side and yellowish on the belly. The female is light brown to olive-green.

E. macrostigma the Large-spotted Killie, is blue-green shading to red-brown on the back, and yellowish on the belly. The side is marked with rows of red to dark brown spots irregular on the posterior of the body. The female is paler than the male and the spots smaller and less distinct.

E. sexfasciatus the Six-banded Killie, is olive-green on the head and back shading to yellowish on the belly. Five to seven, usually six, broad, blue-black bands mark the side below the lateral line. The female is drab.

E. sheljuzhkoi is very similar to *E. macrostigma* but may be distinguished by the regularity of the spots on the posterior of the body.

The genus *Fundulus* is a large one but only a few species are ever introduced into aquaria. They are native to the United States. All will withstand a temperature as low as 13°C, and those from the northern states down to 5°C. On the whole, however, they are best kept at a temperature of about 19°C with some degrees higher or lower, depending on their geographical origin. They are best when fed on living food for in the wild their natural diet is insects and their larvae. All, however, will eat dried food. They are peaceful and make satisfactory community fishes. They breed freely in the regular way of cyprinodonts. The eggs are deposited among fine-leaved plants and incubate in ten to fourteen days at a temperature of 20 to 24°C. The young fishes are quite large and will take finely screened daphnids and newly hatched brine shrimps from the start.

That the genus is represented to aquarists by only four species is probably due to the fact that it is the victim of snobbery. In the United States *Fundulus* species are so common that they are used by American anglers as live bait, just as British anglers use minnows in the same deplorable way.

F. chrysotus the Golden Ear, is found in fresh and brackish waters from South Carolina to Florida. The general colour is a bluish olive-green, lighter on the side and shading to light orange on the belly. The gill cover shows a metallic green spot from which the popular name derives. The female is light brown. It reaches a length of about 2 inches. It enjoys the comparatively high temperature of 23 to 25°C and it is best to keep it in one part sea water to four parts fresh.

F. dispar the Star-head Killie, is native to Missouri, Arkansas, Mississippi and Louisiana. The general colour is olive-green to light yellow. The side is marked with horizontal rows of dark brown spots and ten or eleven vertical bars. A broad stripe crosses the eye. The female is light brown to olive-green and lacks the vertical bars. It reaches a length of 2 or 3 inches. A temperature of 20°C is recommended, which may be reduced to about 16°C in winter.

F. heteroclitus the Zebra Killie, is sometimes known as the Bait Killie because it is the species most widely used by anglers. It is found from Maine to the Gulf of Mexico and Bermuda. The general colour is olive-brown, the back darker and the belly yellow to orange. Some twelve to thirteen vertical, silvery-blue bars, more distinct posteriorly than anteriorly, mark the side. The female is pale brown and the bars on her side less distinct and sometimes absent. It reaches a length of about 5 inches. A mixture of one part sea water to four parts fresh is advised.

F. notatus the Black-striped Killie, is native to Michigan and Texas. The general colour is olive-brown to pale brown with a green sheen. A broad, black stripe extends from the snout, across the eye, to the root of the caudal fin. The female is paler than the male and the horizontal stripe less distinct. It reaches a length of 2 or perhaps 3 inches.

Jordanella floridae the well-known Flagfish, is a small 2-inch fish from the ponds and marshes of Florida. The general colour is yellowish to olive-brown, the back brownish. Every scale is marked with a pale blotch with the result that, by reflected light, the body has a steel-blue to yellow-green iridescent sheen. The female is paler in colour than the male with dark, irregular markings that produce a marbled effect.

This is a hardy fish that may be kept at a temperature of 20°C; 24°C is more satisfactory for spawning. The eggs are sometimes deposited on plants in the regular way of cyprinodonts, but more usually the male makes a depression in the planting medium and the female deposits the eggs in it. The eggs are protected by the male and neither he nor the female eat them nor, after hatching, molest the fry. The young fish need plenty of algae, rotifers and newly hatched brine shrimps for their first food, particularly algae.

On the whole it is an accommodating fish and a pair may be kept in quite a small aquarium. It is best kept out of the community aquarium because it tends to be pugnacious. It eats all the regular living foods and suitable substitutes, will take dried food, and must be given some vegetable food.

Kosswigichthys asquamatus is a small 1- to 2-inch fish that is very closely related to *Aphanius* species. It is native to Turkey. The male fish is dark, paler on the belly and with fifteen to sixteen vertical stripes of a silvery colour on the side. The female is paler than the male, with a silvery belly and thirteen to eighteen irregular blotches on the side.

It is peaceful, eats dried food as well as living food, and may be kept at 20°C, preferably in one part sea water to four parts fresh. It breeds in the regular way of cyprinodonts. The eggs are deposited on fine-leaved plants and at a temperature of 25°C the young fish hatch out in about a fortnight.

Leptolucania ommata is native to Georgia and Florida, where it frequents mud-holes and swamps and is, therefore, known as the Swamp Killie. The general colour is straw-yellow. A broad, dark band extends from the snout, across the eye, to a dark ocellus at the root of the caudal fin. Posteriorly the band is indistinct and five to seven

Opposite page
Above left *Brochis coeruleus*
Above right *Tinca tinca*
Below *Acanthophthalmus kuhlii kuhlii*

Left *Corydoras schwartzi* (An attractive catfish from
western Brazil)
Below *Aphyosemion gardneri*

vertical bars are present. The eye is very large. The female is paler than the male with dark, irregular markings that give a marbled effect; the ocellus is more pronounced. It reaches a length of about 2 inches.

It is an inoffensive and hardy fish that will tolerate a temperature range of 19 to 25°C, and although it will eat dried food it cannot be kept in health without small living food in fair quantities. It breeds in the regular way of cyprinodonts. The eggs are scattered in clumps of plants and, at a temperature of 22°C, incubate in ten to twelve days. The fry are very small and need infusorians for their first food.

The genus *Nothobranchius* embraces about a dozen species that are found in tropical Africa from the east coast to Nigeria. The body is thick-set and slightly compressed; the dorsal and anal fins are well developed; the caudal fin is rounded.

In captivity they are quite hardy provided that they are given the right conditions. Their main requirements are a temperature of about 24°C, a mixture of one part sea water to four parts fresh, no direct sunlight and a diet of earthworms, gnat larvae, whiteworms, bloodworms, and the like.

To distinguish between the sexes is very easy because the female is quite plain but the male is as colourful as a butterfly. What is not so easy is to breed them because, like their South American relations, *Cynolebias* species, they are annual fishes, and breeding must be conducted in the same tricky way.

The genus is represented to aquarists by five species. All are native to the east coast of Africa from Kenya to Mozambique, including the island of Zanzibar. They are fairly small fishes that reach a length of 2 or 3 inches but best kept out of a community aquarium because they tend to be quarrelsome.

N. guentheri is greenish blue, the back brownish, the belly greenish yellow. The scales are edged with red, to form narrow, vertical bars on the posterior of the body. Lines and dots of a deep red mark the gill plate and shoulder. The female is grey-brown shading to cream on the belly.

N. melanospilus is variable in colour. Some specimens have reddish sides with dark-edged scales and black spots on the head and gill cover; others have bluish sides with dark-edged scales. The female is much paler than the male.

N. orthonotus is olive-brown, the scales edged wine-red but some specimens are bluish green and some are light blue, spotted wine-red. The female is brownish red.

N. palmquisti is greenish brown on the back, yellowish on the side. The female is brown.

N. taeniopygus (*rachovi*) is a soft peacock-blue, the back darker. The throat and belly are yellowish orange. About twelve carmine, vertical bars mark the side. The female is a uniform light brown.

Pachypanchax playfairi is native to the Seychelles and the east coast of Africa (including Malagasy) as far south as Mozambique. The male is olive-green with a yellowish tinge particularly on the belly. The side is marked with rows of small, red spots that extend on to the vertical fins. A peculiarity of this fish is that the scales (especially at breeding time) stand out from the body. This must not be mistaken for a symptom of dropsy. The female is light brown and shows a black blotch at the base of the dorsal fin. It reaches a length of about 4 inches.

It is rather a pugnacious fish and best kept out of a community aquarium. For general purposes a temperature of 22°C suits it. It should not be allowed to fall below 20°C and should be raised at breeding time to about 24°C. Breeding is conducted in the regular way of cyprinodonts. The eggs are scattered in clumps of plants and incubate in ten to twelve days. Feeding should consist of living food and suitable substitutes, and it is best to add a teaspoonful of salt to every gallon of water.

Pterolebias longipinnis is native to south-east Brazil and northern Argentina. The male reaches a length of about 3 inches. In colour it is light red-brown, darker on the back, lighter on the belly. The side is marked with numerous sea-green to yellowish spots and two or three dark blotches. The anal and caudal fins are large and flag-like. The female is smaller than the male, both in body and finnage and is of a brownish-yellow colour. It is closely related to *Cynolebias* species and may be kept and bred in the same way.

Rachovia brevis is native to Colombia. The male is olive-brown on the back, greenish blue on the side, yellowish to white on the belly. The scales are edged with violet, giving a reticulated effect. The female is pale brown with no markings. It reaches a length of about 2 inches. It may be kept in the same way as *Cynolebias* species but breeding, as always with annual fishes, is very difficult and the brood fish usually die after spawning.

Rivulus species are widespread in the New World. Their geographical range extends from Florida in the United States, through Central America and the West Indies, to La Plata in South America.

Altogether about ten species and one colour variety are known to aquarists. They are not difficult to recognize because they have a long, cylindrical body, a thick blunt head and small rounded fins, the dorsal and anal set well back on the body. They are typical of surface-living fishes. Indeed it is the practice of *Rivulus* species to hang motionless at the surface of the water for hours on end. Their sluggishness is deceptive, however, for if they are the least active of the killifishes – a group noted for lethargy – they are always on the alert for food and an opportunity to jump clear of the water. Very certainly the aquarium must be kept covered at all times; in the wild some will leave the water for short periods, and they are expert at projecting themselves, like rifle bullets, through quite narrow apertures.

Their natural food is insects and their larvae. They are, however, not fastidious and will eat more or less anything that comes their way. Nor are they particular about temperature. A range of 19 to 27°C suits them well enough, although 20 to 24°C is more satisfactory for normal maintenance, with a rise to 25 or 26°C for breeding.

They are peaceful, active and undemanding in their requirements. The water should be shallow, clear and well matured. The aquarium should be adequately stocked with submerged and floating plants to afford shade.

Rivulus species breed freely in captivity and it is conducted in the usual way of cyprinodonts. It is considered desirable to mate two females with one male. The eggs are scattered among clumps of plants which should be moved to another aquarium for hatching. The period of incubation is about twelve to fourteen days and the young need infusorians for about a week.

Sexing is quite easy. The male is more colourful than the female, and in most but not all species the female (and not the male) shows a round spot or ocellus (popularly known as the rivulus spot) on the upper base of the caudal fin.

R. *cylindraceus* the Green Rivulus, is native to Cuba and Florida. It is sometimes known as the Brown and sometimes as the Cuban Rivulus. The male is olive-green sprinkled with dark green spots and red spots posteriorly. The female is olive-brown with faint red spots and a black on a white ground rivulus spot. It reaches a length of about 2 inches.

R. *dorni* is found in the neighbourhood of Rio de Janeiro. The male is chocolate with a small blue-green spot on each scale, and six or seven dark, vertical bars on the posterior of the body. The female is fawn to ochre with faint dark irregular blotches on the side and no rivulus spot. It reaches a length of about 2 inches.

R. *harti* is native to eastern Colombia, Venezuela and Trinidad. The male is chocolate to olive-brown, with dark red spots arranged in horizontal rows on the side. The female is paler than the male and the rivulus spot is rather indistinct. It reaches a length of about 4 inches and is the largest member of the genus.

R. *isthmensis* is native to Central America, from southern Mexico to Costa Rica and Panama. The male is yellowish to reddish brown, the side marked with red spots. The female is coffee coloured to ochre: the red spots on the side are absent but the rivulus spot is distinct. It reaches a length of about 2 inches.

R. *milesi* the Firetail Rivulus, is native to Colombia. The male is blue-grey to lavender with red spots on the side. The female is brown with a typically well-defined rivulus spot. It reaches a length of about 2 inches.

R. *ocellus* the Ocellated Rivulus, is native to south-east Brazil in the coastal area between Rio de Janeiro and Santos. The male is yellowish green, the side is marked with irregular dark brown to black blotches giving a marbled effect. The female is brownish, the markings on the side lighter than those on the male; the rivulus spot is ocellated. It reaches a length of rather more than 2 inches.

R. *strigatus* the Herring-bone Rivulus, is native to the basin of the Amazon. The male is olive-green with irregular brownish patches on the head, and a number of narrow, light red, V-shaped bars (the angles towards the head) on the side. The female is a light yellow-brown, the V-shaped bars on the side indistinct and no rivulus spot. It reaches a length of about $1\frac{1}{2}$ inches. It is rather more delicate than other *Rivulus* species, not such a ready breeder, and tends to be quarrelsome.

R. *uropthalmus* the Golden Rivulus, is native to the Amazon basin. The male is brownish green with numerous small, red dots on the side in longitudinal rows. The female is brownish, marbled with an ocellated rivulus spot. It reaches a length of about $2\frac{1}{2}$ inches.

A colour variety known as the Red Rivulus, although in fact it is lemon-yellow, with the side marked with red dots, occurs in the wild and has been bred in aquaria where it takes the place of the type species. The female is paler than the male, the red dots on the side are indistinct, and the rivulus spot is faint, sometimes absent.

Opposite page
Xiphophorus maculatus

Above *Aplocheilus lineatus*
Below *Nothobranchius taeniopygus (rachovi)*

R. *xanthonotus* the Yellow-banded Rivulus, is native to the Amazon basin. The male is yellow, the side marked with horizontal rows of red dots that extend on to the unpaired fins. The female is ochre, the red dots on the side are indistinct, but the rivulus spot is well defined. It reaches a length of about 3 inches.

Roloffia occidentalis is a small fish native to western Africa from the delta of the Niger to Cameroun. It is very similar to *Aphyosemion* species and may be kept in the same way.

The colour is very variable but in general the male is a dark reddish brown on the back, shading to yellowish brown on the side and bluish white on the belly. The gill cover is blue with red streaks that extend on to the anterior of the body; the posterior of the body is marked with a few vertical, red bars. The female is a uniform reddish brown. It reaches a length of about 5 inches and is a very hardy fish. The male, however, is very quarrelsome. It is a bottom spawner.

Valencia hispanica is native to south-east and eastern Spain and Greece. The male is grey-brown on the back, shading to greenish blue on the side and yellowish on the belly. The side shows a large dark spot above the base of the pectoral fin and ten to twelve dark brown, vertical bars posteriorly. The female is lighter than the male and the markings of the male are replaced by a light-coloured, horizontal band from the snout to the caudal fin. It reaches a length of about 3 inches.

It is rather a quarrelsome fish not very satisfactory in a community aquarium. It is, however, very hardy and may be kept in an unheated aquarium; it will tolerate a temperature as low as 10°C, though a range of 16 to 24°C is more satisfactory. It will take dried food but like all cyprinodonts prefers living food and certainly should be given some.

It breeds in the usual way of cyprinodonts. The eggs are scattered among clumps of plants and incubate in ten to fourteen days at a temperature of 20 to 22°C. The fry need infusorians for their first food. The brood fish are very greedy eaters of their eggs and young.

Family POECILIIDAE

The Poeciliidae is a family of viviparous (more precisely ovoviviparous) fishes confined to the New World, from Arizona and the Carolinas in the north, through Central America (including the West Indies) and South America east of the Andes, to Buenos Aires in the south.

Members of this family are popularly called live-bearers and are very easily identified because the fore-rays of the anal fin of the male are modified into a gonopodium (the anal fin of the female is fan-shaped). The males are more highly coloured than the females and age for age they are smaller. In some species there are even more pronounced sexual differences, such as the swordtail of the male *Xiphophorus helleri* and *X. montezumae*, and the high dorsal fin (sailfin) of the male *Poecilia latipinna* and *P. velifera*.

Breeding poeciliids is very easy. They are, in fact, generally spoken of as beginner's fishes because it is not difficult to fulfil their requirements. Breeding is best carried out in a standard-sized (24 × 12 × 12 inches) aquarium, well stocked with submerged and floating plants, and under a good light (natural or artificial) to promote the growth of algae that the fishes need in their diet. The water should be shallow, neutral, and at a temperature range of about 24 to 27°C. It is best to mate one male with several females because the male poeciliid is a very hard driver and the female tends to be averse to his attentions. They should be fed on living food.

A few days before delivery the black peritoneum of the female may be seen through the body wall, in the region of the vent. It is commonly spoken of as the gravid spot and is a good indication, but not an infallible one, that the fish is about to deliver. At this stage the female should on no account be handled because, no matter how carefully it is done, it is almost certain to result in a number of premature births. Such fishes can be identified by the fact that they remain at the bottom of the aquarium and may be seen to be carrying abdominally a part of the yolk-sac. The addition of a heaped teaspoonful of kitchen or sea salt to every gallon of water is said to help them recover, but few ever do.

We are not in favour of breeding cages and other devices designed to separate the female from the newly born fish. The male should be removed as soon as he has done his work, and the female after she has delivered; for the rest, if the brood fish are given plenty of living food, not much harm will befall the fry, and virtually none if the aquarium is stocked with sufficient plants to afford them cover.

The fry of the smaller species must be given infusorians as their first food: those of the larger species are able to take small screened daphnids and dust-fine dried food about an hour after birth. Food should be offered about three or four times a day. Growth is rapid and some of the smaller species are ready to breed when only three months old.

With the exception of *Belonesox*, which is strictly carnivorous, and to some extent *Gambusia* species which are mainly so, the poeciliids are omnivorous and will take dried food as well as living food and suitable substitutes. It is essential, however, for them to have some green matter in their diet. Alga is their natural green food but minced and cooked green vegetables from the kitchen, and duckweed, may be given as suitable alternatives. Most are good community fishes but it is best to keep the species apart because some hybridize freely.

Alfaro cultratus from Central America, is best kept out of a community aquarium because, although it is quite a small fish (the male reaches a length of about 2 inches, the female rather more), it is very agile and something of a bully. The general colour is brownish with a bluish-green sheen on the side and a peppering of small black spots. The trivial name *cultratus* and the popular name of the Knifetail Live-bearer stem from the fact that the lower part of the caudal peduncle is compressed to a sharp-edged keel. A temperature of about 24°C is recommended.

Belonesox belizanus is a pike-like species from the Atlantic slope of Central America, from southern Mexico to Honduras. Known as the Pike Minnow, it is quite unsuited for a community aquarium. The male grows to a length of about 4 inches, the female up to 8 inches. It eats an incredible amount of living food, mainly small fishes, and will not take dried food. In captivity it must be fed on tadpoles, large water insects, and the unwanted fry from breeding tanks. Some specimens, but not all, will eat earthworms and pieces of raw meat.

A temperature range of 25 to 30°C is recommended. Breeding is by no means easy. The aquarium should be large and thickly planted, the water clear and well matured, and a teaspoonful of salt to every gallon of water stirred in. The brood fish must be conditioned on living food, and removed as soon as possible or they will greedily eat their young. At birth the fry are about 1 inch long and ready to take small daphnids, whiteworms, and even tiny fishes.

Brachyrhaphis episcopi, popularly known as the Bishop, is native to Panama. The general colour is reddish brown, shading to white or silvery on the belly. The side is marked with dark spots which may be short vertical bars or quadrate spots. The male reaches a length of about 1 inch, the female about 2 inches.

In the wild it is a fairly common fish, occurring mainly in ditches, water holes, and similar places. It is rarely seen in aquaria because in captivity the young are usually born deformed and seldom reach maturity. Brackish water at a temperature range of 24 to 26°C and an aquarium thickly overgrown with algae are to be recommended.

Cnesterodon decemmaculatus is native to southern Brazil and La Plata. It is popularly known as the Ten-spot Live-bearer. It is a small fish (the male reaches about 1 inch, the female rather more), hardy, undemanding in its requirements, and peaceful. The general colour is olive-green to yellow, with a yellow to lavender sheen on the side. The back is darker. The belly is yellow or silvery white. Dark vertical bars, numbering from six to twelve but usually ten, mark the side between the gill cover and the caudal peduncle. Towards the end of her pregnancy the female is very easily frightened; miscarriages are frequent and the young born with bent spines.

The genus *Gambusia* is native to the southern states of North America, Mexico, Central America and the West Indies. Members of the genus are prolific breeders. In captivity, however, few are ever seen because they are not popular fishes with aquarists. They are pugnacious by nature, incorrigible fin nippers, and are not particularly attractive in appearance. Although they will take dried food for want of something better, they are mainly carnivorous. Gnat larvae, *Daphnia*, and similar living foods are their natural diet. They are very partial to mosquito larvae and as a fish is capable of eating its own weight daily, they have been introduced into many parts of the world to help control malarial and other disease-carrying mosquitoes.

Only the two subspecies and one species mentioned below are regularly represented in the aquarium. All are small fishes; the males reach a length of 1 or 2 inches, the females 2 or 3 inches, and they tolerate the fairly wide temperature range of 20 to 29°C.

G. affinis affinis is native to the southern states of the United States from eastern Texas to Alabama. It is popularly known as the Texas Live-bearer. Both sexes are pale grey in colour with metallic-blue reflections. A dark bar crosses the eye. *G.a. holbrooki* is the eastern form of the above. It is found in the Carolinas and southwards, through Georgia and Alabama, to Florida. It is popularly known as the Spotted Live-bearer because the female is identical with that of the foregoing, and the male can be distinguished only by reason of it being irregularly blotched with black.

G. punctata, the Blue Live-bearer, is native to Cuba. The general colour is slate-grey shading to brown on the back and light grey on the belly. In a reflected light there is a pleasing blue sheen. The side is marked with rows of rust-red spots. Unusually among aquarium fishes the eye is blue. The female is paler in colour than the male.

Glaridichthys metallicus, the Yellow Belly, is native to Cuba. It is peaceful and undemanding in its requirements and flourishes well at a temperature range of 22 to 25°C. The general colour is a light metallic yellow, with deep golden tones on the belly. The eyes are golden and gleam in a subdued light. The male reaches a length of about 2 inches and has a very long, double-pointed gonopodium: the female reaches about 3 inches in length.

Heterandria formosa is the well-known Mosquito Fish or Pygmy Live-bearer. It is native to the United States, from North Carolina to Florida. It is the smallest known viviparous fish: when fully grown the male is less than 1 inch long and the female not much more. It is agile and peaceful but best kept out of a community aquarium because even if it does no harm to other fishes, such a small fish is very likely to get eaten by a larger one, and at best pushed away from food. A temperature range of 20 to 24°C and small living food are recommended. The female delivers two or three young daily over a period of ten days to a fortnight, and may be induced by good feeding to a pregnancy about every fourth or fifth week. The general colour is coffee-brown, the back a brownish olive, the belly silvery white. A dark horizontal stripe crossed by eight to twelve dark bars marks the side.

Members of the genus *Limia** are native to the West Indies. A fairly large number of species has been classified but only about seven, mentioned below, are ever introduced into aquaria, and even they are not very popular with aquarists. Why this is so is hard to say because they have many of the attributes that make good aquarium fishes. They are small fishes that reach a length of only 1 or 2 inches at most (the female rather more), peaceful, call for nothing special in the way of temperature (22 to 25°C is recommended), are omnivorous in the full sense of the word and breed readily.

L. caudofasciatus, the Steel-blue Limia, comes from Jamaica; *L. heterandia*, the smallest of the genus, from Haiti and San Domingo; *L. melanogaster*, the Black-bellied Limia, from Jamaica; *L.*

nigrofasciata the Humpbacked Limia, *L. ornata* the Ornate Limia and *L. versicolor* the Olive Limia, from Haiti; and *L. vittata* the so-called Striped Mudfish, from Cuba and perhaps San Domingo. All are very prolific; *L. vittata* in particular: it may deliver between 200 and 300 young at one birth.

*Micropoecilia** species are native to the north-east of South America. The genus is represented to aquarists by two species: *M. branneri* and *M. parae* the Two-spot Live-bearer. Both are essentially for the specialist because they are delicate fishes that, small at the best of times, reach only about halfsize when bred in captivity. They must be kept by themselves and a community aquarium is no place for them. The water should be at a temperature of 24 to 26°C and a teaspoonful of kitchen or sea salt to every gallon of water should be stirred in. Algae in their diet are essential.

M. branneri, from the fresh and brackish waters at the mouth of the Amazon, is dark olive shading to light brown on the side and silvery on the belly. The side is marked with seven or eight dark, vertical bars, and a blue-black spot on the caudal peduncle. The female is less highly coloured than the male and the dorsal fin is rounded; that of the male is extended posteriorly to a point. The male reaches a length of 1 inch; the female rather more.

M. parae, from the fresh and brackish waters of Trinidad, the Guianas, and the Amazon basin, is light olive with silvery reflections. The side has a violet sheen. The belly is white. There is a conspicuous black shoulder spot and the male, but not the female, has a similar spot above the vent and on the caudal peduncle. The male reaches a length of rather less than 1 inch; the female about 1 inch.

The genus *Phallichthys* is represented to aquarists by two species: *P. amates* the so-called Merry Widow, native to Guatemala and Honduras, and *P. pittieri* native to Panama and Costa Rica. They are characterized by a long gonopodium that reaches as far back as the root of the caudal fin: the tip is turned downwards. Both species are peaceful, well suited to a community aquarium, and feed mainly on dried foods and algae. A temperature range of 22 to 25°C is recommended.

P. amates is olive-brown shading to light gold on the belly. The male shows ten to twelve dark bars on the side. The female lacks these bars and is much paler in colour. The male reaches a length of about 1 inch; the female about 2 inches.

P. pittieri is light olive-green, the gill cover,

---

* According to some authorities members of the genus *Limia* should be referred to the genus *Poecilia*.

* According to some authorities members of the genus *Micropoecilia* should be referred to the genus *Poecilia*.

throat and belly silver. The side reflects a blue sheen. Like *P. amates* the male shows ten to twelve dark bars on the side which are absent in the female. The male reaches a length of rather more than 1 inch; the female about 3 inches.

Phalloceros caudomaculatus, popularly called the One-spot Millions Fish, is native to south-east Brazil, Uruguay and Paraguay. The general colour is pale grey with a yellowish or silver belly. The popular name is derived from the fact that the side is marked with a vertical, oval, jet-black spot immediately below the dorsal fin: it is sometimes encircled by a yellow ring. The male reaches a length of about 1 inch; the female about 2 inches.

A number of varieties are known. Some are without markings but the most popular is a speckled or black-spotted variety, *P.c.* var. *reticulatus*, found in the neighbourhood of Rio de Janeiro. Among aquarists it is even more popular than the type species. The general colour is yellowish, the body and fins marked with irregular dark spots.

The best temperature range is 20 to 24°C but the type species is remarkably resistant to low temperature and may be kept in an unheated aquarium at room temperature. All are peaceful and eat dried as well as living foods but food must be small as it is characteristic of the fishes that they have very small mouths.

Phalloptychus januarius the Striped Millions Fish, comes from south-east Brazil and Uruguay. It is not often seen in captivity because it is not a very attractive species and rather delicate. It calls for a well-planted aquarium, not too bright a light, a temperature range of 21 to 25°C, a teaspoonful of sea salt or kitchen salt to every gallon of water, and plenty of algae as well as living food. Broods number about a couple of dozen but many fishes die a few days after birth.

The back is olive-green, the side a metallic blue with eight to twelve vertical, dark stripes. The belly whitish or silvery. The female is a translucent yellowish. The male reaches a length of about 1 inch; the female about 2 inches.

Members of the genus *Poecilia* are native to the New World, from the Carolinas in the north, through Central America, to the La Plata basin in the south. The species best known to aquarists are *P. latipinna*, *P. latipunctata*, *P. sphenops* and *P. velifera* (popularly called mollies because they were once referred to the genus *Mollienesia*), *P. reticulata* (better known under its former name of *Lebistes reticulatus*, the famous Guppy) and *P. vivipara* the One-spot Live-bearer.

Mollies are native to the countries and states of North America that border the Gulf of Mexico. In captivity they require special treatment. For one thing, they are fairly large fishes (some reach a length of 6 inches) and, therefore, must be given plenty of room in which to move. A 2-foot aquarium is about the right size to accommodate a pair. For another thing, in the wild they are not only found in fresh and brackish waters but have been taken far out to sea, and so it is more or less essential to add a teaspoonful of sea salt or kitchen salt to every gallon of water. For a third thing, they are largely herbivorous and although they will eat all the regular living foods and dried foods, it is necessary for them to have a considerable amount of green food. Food should be given to them at least three times daily, and it is as well to stand the aquarium where it will receive sunlight, in order to promote the growth of algae and soft-leaved plants on which they delight to browse.

A temperature range of 24 to 28°C is to be advised and breeding is quite easy. The female fish rarely molests the young but if there are indications that she will, it is better to remove the young fish rather than the mother fish. To move a gravid female nearly always ends in premature or still births and her early death. As the young are about ½ inch long at birth, they are well able to look after themselves.

P. latipinna the Sailfin Molly, is native to the coastal waters of the southern states of North America and north-east Mexico, and *P. velifera* the Giant Sailfin Molly, is native to the coastal waters of Yucatan. They are known to aquarists as sailfin types because they have a very large dorsal fin with twelve to nineteen rays.

P. latipunctata native to the Rio Tamesi system of Mexico, and *P. sphenops* native to the coast and rivers from Texas, southwards through Central America to Colombia, Venezuela and the Leeward Islands, are known to aquarists as short-finned types as they have only eight to eleven rays in the comparatively small dorsal fin.

The wild fish have long been replaced in the aquarium by line-bred varieties. It is true that aquarium-bred specimens rarely, if ever, have such a large dorsal fin as the wild fish but it is equally true that selective breeding over many years has greatly improved the strains, and cross-breeding has produced a number of very fine colour varieties.

In *P. latipinna* the back is olive, the side mother-of-pearl with a pink or blue sheen, the belly silvery. The side is marked with six to eight rows of small dark dots. Short vertical bars cross the shoulder and back. The Black Sailfin Molly is a pure matt-black fish showing no trace of natural coloration, and with the typical high dorsal fin. The Orange-banded Molly is similar to the Black Sailfin but with an even band of orange-yellow along the outer margins of the dorsal and caudal fins.

In *P. latipunctata* the back is light olive-grey. A lateral band of orange dots extends from the gill cover to the root of the caudal fin. Below it the body is silvery with a pink or green sheen.

In *P. sphenops* the coloration varies. A typical form is light grey to various shades of brown with rows of dark dots on the side and, over all, a blue sheen. The belly is a very pale blue or pink. Some specimens show dark, vertical bars on the side. The Black Shortfin Molly is a pure matt-black fish that shows no trace of the natural colour. The Liberty Molly is steel-blue with the dorsal and caudal fins black, yellow and red. The Lyretail Molly is matt-black of body and finnage, the upper and lower rays of the caudal fin extended.

P. velifera is a brilliant blue-green speckled with glittering dots. The throat and belly are brassy to golden. An all-black variety has been developed.

P. reticulata is native to the Lesser Antilles, Trinidad, Venezuela and through Brazil as far south as Santos. It is one of the best known of all aquarium fishes, having been introduced into aquaria in 1908. Its popularity is due in part to the fact that it is very prolific and in part to the fact that it is so remarkably hardy that it will survive and continue to breed despite all the mismanagement that it is subjected to by novices. It is at its best in a temperature range of 22 to 24°C, but will tolerate 15°C for a limited period. It eats dried food as well as living food and suitable substitutes, and breeds readily.

In the wild the female reaches a length of about 2 inches, and is olive-grey, darker on the back and shading to silvery on the belly. The male reaches a length of little more than 1 inch and is of very variable coloration. The most prevalent colours are violet, blue, green and red, in different metallic shades. No two fish ever appear to be marked alike but specimens collected from different areas of the geographical range show dominant colours and markings peculiar to the localities.

In domestication the Guppy has been the subject of intensive line breeding with standards for coloration and the shape of the caudal fin. The Federation of Guppy Breeders Society have drawn up standards for eleven different shapes of the

caudal fin of the male, and the several colour variants. It is outside the compass of this book to describe the line-bred varieties in detail. Those interested should apply to the Federation.

P. vivipara is native to the Leeward Islands and South America from Venezuela to La Plata. The male reaches a length of about 2 inches and varies in colour from olive-brown to silvery grey, shading to silver or yellow on the belly. The whole body, in particular the belly, has a blue sheen. A black spot surrounded by shining gold marks the shoulder below the anterior edge of the dorsal fin. The female reaches a length of 3 or 4 inches and is grey in colour. It is a peaceful fish very suited to a community aquarium. A temperature range of 23 to 25°C is recommended.

Poecilistes pleurospilus is a small fish that is found in the shallow streams and lakes of southern Mexico and Guatemala. The male reaches a length of about 1 inch. The back is olive-grey to brownish, the belly a shiny silver, the sides silvery grey with a violet sheen and marked with a row of four to eight evenly spaced black spots from which the fish derives its popular name of the Porthole Fish. The female grows to about twice the size of the male but in coloration she is similar to him. It is an undemanding, peaceful, omnivorous species that breeds readily at a temperature range of 22 to 24°C.

Quintana atrizona the Black-banded Live-bearer, is found in Cuba and the near-by Isle of Pines. The body, particularly that of the male, is diaphanous and the vertebral column and internal organs can be seen through the body wall. The general colour is light olive-brown, shading to silvery white on the belly. The side is marked with three to nine narrow, dark, vertical bars. The male reaches a length of about 1 inch; the female about 2 inches. Her coloration is similar.

This is a peaceful species quite suitable for a community aquarium. A temperature range of 23 to 28°C is recommended, and a diet of living food and alga. The young are born with the markings and coloration of the adults and, at a temperature of 27°C, reach maturity in about four weeks.

The genus *Xiphophorus* is native to Central America. It is represented to aquarists by four species: *X. helleri* and *X. montezumae* commonly called swordtails because in the male, but not in the female, the lower rays of the caudal fin are extended to form a sword-like appendage; and *X. maculatus* and *X. variatus* commonly called platies, because they were once referred to the genus *Platypoecilus*.

Keeping them in an aquarium does not call for special conditions. They are happy at a temperature range of 20 to 25°C and although they will take dried foods, a diet of vegetable and living foods is to be preferred.

X. helleri is known as the Mexican Swordtail and *X. montezumae* as the Montezuma Swordtail. *X. maculatus* is known as the Common Platy and *X. variatus* as the Variegated Platy. In all four species the males reach a length of 2 to 3 inches and the females 3 to 5 inches.

All four species are native to southern Mexico. The wild fishes, however, are rather drab and for this reason are rarely, if ever nowadays, imported. For all practical purposes they have been replaced by a number of colour varieties which have been developed by selective line breeding from the wild types.

The Federation of British Aquatic Societies recognize the following eleven varieties of swordtails, and ten varieties of platies.

Swordtails: Red, Red-eyed Red, Albino, Golden, Black, London, Berlin, Wiesbaden, Wagtail, Tuxedo and Simpson.
Platies: Red, Black, Yellow, Blue, Spangled, Moon, Sunset, Wagtail, Tiger and Leopard.

Among the swordtails some aquarists include a green variety but it is not so much a colour variety as an improved form of the wild fish.

Swordtails and platies have been extensively hybridized and plenty more colour varieties than those listed by the Federation have been developed. Some are still to be met with: others have had only a fugitive success and are no longer bred. Meanwhile there is plenty of room for the experimentalist. To be worth anything, however, the strains must be kept pure.

Family GOODEIDAE

The family Goodeidae is a small family of viviparous fishes confined to central Mexico. Members of this family are closely related to the poeciliids, but the outstanding difference is that the long gonopodium is replaced by a gonopodium formed by the first two or three rays of the anal fin stiffened and slightly separated into a point. A lack of yolk in the egg necessitates the embryos obtaining their nourishment from the mother who has to be fertilized for each brood. As a result, it may be said that members of this family are truly viviparous species, and not ovoviviparous as is the case with the related families.

Some four genera embracing five species are known, but for all practical purposes the only species known to aquarists is *Neotoca bilineata* from the Rio Lerma basin. The male is greyish with a light green sheen and a black stripe, interrupted by irregular cross bands, that extends from the snout, through the eye, to the base of the caudal fin. The female is much the same as the male in coloration but the longitudinal stripe is edged below with blue-green. The male reaches a length of little more than 1 inch; the female about 2 inches.

This is a quiet and peaceful fish that thrives on any of the foods recommended for omnivorous fishes. Some vegetable food, however, must be given to it. It enjoys water at a temperature range of 22 to 24°C, with periodical additions of fresh water.

Breeding and raising the fry follow the general principles of breeding viviparous species. Under good conditions there are five broods a year, with an average of about twenty-five young at each delivery. If the aquarium is well planted the brood fish do not molest the young, which should be fed on infusorians for about the first fortnight, and after that on microworms, screened daphnids, and the like. Maturity is reached in about three months.

Family HEMIRAMPHIDAE

The family Hemiramphidae is cosmopolitan, its members living mainly in the sea and brackish waters. Only a few species live in fresh water. It is characteristic of members of this family that the upper jaw is short and the lower long, extending beyond the upper jaw to form a long, slender and spear-like half-beak. It is the short upper jaw which moves when food is seized, unlike most fishes.

The freshwater genera are confined to Thailand, Malaysia, Indonesia and the Philippines. Some seven or eight genera and about sixty species are known, but only the genus *Dermogenys* with two species, *D. pusillus* and *D. sumatranus*, are regularly imported.

D. pusillus the Malayan Half-beak, is olive-brown, shading through light olive on the side to white on the belly. The male reaches a length of about 2 inches and the female about 3 inches.

D. sumatranus is very similar to the above but the coloration is more brownish, the pelvic fins are inserted midway between the head and the caudal fin, and it is altogether a smaller fish. The male reaches a length of about 2 inches and the female a little more.

Both species are surface swimmers: their natural food is insects that fall on the water, the fry of fishes, and small aquatic insects and their larvae. Feeding, therefore, must be at the surface for, owing to the construction of the jaws, it is impossible for the fishes to pick up food from the bottom. A temperature range of 18 to 22°C is recommended. The males are very quarrelsome among themselves and should be kept apart because once a fight begins it will continue, always to exhaustion and sometimes to death.

Both species are live-bearers and breeding follows the general principles of breeding viviparous species. It should be conducted in a large, shallow aquarium, thickly planted to offer protection to the fry because the female shows a strong tendency towards cannibalism.

About five to thirty young are delivered at a birth. Still births, however, are very common: a teaspoonful of kitchen or sea salt to every gallon of water is said to improve the chance of success. At birth the young are about $\frac{3}{8}$ inch long and resemble the adult fish except that the lower jaw is not lengthened. As a result, small living food such as screened daphnids and microworms, and finely graded dried food, may be offered to them from the start.

Family THERAPONIDAE
The family Theraponidae is a small family of fishes that ranges from the Red Sea and the east coast of Africa, through the seas of India and Indonesia, to China and the north coast of Australia. Although members of this family are essentially marine they frequently enter rivers during very high tides or in the monsoon season and, cut off from the sea, remain in brackish or freshwater ponds until the next spring tide or the succeeding year's monsoon releases them.

Only one species, *Therapon jarbua*, is represented to aquarists. It is widespread throughout the geographical range of the family. Specimens have been taken as far up the Hooghli as Calcutta and so it may be regarded as a satisfactory fish for the freshwater aquarium although a teaspoonful of salt to every gallon of water is to be advised. It is not a suitable fish for a community aquarium for it is very voracious and eats anything that comes its way. In the wild it reaches a length of 13 or 14 inches and has been known to attack and kill fishes bigger than itself by biting them in the belly.

The general colour is blue-grey, shading to white on the belly. The side is marked with three olive-brown to black lines that curve slightly downwards, and from which the popular name of Targetfish derives.

A temperature of 25°C is satisfactory and the aquarium should be a large one, furnished with strong-rooting plants. It is a very active fish that does a lot of grubbing in the planting medium and when frightened likes to take refuge behind stones and the like. Little is known of its breeding habits although there are reports that it has spawned in captivity.

Family CENTRARCHIDAE
The family Centrarchidae (freshwater sunfishes) is closely related to the Percidae but confined to North America, where its members are found mainly in the central and eastern regions.

The most characteristic feature of the family is the gill plate: in some species the hind edge has two flat points, in others the upper point is enlarged as an opercular flap and hides the lower point from view. In nearly all species there is a black spot on one or other of these points.

Members of this family are by no means difficult

Therapon jarbua

fishes to keep in a large aquarium, but they are strictly carnivorous and must be given living food. Clear, clean water with an acid reaction (pH 4·0 to 5·0) is desirable, and the temperature should not be too high: a range of 16 to 22°C is about right, even cooler in the winter. Some fifteen or more species are known but only about half a dozen are regularly seen in the home aquarium.

Centrarchus macropterus the Peacock-eyed Bass, ranges from Illinois to Florida. In the wild it reaches a length of about 7 inches and although in time it will become quite tame, it is rather too boisterous and untrustworthy for the community aquarium.

Elassoma evergladei from North Carolina to Florida and *E. zonatum* from southern Illinois to Alabama and westwards to Texas, are both very much alike and very suitable for a community aquarium. Commonly known as pygmy sunfishes they grow to no more than 1 inch or so in length.

Lepomis gibbosus from the Great Lakes to Texas

and Florida, is the well-known Pumpkin-seed Sunfish of American aquarists, so called because the head is marked with numerous dark red or reddish-yellow blotches or spots. *L. megalotis* from southern Canada to Mexico east of the Rocky Mountains is popularly known as the Long-eared Sunfish because the gill cover has a large ear-like flap. Both are large fishes that reach 8 inches in the wild.

Mesogonistius chaetodon the Black-banded Sunfish, from New Jersey to Maryland, reaches a length of about 3 inches and is the best-known member of the family.

With the exception of *Elassoma* species, breeding begins by the male making a depression in the planting medium and fanning it with his pectoral fins to clear it of sediment. The female usually deposits the eggs in the depression but sometimes elsewhere, and the eggs are later moved to the depression. At a temperature of 21 to 24°C the fry hatch out in about three days. They remain in the

depression, guarded by the male, for eight to ten days.

Elassoma species build a nest of fine-leaved plants near the bottom. After a nuptial dance the female deposits from forty to eighty eggs in the nest. The performance is repeated and continued for a week or more. At 25°C the fry hatch out in two days.

All sunfishes are able to take comparatively large food, such as the nauplii of *Daphnia*, from the start.

Family PERCIDAE

In the Old World the family Percidae is widespread throughout Europe (including Great Britain) north of the Pyrenees and Alps, and across Asia north of the Himalayas as far east as China. In the New World it is found in the United States from the Mississippi basin eastwards to the Atlantic coast.

It is characteristic of the family that there are two dorsal fins. The first is composed of spinous hard rays, the second of soft rays. In the majority of species the two fins are separate: exceptionally they are united.

Members of this family are by no means easy to keep in a home aquarium but young specimens of *Acerina cernua* the Ruff or Pope, and *Perca fluviatilis* the Perch, will survive if properly cared for. The aquarium must be a large one for in the wild both species reach a length of some 10 inches. The water must be well oxygenated and at a temperature below 17°C. Living food is essential for they are voracious and in the wild eat large quantities of insect larvae, worms and small fishes.

Acerina cernua is native to central and northern Europe. The back is dark grey-green scattered with dark spots and blotches; the belly is yellowish. The two dorsal fins are united.

Perca fluviatilis occurs throughout the geographical range of the family in the New World as well as in the Old. The coloration is very variable. The back may vary from dark green to dark blue-grey or brown. The belly varies from yellowish to silver-white. The side is marked with about six to ten vertical dark-coloured stripes, but except in young fish they are defined only when the fish is excited. The two dorsal fins are separate.

Both species spawn in the spring and early summer but as a very large number of eggs may be produced (a large female Perch may deliver 200,000 eggs), breeding in an aquarium is not very practical.

Family CENTROPOMIDAE

Members of the family Centropomidae occur in

Lepomis gibbosus

salt, brackish and fresh waters. They range from the east coast of Africa, through the seas of India, to Malaysia, Indonesia, Australia and beyond. They are commonly called glassfishes because their most characteristic feature is a strongly compressed and diaphanous body. The skeleton and air bladder can clearly be seen through the body wall. There are two dorsal fins (the first spinous, the second soft) united at the base.

The family is represented to aquarists by the one

genus *Chanda* (once *Ambassis*) and about half a dozen species of which only three (*C. buruensis* the Malayan Glassfish, *C. nama* the Elongated Glassfish, and *C. ranga* the Indian Glassfish) are regularly introduced into aquaria. All are small, oviparous and mainly carnivorous. They will take dried food for lack of something else but small daphnids, finely chopped earthworms, mashed whiteworms and the like, are better for them. A temperature range of 18 to 25°C is recommended

and clear, matured water into which a teaspoonful of sea salt to every gallon of water has been stirred, a fine sandy bottom, and a good light, complete the set-up. They are peaceful fishes and may be introduced into a community aquarium but as they are rather shy, only with those as peaceful as themselves.

For breeding the aquarium should be large (a capacity of at least 20 gallons is advised), with the water about 4 inches deep at a temperature of 26

Perca fluviatilis

or 27°C, and well stocked with plants, particularly
floating plants with long feathery roots because
the female turns on her back and discharges the
eggs upwards. They are minute – like grains of
sand – and stick to the plants. Spawning takes
place over a period of several days in succession.
At 24°C the eggs incubate in about twenty hours
and at 28°C in about eight hours, and so it usually
happens that the first fry will be seen attached to
the plants before the brood fish have finished
spawning. They take no notice of the eggs nor of
the young fish.

The greatest difficulty is feeding the young. Not
only must they be given the smallest of daphnids
(infusorians are not sufficiently nourishing for
them) but in very large quantities, because the
young fish make no attempt to chase food but

snap at it as it passes in front of them.

C. buruensis is native to Thailand, Malaysia, Indonesia and beyond. The general colour is a transparent honey-yellow, very similar to *C. ranga*, but
the fins are hyaline to yellow and the soft dorsal
and anal fins lack the light blue edge. It reaches a
length of about 2½ inches.

C. nama is native to India and Burma. The
general colour is a transparent greenish yellow, the
body peppered with minute black dots and a faint
shoulder spot. It reaches a length of about 4 inches.

C. ranga is native to India, through Burma, to
Thailand. The body is a faint yellow, light blue on
the back with a greenish sheen by reflected light.
The soft dorsal and anal fins are edged with light
blue, less pronounced in the female than in the
male. It reaches a length of about 2 inches.

Acerina cernua

Family TOXOTIDAE

The Toxotidae is a small family embracing a handful of species that are found in the salt, brackish and fresh waters of the coasts of the East Indies, the Philippines, New Guinea and northern Australia.

Members of this family are popularly known as archerfishes. Their main source of food is flies and other insects which they attack by spitting a drop of water at them as they rest on leaves or hover above the surface of the water. If by chance the first drop misses the target, it is followed by a series of drops in quick succession until the insect is brought down. An adult fish can spit as far as six or more feet: young fishes practise by spitting tiny drops of water a few inches.

The feat is made possible by two low ridges

along the middle line of the roof of the mouth. They are set close together and run parallel for most of their length but diverge slightly at the posterior end. The ridges, therefore, form a sort of groove on the palate, and the fish converts it into a tube by the apposition of its tongue. The compression of the gill covers forces water from the pharynx into the groove-tube, and the tip of the tongue (which is paper thin and flexible) serves as a valve to hold the water under pressure. When the tip of the tongue is lowered, the valve is released, so to speak, and a drop of water is shot between the lips. By rapidly lowering and raising the tongue the fish can spit drops of water in quick succession, or in a steady stream of water if the tongue is kept lowered. Even more remarkable is the fact that the fish not only has excellent aerial vision but, when necessary, can allow for the refraction of light. When the water is cloudy or visibility is otherwise obstructed, the fish attacks with its head out of water, but in clear water only the lips are exposed and the eyes remain submerged. The eyes are capable of being moved in all directions except downwards, and the fish is able to swim backwards for a considerable distance. All this helps it to stalk its prey although this method of obtaining food is, in fact, no more than accessory: most of the time the fish feeds on insects found swimming in the water or at the surface, and in captivity it takes all the regular living foods.

The family is represented to aquarists by only one species, *Toxotes jaculator*, widely distributed throughout the geographical range of the family. The general colour varies from olive-grey or green to yellow, or orange. The side shows six black, more or less vertical bars, the first across the eye, the last at the base of the caudal fin. In the wild it reaches a length of about 6 inches but aquarium specimens rarely exceed 4 inches.

It should be provided with a large aquarium, the water at a temperature range of 26 to 28°C and to which a teaspoonful of sea salt or kitchen salt to every gallon of water has been added. Nothing is known of its breeding habits except that it is oviparous.

Family MONODACTYLIDAE

The family Monodactylidae is a small one, represented to aquarists by the one genus *Monodactylus*. The geographical range, however, is a large one: it extends from the coastal waters of western and eastern Africa, through those of southern Asia, to Indonesia and northern Australia.

The most characteristic feature of members of this family are the very deep and strongly compressed body and the elongated and thickly scaled dorsal and anal fins.

The genus is represented in the aquarium by the two species *M. argenteus* and *M. sebae*. Both are rather large fishes that in the wild reach a length of 8 or 9 inches. Aquarium specimens, however, reach only about half this size.

Normally they inhabit salt and brackish waters and the aquarium water, therefore, should consist of one part sea water to four parts fresh. The fishes, however, have the power to adapt themselves to fresh water (it is believed that they enter rivers to breed) and they have been kept in fresh water with some measure of success.

A temperature range of 24 to 28°C and a large

Chanda ranga

aquarium are desirable and as well as all the regular living foods and suitable substitutes, they must have some plant food in their diet. They are very voracious and tend to be very nervous: moving them to a new aquarium has been known to kill them. Their breeding habits are not known.

M. argenteus is native to the east coast of Africa, the Red Sea, and the seas of India, Indonesia and beyond. The colour is silvery with a purplish

sheen, especially in the region of the anal fin. A wide, black band passes from the nape and across the eye; a second from the front of the dorsal fin and over the point of the gill cover to the front of the anal fin.

M. *sebae* is native to the western coast of Africa, from the Senegal to Congo rivers. The body is silvery, light brown on the upper half. A broad, black band extends from the nape across the eye;

another from the tip of the dorsal fin to the tip of the anal; a third over the caudal peduncle.

Family SCATOPHAGIDAE

Members of the family Scatophagidae range along the coasts, in the estuaries and sometimes in the rivers of the east coast of Africa, through southern Asia, to Malaysia, Indonesia, and across the Pacific to the Fiji and Samoa islands.

Toxotes jaculator

The family embraces two genera, *Scatophagus* and *Selenotoca*, characterized by bodies that are strongly compressed, of an angular oval shape, and the spinous and soft dorsal fins nearly divided. The two genera are very much alike but may be distinguished by the fact that in *Scatophagus* there are eleven spines in the dorsal fin and in *Selenotoca* there are twelve.

Members of this family are large fishes that in the wild reach a length of 12 inches and more, although aquarium specimens rarely reach more than 6 or 7 inches. They are quite peaceful but rather too big for a community aquarium, and they do considerable damage to the plants, eating them down to the roots. In fact, they are big eaters that will take anything that comes their way, and their reputation as bullies arises from the fact that they make a point of keeping other fishes away from food.

They have been kept in fresh water with some measure of success but there is evidence to show that in these circumstances they are sometimes attacked by a body fungus that results in their death unless promptly treated.* It is better, therefore, to keep them in brackish water (one part sea water to four parts fresh) at a temperature range of 20 to 28°C. Their breeding habits are not known.

The genus *Scatophagus* is represented by two species: *S. argus* popularly called the Spotted Scat, native to the East Indies; and *S. tetracantha* popularly called the African Scat, native to the east coast

---

* The recommended treatment is to swab the affected part with chlorotone (one tablet dissolved in ½ pint of water) and then place the fish in brackish water and gradually raise it to half-marine strength over a period of a day. The cure takes about a week but the fish should be left in the bath until the scar tissue has peeled off, a matter of about two weeks more.

Monodactylus argenteus

of Africa and Malagasy, and occasionally ranging across the seas of India to Indonesia, northern Australia and beyond.

S. *argus* is the species most usually imported. A number of subspecies and distinct forms – each with a definite geographical range – are known. The coloration is variable. It may be anything from grey to green, or from brassy to salmon-pink. It depends from which area of the wide geographical range the fish has been taken. The body is marked with large dark spots that vary in size, and in coloration from dark green to jet-black. They are most numerous on the back.

S. *tetracantha* is pale yellow overcast with an iridescent bluish-silver tint. The side is marked with a number of vertical, broad, black bands that on young fish extend to the belly, but shrink with age until they are restricted to the upper half of the body on old fish.

The genus *Selenotoca* is represented to aquarists by the species S. *multifasciata* native to the waters of New Guinea, the Celebes and northern Australia. It is a uniform greenish silver in colour, marked on the side with from nine to fifteen vertical dark bars that break up into spots below the lateral line.

Family NANDIDAE

The family Nandidae is of very great importance to geologists for some members of it are confined to the north-east of South America, others to West Africa, and still others to south-east Asia. Most certainly, therefore, they are the survivors of a family that was once more widespread and, as a result, do much to give support to Wegener's Theory of Continental Drift which, at one time decried, is today receiving the support of many leading geologists (see page 39).

Scatophagus argus

Members of this family are characterized by a protrusible mouth which can be opened very widely, and transparent soft dorsal and anal fins and caudal fin, which are almost invisible and in some lights are.

The family is represented to aquarists by five genera each with one species. They are heavy feeders and carnivorous. In the wild they feed largely on small fishes. In the aquarium they can be trained to take *Daphnia*, *Tubifex*, earthworms, and the like. They are not particularly pugnacious, however, and may be kept in a community aquarium provided it contains no small fishes. A temperature range of 24 to 27°C is advised and the light should not be too strong. By nature they are nocturnal or crepuscular and under a bright light they rush for cover.

Badis badis is native to the fresh waters of India and Burma. The coloration is subject to much variation. Specimens from India are differently coloured to those from Assam and Burma, and those taken from clear water are different to those taken from dirty, weedy water. Old fish are differently coloured to young ones. Aquarium specimens are usually yellowish brown with some more or less regular lozenge-shaped black dots. It reaches a length of about 3 inches.

For breeding it is best to choose a female that is bigger than the male because at breeding time the males become extremely vicious. The aquarium should be stocked with plants and a small flower-pot on its side. The water should be mature and the light not too strong. The female deposits the eggs on the upperside of the flower-pot. The female should be removed at once but the male guards the eggs and fry: he should not be removed until they are free swimming. At a temperature of 27°C the period of incubation is two days. Infusorians are necessary as first food for the fry: they will not take fine dried food, powdered egg, or other substitutes.

Monocirrhus polyacanthus is native to the sluggish, overhung streams and ponds of the Amazon basin and Guyana. It is popularly called the Leaf-fish because in coloration it resembles nothing so much as a dead leaf, a peculiarity that is increased by a strongly compressed body, a stalk-like appendage at the mouth, and the practice of drifting idly in the water at varying depths. In the wild it reaches a length of about 4 inches but aquarium specimens are usually much smaller. It breeds in the same way as *Badis badis* and calls for the same care.

Nandus nandus is native to India, Burma and Thailand. It is rather a large fish that reaches a length of 6 or 7 inches; in India it is a recognized food fish. The coloration is variable but usually greenish brown with brassy reflections, vertically marbled with broad, patchy bars. Its breeding habits are not known.

Polycentropsis abbreviata is native to Lagos, Niger and Ogowe. The colour is variable, changing from yellowish or olive-brown to pinkish brown, marbled with a darker shade. It reaches a length of about 3 inches.

The male blows a bubble nest among the floating plants. From time to time the female turns on her back and deposits an egg in it. Up to about 100 eggs are delivered at one spawning. The female should be removed after spawning, but as the male protects the young he should be left until the fry are free swimming. At a temperature of 28°C the young fish hatch out in forty-eight hours, when the male moves them from the bubble nest to a depression in the planting medium.

Polycentrus schomburgki popularly known as the Bobtail, is native to Trinidad, the Guianas and the Lower Orinoco. The colour varies from light brown to blue-black and even to jet-black, superimposed with small jet-black dots with a silvery glint. Three dark brown, wedge-shaped bars radiate from the eye, to the snout, the nape, and the lower edge of the gill plate. In the wild it reaches a length of 4 inches but aquarium specimens reach only 2 or 3 inches. It breeds in the same way as *Badis badis* but not readily.

Family CICHLIDAE

The Cichlidae is a large family of oviparous fishes that inhabit the sluggish and standing waters of subtropical and tropical America and Africa. In the Old World members of the family are found throughout Africa (including Malagasy), Palestine, Syria and southern India (including Ceylon). In the New World they range from the south-east of the United States in the north, through Mexico and Central America (including the West Indies) and South America, to Buenos Aires in the south. Most members of the family are perch-like in appearance but the dorsal fin is single; its spinous part well developed and considerably longer than the soft part. The anal fin has three or more spines.

Cichlids vary greatly in size. Some reach only a few inches, others as much as 18 inches, but with few exceptions all are inclined to be quarrelsome and are best kept in pairs of compatible male and female. Only small species and young specimens of the larger species should be introduced into a community aquarium. Most are carnivorous and must be fed on living food and suitable substitutes for it; some will take dried food, especially if it contains shrimps, insects, and the like; and some must be given green food in their diet. *Tilapia* species and some species of the genus *Cichlasoma* and *Geophagus* need a lot of green food if they are to be kept in health.

As it is the practice of most cichlids to uproot plants, the aquarium should be furnished with stones of various shapes, sizes and quality. If plants are desired for decorative reasons only those that are strong-rooting and have broad leaves should be chosen. Floating plants, however, should always be introduced into the aquarium: they furnish shade (cichlids are not fond of a strong light) and limit the growth of algae.

The water should be matured, neutral or with a slightly acid reaction. The notion that cichlids flourish best in acid water is a fallacy that has long been exploded. For general care and maintenance a satisfactory temperature range is 22 to 25°C. It should be raised to 27 to 29°C for breeding.

The breeding aquarium should be a large one. An aquarium that holds from 10 to 15 gallons of water is by no means too big for a breeding pair of fair size. For bigger fishes an aquarium holding 20 or more gallons should be provided. The bottom of the aquarium should be layered with about 2 inches of coarse sand or fine gravel; on it should be placed two or three pieces of light-coloured stone or some large flat pebbles. Most cichlids show a marked preference for smooth flat surfaces and deposit their eggs on a stone, inside a flower-pot on its side, or a large shell. Some will scrape away the planting medium and deposit their eggs on the bottom glass of the aquarium.

Sexing is by no means easy and is impossible when the fish are young. In adults bolder markings and slightly larger and more pointed dorsal and anal fins usually denote a male; also, age for age, the male is usually larger than the female. What is more certain is that just before breeding time a small white spot may be seen near the vent of both fish. At first it looks rather like a nipple but as it extends it will be seen to be the genital papilla. That of the female (through which the eggs are extruded) is blunter than that of the male (through which the milt is ejected).

Although there are some variations of the breeding pattern, as is only to be expected in a family with such a wide geographical distribution, the differences are not great and in the main breeding follows a regular routine. Typically there is some spreading of fins and intensification of colour, and courtship will sometimes include the interlocking of mouths and a tug-of-war. The place on which the eggs are to be deposited is chosen and very carefully cleaned. The female deposits the eggs in batches of three to eight at a time and they are immediately fertilized by the male. The action is repeated many times. Both brood fish care for the eggs and fan them with their pectoral fins until the young hatch out – a matter of about three or four days. The young fish are then moved to a depression in the sand. It may be a natural one or one specially dug. The parents share the work and move the young several times before they are free swimming.

In general, cichlids protect their young and should not be removed from the breeding aquarium. When the fry are free swimming they shoal with the parents who direct the movements of the shoal, and even help the fry to feed by seizing the larger pieces of food, breaking them up by mastication, and spitting the smaller pieces among the shoal.

Among cichlids many species are mouth-breeders. More correctly, as we have already pointed out (see page 35), the fertilized eggs are taken into the mouth and incubated in the buccal cavity. The eggs are deposited in a depression in the sand and there fertilized. They are then taken up by one of the parents into the mouth. In most species the task is undertaken by the female, but in some (for example *Tilapia heudeloti*) it is undertaken by the male, and in some (for example *Pelmatochromis guentheri*) both parents share.

The period of incubation averages about fourteen days. The young are not released until they are free swimming and even then, at the least sign of danger, they retreat to the protecting mouth. During the period of incubation the brood fish takes no food and becomes very emaciated. Once the fry are free swimming, therefore, it should be allowed to rest and be given plenty of food.

With some exceptions the fry of cichlids are sufficiently large to take newly hatched brine shrimps, finely screened daphnids and mashed earthworms from the start. Mouth-breeders need rotifers and large infusorians for their first food; some will readily take dust-fine dried food.

It is not necessary to remove the brood fish once they have finished spawning, and it seems a pity to break up the shoal. Nonetheless, about a fortnight after the fry have become free swimming, serious consideration should be given whether to leave the brood fish with the fry or move them to another aquarium. There is little

doubt that if the brood fish are moved many more young will be raised to maturity, not only because they will get more to eat, but because there is a tendency for all fishes to turn cannibal if given the opportunity. By contrary, moving the brood fish and breaking up the shoal can be done only at the cost of losing the opportunity to make observations about the behaviour of fishes, of interest to aquarists and, if properly recorded, of value to naturalists.

Acaropsis nassa is native to Guyana and the basins of the Orinoco and Amazon rivers. It is a fairly large fish that in the wild reaches a length of 8 inches; in captivity about 4 or 5. The mouth is very large and protrusible. As a result, it has been given the popular name of the Basket-mouth Cichlid. It is predatory and indeed as well as all the regular living foods, from time to time it must be given small fishes in its diet. It should be accommodated in a large aquarium at a temperature of not less than 22°C and only in company with fishes of its own size. Plenty of hiding-places, such as hollow stones and overturned flower-pots, should be available.

The general colour is grey-green, lighter on the belly. The lower part of the side is marked with silvery-blue spots. A dark band extends from the top of the head, behind the eye, to the point of the gill cover, dividing in old fishes to form two spots. Another band, intensified with a spot in the middle of the body, extends from the eye to the posterior end of the soft dorsal fin. There is a small spot at the origin of the lateral line and another at the root of the caudal fin.

Members of the genus *Aequidens* are native to tropical South America. They are very similar in appearance to *Cichlasoma* species but the head is smaller and the anterior part of the anal fin has only three spines whereas in *Cichlasoma* there are four to twelve.

The genus is represented to aquarists by five species, commonly known as acaras because they were once referred to the genus *Acara*. They may be kept, cared for and bred in the regular way of cichlids. With a few exceptions the smaller species make satisfactory community fishes.

A. curviceps popularly called the Sheep's-head Acara, is native to the Amazon basin. The back is greenish brown, the side silvery blue, the belly light red to golden. The gill cover is peppered with sky-blue dots and streaks. A light stripe extends from above the eye to a dark spot below the dorsal fin. It reaches a length of about 3 inches. It is a peaceful fish and does little damage to plants, but it has the bad habit of usually eating the first batches of eggs; subsequent batches are looked after.

A. maroni native to Guyana, is popularly known as the Keyhole Fish on account of a marking on its side that shows a similarity to a keyhole. The general colour is cream to beige. A broad, dark brown to black band extends from the front of the dorsal fin, across the eye, to the gill cover. It reaches a length of about 4 inches and is peaceful and trustworthy.

A. portalegrensis is native to southern Brazil, Paraguay and Bolivia. It is popularly known as the Brown Acara for although young fish are of a uniform dark olive-green, mature fish darken to rusty brown. The side is marked with a broad stripe that extends from the eye to the base of the caudal fin, where it ends as a black spot edged greenish yellow. Below this stripe some vertical bars are very evident. It is a fairly large fish that in the wild reaches a length of 10 inches and aquarium specimens will grow up to 6 or 7 inches. It is not to be trusted with small fishes.

A. pulcher (*latifrons*) is native to the north of South America from Panama, through Colombia and Venezuela, to Trinidad. Under the name of the Blue Acara it is very popular with aquarists for it is hardy, prolific and does little if any grubbing and damage to plants.

The general colour is turquoise-blue, the belly silvery grey to bluish. The side is marked with eight vertical dark bars and rows of blue-green dots. There is a large dark spot in the middle of the body, a small dark stripe at the root of the caudal fin and another through the eye. The head and gill cover are marked with blue-green stripes and small spots. It reaches a length of about 6 inches.

A. tetramerus the Saddle Acara, is widespread through Central America and the north-east of South America, where it is esteemed as a food fish. It is a large fish that in the wild reaches a length of some 10 inches, and aquarium specimens grow to as much as 8 inches. They tend to bully.

The colour and markings vary. Usually the back is greenish to brownish, the side yellowish to grey, the belly with a rosy tinge. A black stripe extends from the eye to the root of the caudal fin. Above the stripe, the side is marked with three or more very broad bands that vary in colour from light to dark brown. There is a dark spot in the middle of the body and another on the upper part of the caudal peduncle.

Apistogramma species are native to South

Aequidens portalegrensis

America. They are small fishes that reach a length of 2 or 3 inches and are popularly known as dwarf cichlids. We prefer to call them pygmy cichlids, because dwarf suggests the circus freak, with limbs too small for the body, rather than one of diminutive size.

The genus is represented to aquarists by about nine species which commend themselves for a number of reasons. Apart from being small and peaceful, they are colourful and do no damage to plants. They are, in fact, very satisfactory community fishes that may be kept, cared for and bred in the regular way of cichlids. None, however, is prolific even though breeding presents no special difficulties. The female favours an overturned flower-pot in which to deposit the eggs, and the male takes no interest in them once he has fertilized them. An exception must be made for *A. ramirezi*, however, because sometimes the female spawns on the leaves of plants and sometimes the male helps to protect the eggs.

A. agassizi is native to the Amazon basin. The general colour is light brown to olive-yellow. The back is dark violet anteriorly shading to light violet towards the tail. A dark brown stripe extends from the eye to the tip of the caudal fin. Two dark stripes extend from the eye; one to the mouth, the other across the gill cover. The body and head are sprinkled with small, blue spots.

A, cacatuoides of the onomatopoetic name and with the popular name of the Cockatoo Cichlid, is native to the Guianas. The male is a uniform olive-green with a dark stripe from the eye to the base of the caudal fin. The female is yellowish green; a deep yellow when in breeding condition.

A. borelli punningly known as the Umbrella Cichlid, is native to the Matto Grosso and southwards to Argentina. The back is dark olive-brown, the sides paler with a blue sheen. The throat and belly are light brown. A dark stripe extends from the gill cover to the root of the caudal fin. It is rather pugnacious.

A. corumbae (which some authorities tell us should be spelt *commbrae*) is native to the Parana basin. The colour is very variable but aquarium specimens are usually light brown to yellow. The side is marked with a series of dark horizontal bands and vertical bars, sometimes broken up into dotted lines. A black, curved band extends from the nape over the eye. The gill cover is marked with pale green lines and, on the side, brown dots.

A. ortmanni is native to the Guianas and the Amazon basin. The general colour is brown. A dark stripe extends from the snout, through the eye, to a vertical spot at the base of the caudal fin. A black bar extends from the nape, over the eye, to the base of the gill cover.

A. pertense popularly known as the Yellow Cichlid, is native to the Amazon basin. The colour is variable but is usually pale green to golden brown, silvery on the belly. A dark stripe extends from the snout, through the eye, to a vertical spot at the root of the caudal fin. A short stripe extends from the eye to the base of the gill cover. The scales are dark edged, giving a reticulated effect. The head and gill cover are peppered with green and brown irregular lines and small spots.

A. pleurotaenia the Chequered Cichlid, is native to Brazil from the Amazon to La Plata. The basic colour is rusty brown. On young fish a dark stripe extends from the snout, through the eye, to a spot on the caudal peduncle. It is rarely to be seen on mature fish. A dark band runs from the nape across the eye, to the base of the gill cover.

A. ramirezi is native to Venezuela. It is a very colourful and attractive fish that well deserves its popular name of the Butterfly Cichlid. The overall colour is blue with a glint of lavender and sapphire-blue spots. Five or six dark bands extend from the dorsal fin to the lateral line. A black band crosses the eye from the nape to the base of the gill cover. The snout is orange-red; the head and gill cover are marked with electric-blue streaks.

A. reitzigi is native to the Rio Paraguay basin. The back is greenish grey, shading to yellowish grey on the side, and bright yellow on the belly. The gill cover is marked with light green spots and streaks.

Astronotus ocellatus once popularly known as the Marbled Cichlid, is now more usually known as the Oscar. It is native to tropical South America. It is a very handsome fish that reaches a length of 12 or 13 inches, and is rather too large for any except the specialist aquarist. In any case, it must be kept by itself in a large aquarium for even specimens three-quarters grown prefer to eat small fishes than anything else; they will take a 3-inch fish at one gulp.

This species may be kept, cared for and bred in the regular way of cichlids. Sexing is by no means easy; but those specimens that show a few small eye spots on a red field near the base of the dorsal fin are usually males. In captivity it breeds but rarely.

The general colour varies from beige to chocolate-brown. The body is marked with irregular black lines giving a marbled effect and, most conspicuous of all, on the caudal peduncle there

Astronotus ocellatus

is a black eye spot on a copper-red ground. Some bright red spots occur on the head and body.

A number of red forms, and forms that are dark-barred on a red ground, have been developed. They were pioneered by Charoen Pattabongse of Bangkok, who began selective breeding in 1966 and three years later succeeded in fixing the colour and obtaining an all-red strain, now generally known as the Red Oscar.

Members of the genus *Cichlasoma* are commonly known as chanchitoes. The genus is a large one with a geographical range that extends from Mexico in the north, through Central America (including the West Indies) and tropical South America, to Argentina in the south.

All are large fishes, that grow up to 12 inches in length, and are very similar in appearance to *Aequidens* species. They may be distinguished from them, however, by a larger head, a larger and more protractile mouth, and the possession of from four to twelve spines in the anal fin; in *Aequidens* there are only three.

Chanchitoes may be kept, cared for and bred in the regular way of cichlids but as most are pugnacious and even small species are inclined to be bullies, only a few are suited to a community aquarium. Breeding presents no great difficulty but, as is only to be expected, in captivity some species breed less readily than others. Sexing is fairly simple for when the fishes are mature the male is more highly coloured than the female, and the tips of his soft dorsal and anal fins are longer and more pointed. The eggs are deposited on stones; large ones should be provided.

Cichlasoma biocellatum

The species that are mentioned below are the ones more usually to be seen in aquaria, together with white forms of *C. facetum*, *C. nigrofasciatum* and *C. severum*.

C. aureus the Yellow Chanchito, is native to Mexico, Yucatan and Guatemala. The colour ranges from golden yellow to light brown with a pale green sheen. The side is marked with six vertical bars, a large black spot on the middle of the body, and a small one at the root of the caudal fin. It reaches a length of about 6 inches. In the wild it is found in very weedy waters and it is partly herbivorous, and although it cannot be called a peaceful fish neither can it be called a pugnacious one.

C. bimaculatus the Two-spot Chanchito, is native to Trinidad, the Guianas and the Amazon basin. The colour is brownish with a silvery-blue sheen. The side is marked with about eight blue-black, vertical bars, a stripe that extends from the gill cover to the root of the caudal fin, a large dark spot on the middle of the body and another at the root of the caudal fin. It reaches a length of about 8 inches.

C. biocellatum is native to Guatemala and southwards to the Amazon basin. It is very well known to aquarists under the appropriate popular name of the Jack Dempsey. It varies in colour from light brown or dark green to dark brown and even black. The side is marked with six or more vertical bars and a dark stripe that extends from the eye, through a dark spot on the middle of the body, to one at the root of the caudal fin. The lower lip is blue and the gill cover shows a number of blue spots. Each scale is marked with a green spot. It reaches a length of about 8 inches.

C. coryphaenoides the Chocolate Chanchito, is found in the Amazon basin. The popular name is well chosen because the general colour is light to dark brown. The side shows a number of dark vertical bars. There is a dark blotch on the gill cover, another on the middle line of the body, and a third at the root of the caudal fin. It reaches a length of about 8 inches.

C. crassa is native to the Amazon basin. The colour is variable but most aquarium specimens are brown with a greenish or reddish sheen. An irregular band extends from the eye to a small

Cichlasoma festivum

blotch on the caudal peduncle. The side is marked with several rows of spots; they are more conspicuous below the lateral line than above it. It reaches a length of about 8 inches.

C. cutteri is native to Honduras. It is one of the smaller species that reaches a length of only about 5 inches and is usually quite peaceful. The general colour is blue-green to olive-green with a pronounced brassy or coppery sheen. Six dark vertical bars mark the side and extend over the dorsal fin; a seventh crosses the caudal peduncle. There is a dark blotch at the root of the caudal fin.

C. erythraeum is native to Costa Rica. The colour is variable and ranges from pinkish gold to brick-red. It is popularly called the Red Devil because of its colour and its quarrelsome nature but there is a pinkish-white form that is said to be far less of a fighter. It reaches as much as 15 inches in length.

C. facetum is native to north-east Brazil and Paraguay. It is one of the larger species that touches 12 inches. The colour varies from brassy or yellowish brown to dark green or dusky, even black. The side is marked with six or seven vertical dark bars, a dark spot on the middle of the body

and a horizontal stripe from the gill cover to the root of the caudal fin. Sometimes, however, the colour pales to an ash-grey and the markings become almost invisible. For this reason it has been given the popular name of the Chameleon Fish.

C. festivum from Guyana and the Amazon basin, is popularly known as the Barred or Flag Chanchito. It reaches a length of about 6 inches and has the reputation of being peaceful. In fact, it is rather timid and the aquarium should be furnished to provide it with plenty of hiding-places. The general colour is a brassy yellow to green. A black band extends from the corner of the mouth, across the eye, to the front of the soft dorsal fin. The caudal peduncle shows a large black spot.

C. friedrichsthali from Yucatan, Guatemala and Honduras, reaches about 10 inches in the wild. Aquarium specimens are very much smaller and few exceed a length of 6 inches. They are, however, very boisterous. The general colour is yellowish green, the back darker. Seven or eight vertical, dark bars extend from the back and fade into the body colour. A large number of light brown spots

Cichlasoma meeki

form a broken line from gill cover to caudal peduncle; coffee-brown spots pepper the body and fins.

C. maculicauda the Spotted Chanchito, is native to Central America, where it is found in brackish water as well as in fresh. The general colour is yellowish brown on the back, fading to light green on the belly. The side is marked with a number of irregular, vertical, dark bars; a large black blotch that covers most of the caudal peduncle; and numerous dark brown dots. It reaches a length of about 10 inches in the wild – less in captivity – and is as peaceful as may be expected for its size.

C. meeki native to Guatemala and Yucatan, is the well-known and popular Firemouth of the aquarists, so named because the mouth, throat and belly are a rich orange-red. The general colour is bluish green, the side marked with five dark bars and a horizontal black line from gill cover, through a middle spot, to the root of the caudal fin. It is one of the smaller *Cichlasoma* species that reaches only about 5 inches and is usually, but not always, peaceful.

C. nigrofasciatum from Guatemala, Salvador, Costa Rica and Panama, is a fish that reaches only about 4 inches, and although small is a big bully. The general colour is pearly grey with a violet tinge. The side is marked with a number of vertical, dark bars, from which it has been named the Zebra Chanchito, and in the United States, less politely, the Convict Fish. There is an irregular, dark spot on the point of the gill cover. The throat and belly are brown.

C. severum the Sedate Chanchito, is native to Guyana and the Amazon basin. The colour varies from yellowish brown or brassy to bluish green, dark green and blue-black. Young fish show a number of vertical, dark bars on the side but they fade with age and mature fish show only two: one crosses the caudal peduncle, the other just in front of it and connects a large spot on the soft dorsal fin to one on the soft anal. Two black stripes cross the head. It reaches a length of about 7 inches, and small specimens are suitable for a community aquarium.

C. tetracanthus is native to Cuba and Barbados where it is found in brackish as well as in fresh water. The general colour is blue-green, the back darker, the belly yellowish. The side is marked with three black spots on a light field; the head with many irregular dark markings. Colour and markings, however, count for very little because it is a characteristic of the species that it can adopt an almost completely different coloration and marking in a matter of minutes. It reaches a length of about 8 inches.

C. urophthalmus is native to southern Mexico and southwards to Panama. It is brown to yellowish green in colour, the side with about six to eight black, vertical bars and a large black spot on a yellow ground at the root of the caudal fin. It reaches about 7 inches.

The genus *Crenicichla* is native to South America from the Guianas in the north, through Brazil, to La Plata in the south. Some twenty-five species are known to ichthyologists but only three are regularly introduced into the aquarium: *C. dorsocellata* (*notophthalmus*), *C. geayi* and *C. saxatilis*. They may be kept, cared for and bred in the regular way of cichlids but all are rather large fishes that reach a length of 6 to 8 inches, and none is particularly attractive. They are, in fact, fishes more for the specialist than the ordinary aquarist.

The sexes may be distinguished by the dorsal and anal fins: those of the male are more pointed than those of the female. The eggs are deposited either on stones or the leaves of plants, and the brood fish should be removed about a week after the fry are free swimming. They cannot be trusted for longer.

Crenicichla species are commonly known as pike cichlids because they are pike-like not only in appearance but also in behaviour. They are typical predators that lie in wait for their prey and make a lightning rush; fishes only a little smaller than themselves disappear head first in one gulp. *C. dorsocellata* is said to be more peaceful than the others but none can be considered trustworthy enough to be kept other than by itself.

The genus *Etroplus* is represented to aquarists by two species: *E. maculatus* the Orange Chromide, and *E. suratensis* the Green Chromide. They are native to southern India and Ceylon.

E. maculatus is orange or creamy yellow to yellow, the back olive-brown to grey, sometimes almost black. The side is marked with a large black middle spot and sometimes with two smaller ones on each side of it. It is a small fish that reaches a length of about 3 inches, is quite peaceful, and may be kept, cared for and bred in the regular way of cichlids.

E. suratensis is light green. The side is marked with eight vertical bars. Above the lateral line each scale shows a pearly-white spot; the belly is peppered with black spots. It is a large fish that reaches a length of 16 inches in the wild but rarely more than 4 or 5 inches in captivity. In truth it is not often imported and, as far as we know, it has not bred in captivity. It may be kept and cared for as other cichlids but as in the wild it is found in brackish waters, the aquarium water should be a mixture of one part sea water to four parts fresh.

Geophagus species are native to South America from Panama to Argentina. The name means earth-eater, which is not inappropriate, for they spend much of their time chewing over the planting medium and damaging the plants. All are fairly large fishes and quarrelsome, although *G. jurupari* is usually quite peaceful and not given to destroying plants.

In appearance, members of the genus are very like *Aequidens* species but the head is larger, with a long curved upper profile and a straight lower one; the caudal peduncle is noticeably narrow. They may be kept and cared for in the regular way of cichlids and, with the exception of *G. jurupari* which is a mouth-breeder, they breed in the regular way of cichlids. In captivity, however, they breed rarely. The three species described below are those that are most usually seen in aquaria. They reach a length of 10 or 11 inches.

G. acuticeps is native to the Amazon basin. The general colour is olive-green, the belly silvery with a yellowish-green sheen. The side is marked with brilliant blue spots and vertical, dark bars from the back to the lateral line.

G. brasiliensis the Mother-of-pearl Cichlid, is native to eastern Brazil where it is found in brackish as well as fresh water. The general colour is sandy to loam, sometimes grey and often with a greenish sheen. The gill cover is marked with seven to nine mother-of-pearl spots (from which the popular name arises) and the side with small opalescent dots that appear as broken longitudinal lines.

G. jurupari misnamed the Demonfish, is native to the Guianas and north-eastern Brazil. The colour is a dark olive-yellow, the back olive-brown, the belly light yellow. A dark stripe extends from the gill cover to the root of the caudal fin. It is crossed by paler vertical bars. The gill cover is marked with brilliant blue spots. The eggs are deposited on stones. A few hours later they are taken up by the female who incubates them in her mouth for about fourteen days. The male should be removed when the eggs have hatched.

The genus *Haplochromis* is native to Africa, Palestine and Syria. It is represented to aquarists by some half a dozen species, of which the four described below are the best known and the ones most usually imported. They are mouth-breeders and breed quite readily in captivity. They may be

Hemichromis bimaculatus

kept and cared for in the regular way of cichlids. All are small fishes but tend to be aggressive, although *H. multicolor* usually behaves itself. Hard water with a neutral to slightly alkaline reaction is to be advised.

H. callipterus once known as *Pseudotropheus tropheops*, is native to Lake Malawi. It has been given the popular name of the Black-edged Golden Malawi Cichlid, which is no improvement on the scientific name. The general colour is golden with faint greyish barring. The fins are golden yellow, the dorsal, anal and pelvics edged black. It reaches a length of about 4 inches. It needs algae, or other plant matter, in its diet.

H. multicolor (strigigena) is native to the Lower Nile and eastern Africa. It is popularly known as the Small, or Egyptian, Mouth-breeder, and reaches a length of not more than 2 or 3 inches. It is olive-brown to green in colour, the back and side reflect metallic lights. Horizontal and vertical markings on the side are sometimes very pronounced and sometimes disappear.

H. philander (moffati) is widespread throughout tropical Africa from the Congo and Angola to South-west Africa and the Transvaal. The general colour is olive, darker on the back, shading to silvery on the belly. A dark line runs from the mouth to the eye and horizontally from the eye to the edge of the gill cover. The side is marked with a number of horizontal lines, and a peppering of copper-coloured dots above the lateral line and light blue ones below it. It reaches a length of about 4 inches.

H. wingatei is native to Nigeria and, therefore, has been given the popular name of the Nigerian Mouth-breeder. The side is a silvery grey-blue with a horizontal stripe from gill cover to caudal peduncle, crossed by about seven vertical, dark bars. Red spots occur on the anal fin of the male. It reaches a length of about 4 inches.

Members of the genus *Hemichromis* are popularly known as jewelfishes. They are native to tropical Africa from the Nile, southwards to the Congo and Angola. Only two species are known: *H. bimaculatus* the Red Cichlid or Jewelfish, and *H. fasciatus* the Five-spot or Banded Jewelfish. They may be kept, cared for and bred in the regular way of cichlids, but they are aggressive fishes, unsuited to the community aquarium. The aquarium should be furnished with shelter for the female for at breeding time she needs to be protected from the male.

H. bimaculatus is olive-brown, darker on the back, and shading to yellow on the belly. The side is marked with a dark horizontal stripe, a few faint vertical bars, a dark spot below the dorsal fin and another on the caudal peduncle. A dark line crosses the eye. During the breeding season the underside becomes a brilliant lacquer-red, the markings on the side blue-black, and the whole body sparkles with metallic-blue spots. It reaches a length of about 4 inches.

H. fasciatus is olive to yellow with a green sheen. The side shows five distinct dark spots equally spaced from just behind the gill cover to the root of the caudal fin. Vertical bars, tapering towards the belly, pass through each spot. During the breeding season the colour of the fish deepens to brassy yellow with a reddish sheen on the back; the belly blood-red. It reaches a length of about 10 inches.

Herichthys cyanoguttatus the Freshwater Sheep's Head, sometimes known as the Texas Cichlid, is the only member of the family in the United States.

It is native to Texas and Mexico. Young fish are orange-yellow to olive-green with seven dark, vertical bars, the third showing a dark blotch below the lateral line. Mature fish are pearly grey with light blue spots on the head, body and vertical fins. In the third year the male (but not the female) develops a nuchal hump. In the wild it reaches a length of 12 inches, but in captivity only about 6 inches. It may be kept, cared for and bred in the regular way of cichlids. Due to its geographical distribution it will tolerate a temperature lower than most cichlids; a range of 14 to 16°C does it no harm.

Members of the genus *Julidochromis* are native to Lake Tanganyika. They are represented to aquarists by two species: *J. ornatus* that reaches a length of about 3 inches, and *J. marlieri* that reaches about 4 inches. Both call for the same living conditions: hard and alkaline water at a temperature of about 24°C, large stones to provide shelter and small worms and vegetable matter in the diet. They are not difficult to breed. The eggs are deposited on stones previously cleaned by the brood fish.

J. ornatus is lemon-yellow with three black stripes that extend from the head to a dark blotch on the caudal peduncle.

J. marlieri is chocolate-brown with a row of oval, white spots above the lateral line and ivory to white below it. The unpaired fins have blue margins.

The genus *Labeotropheus* is native to Lake Malawi. It is represented to aquarists by two species: *L. fuelleborni* and *L. trewavasae* known as the Red-top Cichlid. Both are small fishes that eat most things and need some plant matter in their diet if they are to remain in health. A temperature of about 24°C suits them and the water should be hard and alkaline. They are mouth-breeders.

L. fuelleborni has a brilliant light blue body with dark blue vertical bars on the side. The fins are blue, the soft dorsal and anal with orange spots. It is peaceful but best kept with fishes of its own size.

L. trewavasae is a very handsome species. The male is blue with about twelve dark blue vertical bars on the side and a bright red long-based dorsal fin. The female is grey to light olive with brown to orange markings. It is an aggressive fish and during the breeding season the males bully the females.

The genus *Nannacara* is native to South America. It is represented to aquarists by two small, or pygmy, species that, like *Apistogramma* species, are popularly known as dwarf cichlids. *N. anomala*,

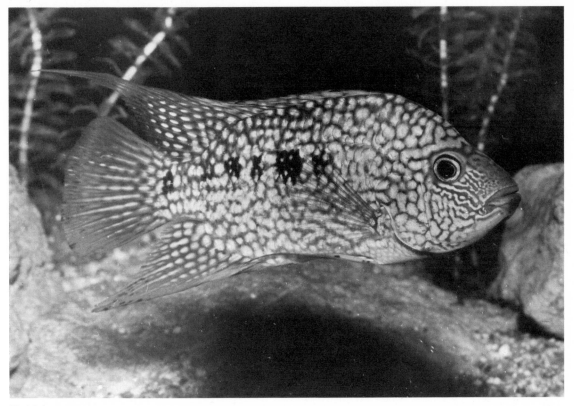

Herichthys cyanoguttatus

the Golden-eyed Dwarf Cichlid, is native to Guyana, *N. taenia* the Lattice Dwarf Cichlid, is native to the Amazon.

In appearance they are very like *Aequidens* species but are very much smaller and the lateral line runs close to the dorsal fin. They make satisfactory community fishes as they are quite peaceful and may be kept, cared for and bred in the regular way of cichlids. The female is smaller than the male and favours a flower-pot on its side in which to deposit the eggs.

N. anomala is olive-brown on the head and back, sometimes with black spots anteriorly. The side is a metallic green with a golden tinge. Each scale is marked with a triangular olive-brown dot. The gill cover shows irregular, green markings. The iris of the eye is orange, red towards the pupil. The male reaches a length of about 3 inches.

N. taenia varies in colour from greenish grey-brown to light yellow. A dark, horizontal stripe extends from the eye to the root of the caudal fin and six narrow lines run parallel to it; three above and three below. When excited vertical bars appear on the side and produce the lattice effect that has

given the fish its popular name. The male reaches a length of about 2 inches.

Nannochromis is a genus of small, or pygmy, cichlids, popularly called dwarf cichlids, native to the Congo. The genus is represented to aquarists by two species: *N. dimidiatus* and *N. nudiceps*. The males reach a length of about 3 inches; the females about an inch less. They may be kept, cared for and bred in the regular way of cichlids and, like other pygmy cichlids, the female favours an overturned flower-pot in which to deposit the eggs. They are peaceful and as they do no damage to plants they are very suitable for a community aquarium. Like many other cichlids, however, they take their stand over a definite area and defend it against all comers. Soft, neutral to acid water is advised.

N. dimidiatus is purplish brown with dark blotches on the side and some red in the dorsal and caudal fins.

N. nudiceps is ochre, the side pale blue, the belly enamel-green. The dorsal fin is orange-brown, the caudal ochre, the anal violet to green.

Pelmatochromis species are native to Africa. They

Labeotropheus fuelleborni

are very handsome fishes (much like *Haplochromis* species) particularly when in their breeding liveries. As they are fairly small fishes that reach about 4 inches at most, peaceful and not given to destroying plants, they make suitable community fishes, kept and cared for in the regular way of cichlids. Seven species are represented to aquarists. With the exception of *P. guentheri*, which is a mouthbreeder, they breed in the regular way of cichlids. Each egg is attached to a flat stone or overturned flower-pot by means of a filament.

P. annectens from western Africa, is grey to yellow-brown with a blue sheen, and three horizontal stripes and six vertical bars on the side. *P. arnoldi* from western Africa, is light olive-green with silvery reflections, the side marked with five round, black spots which sometimes expand into indistinct vertical bars.

P. guentheri from Ghana to Gabon, is blue-green, the back darker, the belly lighter, the side marked with a horizontal stripe from the eye to the root of the caudal fin and a curved stripe from the mouth, through the eye, and following the contour of the body to the caudal peduncle.

P. kribensis from western Africa, is variable in colour and markings but usually the back is brownish with a bluish to violet sheen, the side and belly ivory with greenish areas. During the breeding season the belly is flushed pink, a pronounced red in the female.

P. pulcher from the delta of the Niger, is dark green on the back, paler on the side, reddish on the belly. The gill cover is marked with greenish-blue stripes and a large dark blotch.

P. subocellatus from western Africa, the Niger to the Congo, is light brown to brownish yellow, the back dark olive-green, the belly yellowish with a rosy sheen. The side is marked with a dark brown longitudinal line and vertical bars.

P. taeniatus from Nigeria, is characterized by a broad olive-blue stripe from the snout to the root of the caudal fin, above which the side is yellowish grey to blue-grey and below it yellowish brown with a greenish sheen.

The genus *Pseudotropheus* is native to Lake Malawi. It is represented to aquarists by three species: *P. auratus* the Malawi Golden Cichlid, *P. elongatus* the Malawi Slender Cichlid, and *P. zebra* the Malawi Blue Cichlid. All are small fishes that reach a length of 3 or 4 inches but they are aggressive. They are at their best in hard and alkaline water, eat anything, and may be kept and cared for in the regular way of cichlids. *P. auratus* and *P. zebra* are mouth-breeders and have bred in captivity. Nothing is known of the breeding habits of *P. elongatus* but it may be supposed to be a mouth-breeder also.

P. auratus is golden yellow with two black stripes bordered blue from head to caudal peduncle. The fins are yellow, the upper lobe of the caudal with black spots.

P. elongatus is blue, the male inky-blue with darker cross bars, the female a paler blue.

P. zebra is of variable coloration but most specimens are slate-blue with darker cross bars and blue fins. The anal fin shows some yellow spots.

Members of the genus *Pterophyllum* are native to the Amazon and Orinoco basins. They are well known to aquarists under the popular name of angelfishes, so called on account of a body so laterally compressed that it is discoid, and extended dorsal and anal fins rather longer than the body, and filamentous pelvic fins.

The genus is represented by three species: *P. altum*, *P. eimekei* and *P. scalare*. For all practical purposes, however, only the last needs to be considered. It is doubtful that *P. altum* has ever been imported into England and according to some authorities *P. eimekei* is no more than a synonym for *scalare*. In any case, all three species are so much alike that only a trained taxonomist can tell them apart.

P. scalare is metallic silvery to olive-grey, the back brownish to olive-green. The side is marked with four vertical bars that are sometimes ink-black and sometimes barely visible. The first crosses the eye, the last the root of the caudal fin; the broadest extends from the tip of the dorsal fin and crosses the body to the tip of the anal fin. It reaches a length of about 5 or 6 inches. It is quite peaceful with fishes of its own size, and small specimens may be introduced into a community aquarium with confidence. It may be kept and cared for in the regular way of cichlids.

Sexing is by no means easy. The most reliable method is to observe the genital papilla (see page 130) which becomes visible at breeding time; that of the female is thicker than that of the male.

Breeding occurs in the regular way of cichlids but the aquarium must be a very large one for in the wild the fish frequent water that may be anything from 3 to 10 feet deep. It should be furnished with bamboo canes, opaque glass rods or strips of slate, vertically secured, because in nature the female deposits the eggs on reeds. The light should be subdued and 1 ounce of sea salt or kitchen salt to every 20 gallons of water is considered beneficial.

A number of colour varieties have been developed. In one the normal metallic silvery to olive-green ground colour has been replaced by pale blue, and in another by pale yellow or a golden tint. An all-black variety is a deep velvety black and the vertical bars more or less invisible. The lace variety is darker than the type species and the fins have a black lace pattern. The veiltail variety has elongated fins. A popular variety is marbled silver and black.

The genus *Symphysodon* is native to the Amazon. It is represented in the aquarium by the species and subspecies: *S. aequifasciata aequifasciata* the Green Pompadour, *S.a. axelrodi* the Bronze Pompadour, *S.a. haroldi* the Blue Pompadour, and *S. discus* the Pompadour. All are remarkably handsome fishes with beautifully coloured disc-shaped, strongly compressed bodies reaching a length of from 5 to 8 inches. They are peaceful fishes. They may be kept and cared for in the regular way of cichlids but they are rather specialized feeders and they cannot tolerate uncleanliness.

In captivity *S. discus* has bred several times. The eggs are deposited on stones or the leaves of large plants and incubate in about fifty hours. The fry have very small mouths and for about the first fortnight they feed on the body mucus of the brood fish, usually that of the female. Later they must be given the smallest of living food.

S. aequifasciata aequifasciata is greenish brown with nine vertical dark bars and some horizontal blue stripes anteriorly and posteriorly. *S.a. axelrodi* is light to dark brown with nine bluish bars across the body and head. *S.a. haroldi* is variable in colour but most aquarium specimens are light brown with horizontal, wavy blue lines over the whole body and three dark vertical bars.

S. discus is brassy or orange to deep brownish red or dark blue-green, with eight vertical bars and the head, nape and gill cover marked with grey to green wavy lines.

The genus *Tilapia* is native to Africa, Palestine and Syria. In general appearance these fishes approach very closely to *Cichlasoma* species but may be distinguished from them by a dark spot on

Opposite page
Xiphophorus helleri var. Red and Green Swordtails

Above *Dermogenys pusillus*
Left *Polycentrus schomburgki*

Pterophyllum scalare

the point of the gill cover and two incomplete lateral lines.

Altogether over a hundred different species are known but only about ten are regularly introduced into the aquarium. They are rather large fishes (some grow up to 20 inches) and only small specimens should be chosen for the aquarium. They are very voracious and greedy, and as they are largely herbivorous, they do much damage to plants. Old fishes are rather coarse. They may be kept and cared for in the regular way of cichlids and it is in their favour that they are tolerant of a temporary drop in temperature.

In captivity they are not ready breeders. *T. guinasana, T. guineensis, T. sparrmanii, T. tholloni* and *T. zillii* breed in the regular way of cichlids; the other species are mouth-breeders.

T. galilaea is believed the fish of the New Testament. It is widespread from the Jordan, across Africa, to Liberia. It reaches a length of about 16 inches. *T. guinasana* is from Lake Guinas in South-west Africa. It is a comparatively small fish that reaches no more than 5 or 6 inches. *T. guineensis* is found in the brackish lagoons of the countries bordering the Gulf of Guinea. It reaches a length of about 8 inches. *T. heudeloti* (*dolloi* and *macrocephala*) is found in the coastal districts (sometimes in brackish waters) from Senegal to the Congo. It reaches a length of 12 inches. *T. lepidura* is found in Angola and the Congo in brackish as well as in fresh water. It reaches a length of about 8 inches. *T. mossambica* is native to the coast of eastern Africa where it is found in brackish and fresh water. It reaches a length of 14 inches. *T. nilotica* is widespread from Syria, through Egypt and eastern Africa, to the Congo and western Africa. It is found in brackish as well as in fresh water and grows to as much as 20 inches. *T. sparrmanii* is widespread through southern Africa. It reaches a length of 7 or 8 inches. *T. tholloni* is native to western Africa from Cameroun to the Congo. It reaches a length of about 7 inches. *T. zilli* is native to Jordan, Syria and Africa north of the Equator. It reaches a length of 12 inches.

Family ELEOTRIDAE

Members of the family Eleotridae, popularly known as sleepers, inhabit the seas and brackish waters of the tropics and subtropics: a mere handful are freshwater species. They are closely related to the Gobiidae but the pelvic fins are separated and not united to form a sucking disc as in the true gobies.

Only a few species have been introduced into

Opposite page
Above left *Apistogramma ramirezi*
Above right *Hemichromis bimaculatus*
Below *Pseudotropheus auratus*

Left *Symphyosodon aequifasciata axelrodi*

Tilapia mossambica

the aquarium. All call for much the same care and treatment. A temperature range of about 18 to 25°C and medium-hard water is required. They are extremely voracious and will eat most things that come their way: feeding should be plentiful as some will eat as much as their own weight each day. As they are nocturnal the aquarium must be furnished with hiding-places, and a sandy planting medium into which they can dig.

The genus *Dormitator* is represented to aquarists by two species: *D. latifrons* the Broad-headed or Western Sleeper, and *D. maculatus* the Spotted Sleeper. Both are fairly large fishes that reach a length of 10 inches in the wild and 5 or 6 inches in captivity. They cannot be kept in pure fresh water; a mixture of one part sea water to four parts fresh is essential.

Breeding is by no means difficult. The eggs are deposited on stones previously cleaned by the brood fish. At a temperature of 25°C they incubate in about twenty-four hours. The brood fish should be removed and the fry raised on infusoria and later on small rotifers, screened daphnids and the like. Some green food is to be advised.

D. latifrons is native to the Pacific coasts of Mexico and Central America. The general colour is brownish to red-brown with a greenish sheen. The back darker, the side lighter and marked with five or six longitudinal rows of bright, red-brown spots. The belly is yellowish to reddish. The vertical fins are marked with red-brown spots on an almost colourless background.

D. maculatus is native to the Atlantic coast of America, from the Carolinas to Brazil. In appearance and coloration it is very similar to the above but the head is markedly smaller, and the caudal fin shows an iridescent blue blotch.

The genus *Eleotris* contains about ten species but most are unsatisfactory fishes for the aquarium. They must be kept in brackish if not in pure sea water; they are voracious and predatory, burrow in the planting medium and in captivity rarely, if ever, breed. An exception may be made for *E. lebretonis*, a small 4- to 5-inch fish from equatorial West Africa, where it is found usually in fresh water.

Its body is yellowish to olive-brown, darker on the back, the belly yellowish. There is a large, brilliant bluish blotch behind the gill cover and every scale is marked with a dark spot. It breeds readily in captivity and is very prolific. The eggs are scattered among fine-leaved plants. The fry should be fed with infusorians, and later with screened daphnids and the like. Some green food should be given them.

Hypseleotris cyprinoides the Chameleon Goby, native to the Philippines and Sumatra, is classified by some authorities as a colour variety of *H. modestus*. The body is a deep olive-green with a broad, black band from gill cover to base of the caudal fin; below it the body is white. It reaches a length of about 3 inches, is quite peaceful, and has bred successfully in captivity.

Mogurnda mogurnda the Sleepy Trout, is native to the rivers and coastal fresh waters of central, northern and eastern Australia, and New Guinea. The general colour is olive-green to brown with a purple sheen. The sides and fins are marked with irregular trout-like spots of red, yellow and purple. In the wild it reaches a length of about 7 inches but aquarium specimens are very much smaller and some cease to grow beyond a length of 2 inches.

In captivity it breeds quite readily. Several males should be mated with one female, who deposits from 100 to 150 eggs in successive batches. They are attached to large stones, or the glass of the aquarium, by a filament and brushed, rather than fanned, by the male with his pectoral and anal fins. At a temperature of 22 or 23°C the eggs incubate in about five days. The brood fish should be removed and the fry fed on infusoria and finely shredded earthworms forced through a cotton bag. Growth is rapid and within a week the young fishes are ready to take small brine shrimps, freshly chopped whiteworms, and the like.

Oxyeleotris marmoratus the Marbled Sleeper, is native to Malaysia and Indonesia. The general colour varies from dark brown to light chocolate, with a marbling of ivory-white. The fins show dark spots scattered at random. It is a large fish that reaches 20 inches in the wild. Aquarium specimens average only about 6 inches. The mouth, however, is large and the stomach capacious: a 4-inch specimen will swallow a fish half its size with ease and relish. Such a fish must be kept by itself.

Family GOBIIDAE
Members of the family Gobiidae are to be found in all temperate and tropical regions.

The most characteristic features are the large mobile eyes and the pelvic fins which meet on the underside of the body to form a nearly circular sucking disc by which the fish clings to solid objects.

Most gobies are small fish; few exceed 5 or 6 inches, and some are no more than 1 inch long. In nature they frequent shallow coastal waters and the brackish waters at the mouths of rivers. Only a few species penetrate into fresh water. As a result, they are best accommodated in a small aquarium, filled to a depth of about 6 inches, and at a temperature range of 22 to 30°C. *Brachygobius* and *Stigmatogobius* species are best kept in slightly brackish water, and *Periophthalmus* species in a mixture of one-third sea water and two-thirds fresh. *Paragobiodon echinocephalus* has the power to adapt itself to fresh and sea water.

All are carnivorous with a preference for daphnids, *Tubifex*, *Enchytraeus*, and similar living food. Some will take dried food if it contains a large amount of animal matter such as shrimp.

In captivity only *Brachygobius* has spawned. The water should not be more than 5 inches deep and the aquarium furnished with an overturned flowerpot. About 50 to 150 eggs are deposited on the inside of the pot, and fertilized by the male. He fans the eggs until they hatch – a matter of about a week at a temperature of 24°C, and about five days at 27°C – and neither eats them nor the newly hatched fish. The young fish need the smallest of infusorians and powdered egg pressed through fine linen-cloth, as their first food. After about a week they are ready to take newly hatched brine shrimps.

The genus *Brachygobius* is represented to aquarists by the species *B. aggregatus*, *B. nunus* and *B. xanthozona*. All are very similar in appearance. The general colour is a golden yellow, the body, from head to caudal peduncle, encircled by four broad dark brown to black bands. They are small fishes that reach a length of barely 2 inches and are appropriately known to aquarists as Bumblebee or Waspfishes.

B. aggregatus is found in north Borneo and the Philippines. *B. nunus*, which is the species most usually imported, is widespread in Thailand, Malaysia and Indonesia; *B. xanthozona* is found only in Sumatra, Java and Borneo.

Paragobiodon echinocephalus the Prickle-headed Goby, is native to the Red Sea and eastwards, through the East Indies and Philippines, to the coast of China and Polynesia. In sea water the body is chocolate-brown, the head a pale yellow. In fresh water the colours are much darker: the body is almost black, the head brown. The head is covered with many small prickle-like papillae. It reaches a length of about 1½ inches.

The genus *Periophthalmus* is native to the east coast of Africa and Malagasy, and eastwards through the Red Sea, India and south-east Asia, to Australia and the South Seas. Several species have been identified but *P. barbarus*, popularly known as the Mudskipper, is the one usually seen in the aquarium. *Boleophthalmus* and *Scartelaos* are very closely related genera.

The Mudskipper is essentially a fish for the specialist aquarist. It is by no means easy to keep in captivity: it requires an aquarium at least 3 feet

Right *Stigmatogobius sadanudio*
Below *Betta splendens*

Opposite page *Pterophyllum scalare*

Above *Belontia signata*

Below *Anabas testudineus*

in length and furnished so that about three-quarters is land and the rest water. The water should be about 3 or 4 inches deep and saline. The land should be of sand or fine grit, well stocked with marsh plants, large stones, and small logs of wood at different levels. In the wild the Mudskipper enjoys nothing more than to cling with its pectoral fins to a stone or log of wood, and remain there motionless contemplating (if a fish can contemplate) its surroundings.

A temperature of about 27°C is to be advised and the aquarium must be kept tightly covered at all times. A sudden change of temperature cannot be endured and dry air is fatal. On the other hand, feeding presents no difficulty. Flies and other small insects, earthworms, gentles, tadpoles, whiteworm and shrimps, are all eaten with relish. Its breeding habits are unknown but it is supposed that in its natural habitat it breeds in the mudhole in which it takes refuge during the dry season.

P. barbarus is found throughout the geographical range of the genus. The general colour is olive-brown, the back darker, the side lighter, the belly pale brown to yellowish. The side is marked with some irregular transverse bars. The two dorsal fins are steel-blue; the first, which is sail-shaped, has a dark edge and an intramarginal band of white. It reaches a length of 5 or 6 inches. Many colour varieties occur in nature.

Stigmatogobius sadanundio is popularly known as the Marbled Goby. It is native to India and eastwards to the Philippines. In colour it is slate- to olive-grey with numerous small, round, black dots, often edged white, peppered over the body. It reaches a length of about 3 inches.

Family
CHANNIDAE (OPHICEPHALIDAE)

The family Channidae, the snakeheads of the aquarist, is native to equatorial Africa, and southeast Asia from India, through Malaysia and Indonesia, to northern China.

It is represented by two genera: *Channa* and *Ophicephalus*. They are characterized by eel-like bodies, snake-like heads, and an ability to leave the water and travel overland in search of more favourable water. Like the Anabantidae to which they are closely related, they possess an accessory – though not so highly developed – breathing organ, enabling them to breathe atmospheric air. Movement overland is effected in a serpentine manner, by alternate advancement of the pectoral fins, and the help of the caudal fin.

All are very pugnacious and must be kept by themselves. They are also very voracious and must be given food in quantity. This is by no means easy because their natural food is living fishes, and it is only small, young fishes that will take earthworms, tadpoles, and the like. Temperature, however is of little importance for adult fishes will tolerate a range of from 10 to 35°C.

Some species have bred in captivity. The eggs are large and non-adhesive. No bubble nest is built but by virtue of a droplet of oil in each egg, they float at the surface in a mass. At a temperature of 26 to 28°C they incubate in two or three days and the fry are free swimming about four days later. Newly hatched fish feed readily on infusoria, later on screened daphnids and finely chopped earthworms. Finely graded dried food will also be taken.

In the wild these fishes grow to a very large size and are esteemed in the Far East as food fishes. *C. asiatica* the species that is most usually imported reaches about 1 foot in length. *O. marulius* grows to 4 feet, and *O. striatus* to 3 feet. By contrary, *O. guacha* reaches a bare 6 inches, but is rare.

C. asiatica the Chinese Snakehead or Walking Fish, is native to southern Asia, chiefly south China. The colour is dark olive-green on the back, shading to a dirty grey to white on the belly. The side shows a zigzag line of silvery spots, ending at a large black ocellus surrounded by silvery dots at the root of the caudal fin. The dorsal and anal fins are long; there are no pelvic fins. Aquarium specimens usually reach a length of 6 or 7 inches.

The genus *Ophicephalus* is represented by about half a dozen species. *O. africanus* the African Snakehead and *O. obscura* are from Africa; *O. guacha*, *O. lucius*, *O. marulius* the Murrul, *O. pleurophthalmus* and *O. striatus* are from Asia. They are rarely imported.

Family ANABANTIDAE

The family Anabantidae is a fairly large one that is represented to aquarists by about forty species and subspecies and one or two colour varieties. In Asia members of the family extend from India, through Malaysia and Indonesia, to China and Korea, and in Africa from approximately latitude 20° N. southwards to the Cape, excluding the Sudan, Tanzania and Malagasy.

Anabantid fishes are sometimes called labyrinth fishes because they are characterized by the presence of a labyrinth-like accessory breathing organ on each side of the head, which enables them to breathe atmospheric air. The organ consists of three or more concentrically arranged bony

Opposite page
Above *Helostoma temmincki*
Below *Colisa lalia*

Below *Melanotaenia fluviatilus* (One of the rarer Australian rainbow fish)
Bottom *Macrognathus aculeatus*

plates with frilled margins, attached to a bony base that is attached to the upper end of the fourth gill arch, and enclosed in a dorsal enlargement of the gill cavity. The vascular membrane, which covers the organ, is supplied with venous blood by a branch of the fourth afferent branchial artery, and the efferent vessel for the organ joins the dorsal aorta. Under normal conditions the fish takes about four gulps of air every minute. The gulp of air is automatically pressed into the labyrinth; the oxygen is absorbed directly into the bloodstream and the deoxygenated air is expelled as a single bubble.

With a few exceptions, anabantids are not suitable for a community aquarium. Most of them are bullies, and many of the larger species go about looking for trouble. The well-known Paradisefish, for example, will often bite the head off a Guppy. Much damage is done at night when many fishes are dormant. On the other hand, anabantids are comparatively easy fishes to keep; they are omnivorous, with a marked preference for meat, and on account of their accessory breathing organ are able to tolerate a crowded aquarium and polluted water. Most species are fairly long-lived, and with the exception of *Macropodus* species, which will endure a temperature range of 15 to 30°C, most flourish well in a range of 23 to 26°C.

With some exceptions, anabantids are bubble-nest builders. The nest varies in size from about $1\frac{1}{2}$ to 5 inches in diameter and is dome-shaped, sometimes rising 2 inches above the surface of the water. Nest-building takes place at any time of the year, and if no female is present the male should be moved to an aquarium already occupied by a female. From time to time the male will parade in front of the female with outspread fins and intensified colours, and if the female is unready to mate, the male will jostle her, sometimes so viciously that unless the aquarium is a large one and thickly planted to provide shelter, she will be killed. If, however, the female is ready to mate, she takes up a position below the nest and sways her body from side to side. The male wraps his body round hers – head touching tail – the pair sink slowly in the water, and the female is turned on her back. With a quivering of the bodies and a tightening of the embrace, the female releases a shower of eggs which are immediately fertilized by the male; the male and female separate, gather the eggs in their mouths, and blow them into the nest. In some species, however, the eggs, by virtue of containing droplets of oil, float upwards into the nest.

The performance is repeated, perhaps a dozen or more times, until the female has released all the eggs. The male now becomes vicious and divides his time between driving the female away from the nest and blowing bubbles to keep it in repair. At this stage it is best to remove the female.

At a temperature of 25 or 26°C the eggs hatch in about three or four days. The young fish remain in the nest until it breaks up – a matter of some three days – after which they must be fed with rotifers, infusorians and dust-fine dried food. Before the nest breaks up some of the young fish will occasionally spiral away from it. They are immediately picked up by the male and blown into the nest.

Once the fry are free swimming the male should be removed. The surface of the water should be kept clear of dust and scum, and gentle aeration is a great help towards keeping the aquarium in good condition. Young anabantids need well-oxygenated water if they are to survive; the labyrinth organ does not develop until two to four weeks after birth. At this stage the young are very sensitive to low temperature and the aquarium should be kept covered at all times and away from draughts. Excess food, likely to foul the water, must be siphoned off daily.

Anabas testudineus is widely distributed through south-east Asia, from India and Ceylon, through Malaysia and Indonesia, to southern China and the Philippines. It is popularly known as the Walking Fish because it frequently leaves the water and undertakes journeys overland. In the hot months it has been found aestivating. Progress out of the water is accomplished by specialized spines that extend from the edge of the gill cover. By spreading the gill covers and rocking the body from side to side, the fish digs the spines into the ground and pulls itself slowly forward. It is sometimes known as the Climbing Fish because specimens have been found high up among the branches of trees, and it was supposed that the fish climbed there. The name, however, is a misnomer; it is now known that the fish cannot climb a vertical surface and those that have been found high up in trees have been carried there by birds to be eaten later at leisure.

In the wild it grows to a length of 10 inches and in India it is a recognized food fish. Sometimes it is eaten raw. In the aquarium it rarely grows to more than 5 inches. The coloration is variable but aquarium specimens are usually brownish to olive-green, lighter or silvery below.

It is a very hardy fish that will tolerate a temperature range of from 18 to 32°C, and is a hearty eater not very particular about food, but preferring meaty foods to all else. It is not a bubble-nest builder. Breeding in captivity is rare but from all accounts the eggs are scattered at random and rise to the surface of the water. As it is a nocturnal species, in the aquarium it is shy and pugnacious and, therefore, unsuited to a community aquarium.

Belontia signata from Ceylon, is popularly known as the Combtail, because the rays of the caudal fin extend about 1 inch, to form a fringe or comb. The male is purplish red on the back, shading to greenish blue on the belly. The female is a uniform olive-brown. It reaches a length of 4 or 5 inches. It may be kept and cared for in the regular way of anabantids.

It is not a bubble-nest builder. The eggs float at the surface among the floating plants, loosely kept together with a few bubbles. At a temperature of about 29°C the fry hatch out in about three days and are free swimming about two days later.

The genus *Betta* contains altogether about twenty-five species, of which only about six are regularly introduced into the aquarium. They are native to eastern India and through Malaysia and Indonesia to southern China.

B. brederi from Java and Sumatra, *B. pictum* from Singapore, Sumatra and Java, *B. pugnax* from Penang, are mouth-breeders, and *B. taeniata* from Sumatra and Borneo, probably is. *B. fasciata* from Sumatra and *B. splendens* from Thailand and Malaysia, are bubble-nest builders.

All are very pugnacious and popularly known as fighting fishes; in its native Thailand, *B. splendens* has earned such a reputation as a fighter that it was, if no longer, specially bred for its fighting qualities.

All six species may be kept and cared for in the regular way of anabantids. They are, however, rather unpredictable in their breeding. The two main considerations (apart from the fact that the brood fish must be a matched pair) are a high temperature (28 to 30°C) and living food (particularly gnat larvae) in large quantities.

Many young fish are lost during the first three weeks after hatching, and incorrect feeding seems to be the chief reason. As soon as the fry are free swimming (a matter of about four days after spawning) they need to be given infusorians in large quantities, until they are ready to take brine shrimps, screened daphnids, and the like. They are best retained in a large aquarium, filled to a depth of about 8 or 9 inches, with matured water with an acid reaction (*p*H 6·8) and a fair amount of sediment on the bottom. A bright light is essential for the development of the fry, and we cannot stress too strongly the need to keep the aquarium covered so that the surface of the water is kept free of dust and scum, until the labyrinth organ has developed.

B. brederi is a uniform brown to yellowish brown with irregular transverse bands on the side, the head and nape mottled. It reaches a length of about 3 inches.

B. fasciata the Striped Fighting Fish, is blue-black to dark green, sometimes reddish, in colour. Some indistinct transverse bands mark the side; the scales each with an indistinct greenish spot. It reaches a length of about 4 inches.

B. pictum is very variable in colour and ranges from clay to dark brown, sometimes reddish brown. The side is marked with three narrow, horizontal bands. It reaches a length of about 2 inches.

B. pugnax varies in colour from grey-blue to red-brown, with several dark transverse bands and a horizontal stripe that extends from the snout to the root of the caudal fin. It reaches a length of about $3\frac{1}{2}$ inches.

B. splendens is the well-known Siamese Fighting Fish. The wild fish is reddish brown with a blue-green sheen and numerous metallic spots arranged in rows. These are usually green but sometimes blue or red. It reaches a length of about $2\frac{1}{2}$ inches.

In the aquarium, however, the wild fish is rarely, if ever, seen. Its place is taken by a number of colour varieties. The Federation of British Aquatic Societies recognizes five varieties: Red, Blue, Green and indigo (called Black) whose bodies and fins are of equal intensity of colour, and the Cambodia which has a cream-coloured body and red fins.

B. taeniata is usually brown to yellowish brown in colour, sometimes fawn. A dark band extends from the snout, across the eye, to a dark blotch at the root of the caudal fin, and another from the lower edge of the gill cover to the blotch at the root of the caudal fin. It reaches a length of 3 or 4 inches.

The genus *Colisa* is native to northern India, Assam, Burma, Singapore and Borneo. It is represented to aquarists by four species that are very similar to *Trichogaster* species but from which they may be distinguished by the pelvic fins. They are reduced to single, elongated, filiform rays which the fish uses as tactile organs.

All four species are hardy and prolific. They may be kept and cared for in the regular way of anabantids, and bred in the regular way of bubble-nest builders. Females may be distinguished from males by their paler coloration. They are satisfactory community fishes but allowance must be made for them being shy and of retiring disposition.

C. chuna the Honey Gourami, is widespread in northern India. The body is a uniform tan that deepens to honey-gold at breeding time, with some bars that come and go. The head is brown deepening to golden red. It reaches a length of about $2\frac{1}{2}$ inches.

C. fasciata the Striped Gourami, is native to northern India, Assam and Burma. The general colour is brownish yellow to brownish olive with a suffusion of sky-blue. The side is marked with fourteen or more dark, vertical bands. The gill cover shows a bluish-green metallic spot. It reaches a length of from 4 to 5 inches and is sometimes known as the Giant Gourami.

C. labiosa the Thick-lipped Gourami, is native to southern Burma. The back is rusty brown in colour, the sides green to olive-green suffused with a dark violet sheen. Eight to ten red vertical bars mark the sides, and a wide longitudinal stripe extends along the side from the mouth to the base of the caudal fin, where it ends as a metallic-blue spot. The lips are characteristically negroid. It reaches a length of about $3\frac{1}{2}$ inches.

C. lalia native to Bengal and Assam, is popularly known as the Pygmy or Dwarf Gourami, because at best it reaches no more than 2 inches, and rarely that in domestication. It is brilliantly coloured, a dark red with oblique bars of metallic blue or green on the side. The throat and belly are indigo. The vertical fins are peppered with red dots and outlined crimson.

The genus *Ctenopoma* is native to tropical Africa. It is represented to aquarists by ten species, popularly known as African Walking or Climbing Fishes, because they are similar to *Anabas testudineus* in appearance and have the same habit of leaving the water and making journeys overland.

Essentially they are fishes for the specialist aquarist; they must be kept at a temperature about 14°C and are very voracious feeders that need living food, particularly small fishes, in their diet.

C. acutirostre from the Congo basin, *C. argentoventer* from the Niger basin, *C. kingsleyae* from Senegal to the Congo, *C. multispinis* from the Zambezi basin, and *C. nigropannosum* from the Niger to the Congo, are fairly large and pugnacious fishes that reach a length of from 6 to 8 inches and must be kept by themselves.

Of the smaller species that are peaceful, mention may be made of *C. ansorgei* from West Africa, *C. congicum* and *C. fasciolatum* from the Congo basin, *C. nanum* from Cameroun, and *C. oxyrhynchus* from the Lower Congo. All reach a length of no more than 3 or 4 inches.

Little is known about their breeding habits. *C. oxyrhynchus* is said to scatter its eggs at random which float at the surface among the floating plants; the others are said to be bubble-nest builders. Like the larger members of the genus they will not tolerate a temperature below 24°C, and feeding should consist of living food such as earthworms, gnat larvae, bloodworms, and the like.

The genus *Ctenops* (*Trichopsis*) is native to India and eastwards, through Thailand and South Vietnam, to Malaysia and Indonesia. In general appearance members of the genus are very similar to *Betta* species but may be distinguished from them by the presence of two to six spines in the dorsal fin (*Betta* species have only one or none), and four to eight spines in the anal fin (*Betta* species have usually one to four). Unlike *Betta* species, however, they are peaceful fishes, quite suitable to be introduced into a community aquarium, and the brood fish need not be separated from their young.

They are bubble-nest builders that breed in the regular way of anabantids, but the fry are small and must be supplied with very small infusorians as their first food. Breeding is best conducted in a sunny situation, the water not more than 8 or 9 inches deep and at a temperature range of 27 to 30°C.

The genus is represented to aquarists by four species (the females are less brilliantly coloured than the males) that are given the popular name of croaking gouramies. During the breeding season they produce a faint but audible croaking sound.

C. nobilis from India, south-east Bengal and Assam, is brownish with a white stripe that extends from the head to the base of the caudal fin, and another from the root of the pectoral fin to that of the caudal. It reaches a length of about 4 inches.

C. pumilus from Thailand, Cambodia and Malaysia, is olive-green, darker on the back, lighter on the side; the side marked with a row of blue-black spots from the snout to the base of the caudal fin. It reaches a length of little more than 1 inch.

C. schalleri from Thailand, is yellowish to brownish, the side marked with three horizontal stripes from the snout to the base of the caudal fin. It reaches a length of about $2\frac{1}{2}$ inches.

C. vittatus from Thailand, South Vietnam and Malaysia, is yellowish brown to reddish brown, the back greenish, the belly yellowish white to white. The side is marked with three dark, horizontal stripes. It reaches a length of about 1½ inches.

Helostoma temmincki is native to Thailand, Malaysia and the Sunda Islands. It has been given the popular name of the Kissing Gourami. It is characteristic of the species that it has heavy, protruding lips furnished with fine teeth, designed by nature to help it remove algae from stones, and from time to time two fish appear to kiss each other. This is not a prelude to mating and, according to some authorities, is purely a form of threat display.

The general colour is light olive-green, silvery on the belly, the side marked with narrow, horizontal, undulating stripes. There is a dark bar at the base of the caudal fin. In the wild it reaches a length of 12 inches, and is much esteemed as a food fish; aquarium specimens rarely exceed 4 or 5 inches.

It may be kept and cared for in the regular way of anabantids but must be given some green food in its diet, and the temperature should not be allowed to fall below 24°C.

In captivity it breeds rarely. From the available records we understand that no bubble nest is built. There is a nuptial embrace and the eggs are scattered at random, to float to the surface of the water. The brood fish must be removed as they are greedy eaters of the eggs. The water should be about 12 inches deep, at a temperature of 26 to 29°C, and with a *pH* reaction of 7·4 or 7·6. The eggs hatch in about three days, and the young fish thrive well on infusorians and powdered dried food for about a week or ten days; after this they are ready to take brine shrimps, microworms, and the like.

Members of the genus *Macropodus*, popularly called paradisefishes, are native to Korea, and southwards to Tonking, Formosa and Hanoi, and westwards to India. They are found mainly in estuaries and shallow waters within, or not far from, tidal influence.

The genus is represented to aquarists by two or three species and some subspecies, of which *M. opercularis* is of historical interest. It was the first tropical fish to be introduced into the home aquarium, and there is reason to believe that it was the fish seen by Samuel Pepys when, under date of 28 May 1665, he wrote in his *Diary*; 'Thence home and to see my lady Pen, where my wife and I were shown a fine rarity: of fishes kept in a glass of water, that will live so for ever, and finely marked they are being foreign.'

All members of this genus are bubble-nest builders and their breeding follows the general principles for breeding anabantids. They are fairly prolific and very hardy. They breed readily at 24°C and *M. cupanus* and *M. opercularis* have been known to breed at 21°C. As already stated, they will live at a temperature range of 15 to 30°C. They are small fishes that reach a length of not more than 3 to 3½ inches, but they are pugnacious.

M. chinensis the Round-tailed Paradisefish, is found from Korea to southern China. The general colour is olive-brown, darker on the back, lighter on the side, overcast with a greenish tinge. The side is marked with dark, vertical, irregular bars.

M. cupanus cupanus the Spike-tail Paradisefish, is native to India and Ceylon. The general colour is light brown. The head, shoulder and gill cover are a metallic olive-green. There is a round black spot at the base of the caudal fin.

M. cupanus dayi the Brown Spike-tail Paradisefish, is native to Malabar, Burma and South Vietnam. The back is coffee-brown, the side chestnut, the throat and belly vary from brownish red to deep red. The head is peppered with small brown dots, the side marked with two brown stripes that extend from the gill cover to the root of the caudal fin.

M. opercularis opercularis the well-known Paradisefish of the aquarists, is native to Korea, China, South Vietnam and Formosa. The general colour is greenish brown to grey, the top of the head and anterior part of the back mottled black. The side is marked by about twelve metallic bars, alternating red and blue. The gill cover shows a large blue-green metallic spot edged orange. An albino variety, known as the White Paradisefish, has been developed. The general colour is a fleshy white, the sides marked with deep pink and light blue-green vertical bars. The eyes, as in all albinos, are pink.

M. opercularis concolor the Black Paradisefish, is native to Malaysia and Indonesia. The general colour is cyclamen-blue, each scale edged navy-blue giving a reticulated effect. A dark horizontal line extends from the eye to the edge of the gill cover.

Osphronemus goramy is native to Malaysia, Thailand and the Sunda Islands. It is a very large fish that in the wild reaches a length of 2 feet and makes excellent eating. Only young specimens are suitable for the aquarium. Young fish are reddish brown with a green tinge. The belly is whitish with brown dots. The throat a light blue. The side is marked with seven to ten dark vertical bars. Old fish are a uniform olive-green. It may be kept

Trichogaster leeri

and cared for in the regular way of anabantids but some green food is necessary in the diet. It is a bubble-nest builder but rarely breeds in captivity, and no result may be expected unless the aquarium is a large one.

Parosphronemus deissneri is native to Malaysia and the Sunda Islands. The general colour is rose-pink to yellow-buff. The side is marked with broad, dark, horizontal bands that extend from the snout to the caudal peduncle. It is a small fish that reaches no more than about $1\frac{1}{2}$ inches in length. It may be kept and cared for in the regular way of anabantids but a high temperature is to be recommended for in the wild it frequents shallow, weedy ditches where the temperature may be as high as 32°C. Little is known about it, however, as it is not very often imported. It is known to be rather shy and timid, and believed to be a bubble-nest builder that breeds in the same way as most anabantids.

Sphaerichthys osphronemoides the Chocolate Gourami, is native to southern Malaysia and Sumatra.

The general colour is dark chestnut-brown to black. The side is marked with four or five silvery-white bars. The dorsal, pelvic and anal fins are black, sometimes flecked with gold. It reaches a length of about 3 inches. It is a rather delicate fish and must be kept in well-matured water, soft, with a slightly acid reaction, and at a temperature range of 26 to 30°C. Living food is recommended.

The genus *Trichogaster* is native to northern India, through Bengal, Assam and Burma, to Thailand, Malaysia and beyond. Members of this genus are very similar in appearance to *Colisa* species but may be distinguished by the pelvic fins, which are reduced to elongated filaments to which a vestigial spine and two or three rudimentary rays are attached. All members of the genus are bubble-nest builders and may be kept and cared for in the regular way of anabantids. Males may be distinguished from females by a larger and more pointed dorsal fin, and a deeper anal fin.

T. leeri popularly known as the Pearl or Mosaic Gourami, is native to Malaysia and Indonesia. The

general colour is light olive with an iridescent mother-of-pearl sheen. The body and fins are peppered with pearly dots. The throat and belly are a clear enamel-white. The side is marked with an interrupted dark line from the snout to the root of the caudal fin. It reaches a length of about 4 inches.

T. microlepis the Moonlight Gourami, is native to Thailand. The general colour is a uniform silky bluish silver. The scales are very small. Young fishes are marked with longitudinal rows of dark spots that are sometimes rather faint. It reaches a length of about 6 inches.

T. pectoralis the Snake-skin Gourami, is native to Malaysia, Thailand and South Vietnam. The general colour is bluish green. The side is marked with a heavy brown line that zigzags from the snout to the base of the caudal fin. Oblique, irregular dark bars cross the body. In the wild it reaches a length of 10 inches but aquarium specimens rarely exceed 6 inches.

T. trichopterus trichopterus is native to Bengal, Burma, Thailand, Malaysia and Indonesia. The general colour is an iridescent silvery olive, the back darker, the belly lighter. Faint oblique bands sometimes mark the sides. There is a large black spot on a white ground on the middle of the side, and another on the caudal peduncle. The popular name of the Three-spot Gourami stems from the fact that the eye of the fish is counted as a spot, but those who refer to it as the Two-spot Gourami are more precise. It reaches a length of about 6 inches.

T. trichopterus sumatranus the Blue Gourami, is native to Singapore and Malaysia. The general colour is grey-blue on the back, shading to pale blue on the side and silvery white on the belly. It reaches a length of about 5 inches.

A colour variety, known as the Opaline Gourami, was developed some twenty years ago by an American breeder. The general colour is blue, the sides are marked with some blue-black blotches and an irregular dark, horizontal stripe along the middle of the body.

Family LUCIOCEPHALIDAE

The family Luciocephalidae is represented to aquarists by the one species *Luciocephalus pulcher* popularly called the Pretty Pike-head, a 7-inch fish native to Malaysia and Indonesia.

It is characterized by a pike-like head and although it is closely related to the Anabantidae, and like members of this family has an accessory breathing organ, it may be distinguished from them by the absence of spinous dorsal and anal fins.

In the wild it frequents running water, where it drifts with the current, snapping up insects and other suitable foods. As a result, it is not a very satisfactory aquarium fish and is rarely imported. Little is known about it except that it is best kept by itself in a large, well-planted aquarium, at a temperature range of 22 to 24°C, needs living food, and is probably a mouth-breeder.

The general colour is olive-green to reddish, the side marked with two white stripes, edged with black above and below, that extend from the eye to the base of the caudal fin. The belly is a dirty white to pink. The vertical fins have red markings.

Family ATHERINIDAE

The family Atherinidae, the silversides, is a large one, and members of it are to be found in nearly all temperate and tropical coastal waters. Some are to be found in brackish waters; a few penetrate into fresh waters.

Trichogaster trichopterus sumatranus

The four species described below are among the latter. They flourish quite well in a large aquarium at a temperature of about 24°C and are sufficiently peaceful to be introduced into a community aquarium. They are undemanding in their requirements. Some direct sunlight and a mixed diet of dried, living and vegetable foods are all that are necessary to keep them in good health.

Silversides breed in the regular way of oviparous species. The eggs are scattered at random among thickets of submerged plants to which they cling by means of a short filament. At a temperature of about 25°C the eggs incubate in seven to ten days. The young fish should be fed on dust-fine dried food for about a fortnight: after that they may be given screened daphnids and algae.

Bedotia geayi the Madagascar Rainbowfish, is native to the coastal water of Malagasy from sea-level up to about 2,500 feet. The general colour is a greenish olive; a dark stripe extends from the eye to the base of the caudal fin. The vertical fins are yellowish with dark edges, and those of the male (a more colourful fish than the female) show some red. The first dorsal fin is short-based, the second long-based. It reaches a length of $2\frac{1}{2}$ to 3 inches.

The genus *Melanotaenia* is native to the coastal streams of Australia and New Guinea. It is represented to aquarists by *M. maccullochi* the Pygmy or Dwarf Rainbowfish, from north-eastern Australia, and *M. nigrans* the Australian Rainbowfish, that is found throughout the geographical range of the genus.

M. maccullochi is brown on the back, yellowish green on the belly. The side is marked with seven dark brown stripes that extend from head to caudal peduncle; the scales between each stripe are a silvery gold. The gill plate is green with a bright red blotch edged with gold. It reaches a length of about $2\frac{1}{2}$ inches.

M. nigrans is dark olive-green, shading to silvery on the belly, the scales reflect blue, green and violet tints. The side is marked with red and yellow horizontal stripes. There is an intense red spot on the gill plate. It reaches a length of about 4 inches.

Telmatherina ladigesi is native to Celebes and is popularly known as the Celebes Rainbowfish or Sailfin. The general colour is olive, shading to yellow with a brilliant iridescent sheen. The side is marked with a faint blue stripe that extends from behind the first dorsal fin to the root of the caudal. The first dorsal fin is small: the second is large, and in the male is very large with the front rays black and drawn out. The peculiarity is repeated in the anal fin. It reaches a length of 2 or 3 inches.

Trichogaster trichopterus sumatranus var. Opaline Gourami

Family COTTIDAE

Members of the family Cottidae are native to the Northern Hemisphere. The majority are marine: very few penetrate into fresh water, and the only species represented to aquarists is *Cottus gobio* the well-known Miller's Thumb or Bullhead. It is widely distributed throughout Europe, Siberia and Asia Minor, in the clear water of mountain and lowland streams running over gravel bottoms.

The head is flat and broad, the mouth wide. There is a short, upturned spine on the gill cover.

Seen from above the body is wedge-shaped. There are two dorsal fins joined by a low membrane. The pectoral fins are large; the anal long. The coloration is very variable and depends largely on the intensity of the light. Usually it varies from brown to yellowish brown, blotched and spotted with black. The belly is nearly white. It reaches a length of 6 or 7 inches.

This is rather too quarrelsome a fish to be introduced into a community aquarium and is best kept in a large aquarium with a gravel bottom, the

from 100 to 200 eggs in clusters. They are fanned by the male and incubate within six weeks.

Family GASTEROSTEIDAE

Members of the family Gasterosteidae, popularly known as sticklebacks, are found in the temperate seas and fresh waters of the Northern Hemisphere. Most species are native to North America, but *Gasterosteus aculeatus* the Three-spined Stickleback, is widespread in the fresh waters of Europe (excluding the basin of the Danube), Algeria, northern Asia and North America. It is also found in brackish waters. It is the species usually introduced into aquaria.

The general colour is greenish to brownish on the back, sometimes blue-black and often marbled. The belly is silvery. During the breeding season, the back is sea-green, the belly orange-red. There are three erectile spines, each supporting a short fin-membrane, in front of the dorsal fin. It reaches a length of about 4 inches.

It flourishes well in a large and well-planted aquarium. The temperature should never exceed 22°C, and in winter should be reduced to a range of from about 5 to 8°C. In the wild it feeds on worms, bloodworms, shrimps, the eggs and fry of fishes, and the like.

The breeding season is from April to June. Several females should be placed in the same aquarium as one male. The male builds a nest among the water plants, using short lengths of leaf and similar material, cemented together by a discharge from the kidney. When the nest is completed, a female is enticed into it to deposit her eggs. Once the eggs have been laid and fertilized, the female breaks out at the back of the nest. The performance is repeated many times, sometimes with more than one female. Once they have spawned, the females should be removed, but not the male who fans the eggs until they hatch – a matter of about ten to fourteen days – and then protects the young fish.

Family TETRAODONTIDAE

Members of the family Tetraodontidae are popularly known as puffer, or globe fishes. They are so called because their chief characteristic is an ability to inflate themselves with air or water. This they do when frightened until the belly becomes as round and as hard as a tennis ball, and even the vent is turned inside out to a fine point. If the fish inflates itself at the surface of the water, it does so by taking air into the mouth in noisy gulps, and when inflated it floats. If the fish inflates itself

water shallow and unheated. As it is crepuscular, the aquarium should be furnished with hiding-places into which it can retire during the hours of daylight. Feeding is not difficult because it eats most things that come its way, with a marked preference for bloodworms and freshwater shrimps.

In the wild it breeds from February to the end of April or beginning of May. The male prepares a shallow depression between two stones, or under an overhanging stone, in which the female deposits

Gasterosteus aculeatus

when submerged, it does so with water. It remains at the bottom, right way up, but if brought to the surface, or if it rises of its own accord, it ejects the water and fills itself with air. This unique behaviour is a form of self-protection.

Another characteristic of these fishes is the fused front teeth (two above, two below) forming a beak with a sharp edge. Since most species are pugnacious by nature and capable of dealing a nasty bite, they should be kept apart from other fishes.

The family is not a large one but members of it are widely distributed. Most are marine and represented in nearly all tropical and subtropical seas and estuaries throughout the world. A few species are confined to tropical fresh waters.

Puffer fishes are considered a great delicacy by the Japanese but great care has to be exercised because the flesh of most is poisonous; that of the Shaggy Puffer (*Tetraodon hispidus*) kills in a matter of hours. Some are poisonous only at certain seasons and others are poisonous when taken from certain waters but not from others. The reason for this is the food that the fish have been eating. The plain truth is that the clean meat on the back of the fish is excellent eating, but the fish is dangerous to eat because its flesh is permeated with certain alkaloids, called leucomaines, that form a dangerous poison when they combine with other alkaloids, called ptomaines, due to the action of bacteria in the decomposing tissues. If eaten at all, therefore, puffer fishes must be eaten at their absolute freshest, and in Japan the precaution is taken to sell the fishes alive in the food markets, to be killed just before cooking. Japanese cooks, however, are sometimes no more successful than English doctors. The first symptoms are violent spasms of the stomach, later of the whole body. There is no known antidote. The only treatment is to adminster strong emetics and stimulants to prevent collapse. Death results from paralysis of the heart and asphyxiation.

In the aquarium the family is represented by four species of the genus *Tetraodon*. They may be kept in fresh water at a temperature range of 21 to 27°C and the aquarium must be a large one as they are active fishes. By nature they are scavengers and will eat most things that come their way. Their favourite foods, however, appear to be earthworms and snails. Few will take dried food. They are oviparous. The eggs are deposited on stones where they are protected by the male. The period of incubation is from six to eight days.

T. cutcutia the Common Puffer, and *T. fluviatilis* the Green Puffer, are native to the fresh and brackish waters of India and eastwards to Indonesia. Both are fairly large fishes that reach a length of 6 or 7 inches, and are quarrelsome.

T. schoutedeni is native to the Stanley Pool in the Lower Congo. It reaches a length of about 3 inches and is peaceful.

T. somphongsi is native to the fresh waters of Thailand. It reaches a length of about 2½ inches and is peaceful.

Family MASTACEMBELIDAE
The family Mastacembelidae is native to the fresh and brackish waters of Africa (excluding Malagasy) south of the Sahara, and in Asia to Syria and eastwards, through India, Ceylon and Burma, to Malaysia and Indonesia. Members of the family are characterized by their eel- or snake-like appearance and a snout that tapers to a point.

By nature they are crepuscular and inhabit weedy waters over a sandy or muddy bottom. Most live well in an aquarium, provided it is furnished with plenty of hiding-places, the water is brackish (one part sea water to four parts fresh) and at a temperature range of 22 to 28°C. Earthworms, bloodworms, shrimps, and other living food is recommended. The larger species must be kept by themselves.

Macrognathus aculeatus the Arrownose, is widely distributed throughout south-east Asia, from India to Borneo and the Moluccas, although it appears to be absent from the Malabar coast. It is brownish or greenish in colour – the back marbled – shading to yellowish on the belly. A light band extends along the body just above the lateral line. There are two dorsal fins; the first consists of a row of spines, the second is soft. It reaches a length of 14 inches in the wild but aquarium specimens reach only 7 or 8 inches.

The genus *Mastacembelus* is represented in the aquarium by about half a dozen species but only two or three are regularly imported.

M. armatus the Tyretrack Eel, is greyish brown, shading to yellowish on the belly. Dark zigzag markings, branching alternatively towards the dorsal and anal fins, give the effect of a tyre track. *M. erythrotaenia* the Fire Eel, is dark brown to blackish, marked with red streaks and dots. *M. maculatus* the Spotted Spiny-eel, is light olive-green with some eye spots along the base of the dorsal fin. All three species are native to south-east Asia, from India and Ceylon, through Thailand, to southern China and Sumatra, and all three are large fishes that, in the wild, reach a length of from 18 upwards to 36 inches.

Further Reading

The hobby of keeping fishes in aquaria has attracted to itself a very large literature. The books mentioned below do not constitute a bibliography. Rather it is a list of those books that the authors have consulted; designed to serve the double purpose of a guide to further reading and an acknowledgement of some of the obligations of the present writers.

The date of a book is that of the edition consulted; it is not necessarily the date of the first or the most recent edition.

Most of the books mentioned are major works, available at libraries if out of print, and many contain bibliographies that will direct the reader to more specialized works.

ANGEL, F. *Poissons Exotiques et d'Aquariums*. Boubée, Paris, 1949.
ARNOLD, J. P. and AHL, E. *Fremdländische Süsswasserfische*. Wenzel, Brunswick, 1936.
AXELROD, H. R. and SCHULTZ, L. P. *Handbook of Tropical Aquarium Fishes*. McGraw Hill, New York, 1955.
AXELROD, H. R. and VORDERWINKLER, W. *Encyclopedia of Tropical Fishes*. Sterling and T.F.H. Books, Jersey City, 1961.
BADE, E. *Das Süsswasser Aquarium*. Pfenningstorf, Berlin, 1923.
BRÜNNER, G. *Aquarium Plants*. Trans: G. Vevers. Studio Vista, London, 1966.
BRYMER, J. H. P. *Guide to Tropical Fishkeeping*. Iliffe Books, London, 1967.
DE WIT, H. C. D. *Aquarium Plants*. Blandford Press, London, 1964.
DUIJN, C. Van. *Diseases of Fishes*. Iliffe Books, London, 1967.
EDDY, S. *Freshwater Fishes*. Brown, Dubuque, 1957.
EMMENS, C. W. and AXELROD, H. R. *Fancy Guppies for the Advanced Hobbyist*. T.F.H. Publications, Jersey City, 1967.
Gouramies in Colour. T.F.H. Publications, Jersey City, 1967.
EVANS, A. *Aquariums*. Foyle, London, 1967.
FRANÇOIS, M. *Décors Exotiques et Plantes d'Aquariums*. Desseaux, Colombes, 1951.
FREY, H. *Illustrated Dictionary of Tropical Fishes*. Trans: A. V. W. Schultz. T.F.H. Books, Jersey City, 1961.
GHADIALLY, F. N. *Advanced Aquarist Guide*. Pet Library, London, 1969.
HERVEY, G. F. and HEMS, J. *Freshwater Tropical Aquarium Fishes*. Spring Books, London, 1963.
The Goldfish. Faber and Faber, London, 1968.
INNES, W. T. *Complete Aquarium Book*. Blue Ribbon Books, London, 1937.
Exotic Aquarium Fishes. Innes Publications, Philadelphia, 1959.
JOCHER, W. *Food for the Aquarium and Vivarium*. Trans: G. Vevers. Studio Vista, London, 1966.
KRAMER, K. and WEISE, H. *Aquarienkunde*. Wenzel, Brunswick, 1943.
KYLE, H. M. *The Biology of Fishes*. Sidgwick and Jackson, London, 1926.
McINERNY, D. and GERRARD, G. *All About Tropical Fish*. Harrap, London, 1969.
NORMAN, J. R. *A History of Fishes*. Benn, London, 1947.
NORTON, J. *Fancy Platies*. T.F.H. Publications, Jersey City, 1967.
PINCHER, H. C. *A Study of Fishes*. Jenkins, London, 1948.
ROE, C. D. *Manual of Aquarium Plants*. Shirley Aquatics, Solihull, 1964.
ROE, C. D. and EVANS, A. *Koi*. Petfish Publications, London, 1969.
SCHEEL, J. *Rivulins of the Old World*. T.F.H. Publications, Jersey City, 1968.
SCHNEIDER, E. and WHITNEY, L. F. *Complete Guide to Tropical Fishes*. Nelson, New York, 1957.
SCHUBERT, G. *Diseases of Aquarium Fish*. Trans: G. Vevers. Studio Vista, London, 1967.
STERBA, G. *Aquarium Care*. Trans: G. Vevers. Studio Vista, London, 1967.
Freshwater Fishes of the World. Trans: D. W. Tucker. Studio Vista, London, 1967.
STODOLA, J. *Encyclopaedia of Water Plants*. T.F.H. Publications, Jersey City, 1967.
STOYE, F. H. *Tropical Fishes for the Home*. Stoye, Sayville, 1935.
WACHTEL, H. *Aquarium Hygiene*. Trans: G. Vevers. Studio Vista, London, 1966.
WAINWRIGHT, N. *Coldwater Aquariums and Simple Outdoor Pools*. Warne, London, 1969.
WEIGEL, W. *Planning and Decorating the Aquarium*. Trans: G. Vevers. Studio Vista, London, 1966.
WICKLER, W. *Breeding Aquarium Fish*. Trans: D. W. Tucker. Studio Vista, London, 1966.

Index